MTTC 82 Early Childhood Education
Teacher Certification Exam

By: Sharon Wynne, M.S
Southern Connecticut State University

XAMonline, INC.
Boston

Copyright © 2007 XAMonline, Inc.
All rights reserved. No part of the material protected by this copyright notice may be reproduced or utilized in any form or by any means, electronic or mechanical, including photocopying, recording or by any information storage and retrievable system, without written permission from the copyright holder.

To obtain permission(s) to use the material from this work for any purpose including workshops or seminars, please submit a written request to:

XAMonline, Inc.
21 Orient Ave.
Melrose, MA 02176
Toll Free 1-800-509-4128
Email: info@xamonline.com
Web www.xamonline.com
Fax: 1-781-662-9268

Library of Congress Cataloging-in-Publication Data

Wynne, Sharon A.
 Early Childhood Education 82: Teacher Certification / Sharon A. Wynne. -2nd ed.
 ISBN 978-1-58197-974-9
  1. Early Childhood Education 82.   2. Study Guides.   3. MTTC
  4. Teachers' Certification & Licensure.   5. Careers

Disclaimer:
The opinions expressed in this publication are the sole works of XAMonline and were created independently from the National Education Association, Educational Testing Service, or any State Department of Education, National Evaluation Systems or other testing affiliates.

Between the time of publication and printing, state specific standards as well as testing formats and website information may change that is not included in part or in whole within this product. Sample test questions are developed by XAMonline and reflect similar content as on real tests; however, they are not former tests. XAMonline assembles content that aligns with state standards but makes no claims nor guarantees teacher candidates a passing score. Numerical scores are determined by testing companies such as NES or ETS and then are compared with individual state standards. A passing score varies from state to state.

Printed in the United States of America
MTTC: Early Childhood Education 82
ISBN: 978-1-58197-974-9

TEACHER CERTIFICATION STUDY GUIDE

Project Manager: Sharon Wynne, MS

Project Coordinator: Victoria Anderson, MS

Content Coordinators/Authors: Fran Stanford, MS
Victoria Anderson, MS
Christina Godard, BS
Kimberly Putney, BS
Vickie Pittard, MS
Deborah Suber. BS
Kelley Eldredge, MS

Sample test: Shelley Wake, MS
Deborah Harbin, MS
Christina Godard, BS
Kim Putney, BS
Carol Moore, BS
Vickie Pittard, MS

Editors: Managing   Dr. Harte Weiner, PhD
Proof reader   Deborah Harbin, MS
Copy editor   Deborah Harbin, MS
Sample test   Shelley Wake, MS
Production   David Aronson

Graphic Artist   Jenna Hamilton

TEACHER CERTIFICATION STUDY GUIDE

Table of Contents

SUBAREA I   **CHILD DEVELOPMENT AND LEARNING**

COMPETENCY 1.0   UNDERSTAND THE PROCESSES OF CHILD GROWTH AND DEVELOPMENT (AGES BIRTH – 8) AND THE INTEGRATED NATURE OF DEVELOPMENT ACROSS ALL DOMAINS 1

Skill 1.1   Physical growth and development, social-emotional development, cognitive development, language development, and aesthetic development 1

Skill 1.2   Chronological age versus developmental age 4

Skill 1.3   Individual differences in development 5

Skill 1.4   The effect of development in one domain on development in other domains 6

COMPETENCY 2.0   UNDERSTAND HOW YOUNG CHILDREN DIFFER IN THEIR DEVELOPMENT AND APPLY THIS UNDERSTANDING TO SUPPORT THE DEVELOPMENT AND LEARNING OF INDIVIDUAL CHILDREN 7

Skill 2.1   Conditions that affect children's development and learning (e.g., risk factors, developmental variations, developmental patterns) 7

Skill 2.2   Strategies to create and modify environments and experiences to meet the individual needs of all children, including those with disabilities, developmental delays, and special abilities 9

COMPETENCY 3.0   UNDERSTAND THE SIGNIFICANCE OF DIVERSITY FOR CHILD DEVELOPMENT AND LEARNING 14

Skill 3.1   Recognition that children are best understood in the contexts of family, culture, and society 14

Skill 3.2   The interrelationships among culture, language, and thought 14

Skill 3.3   The function of home language in the development of young children 15

Skill 3.4   The importance of creating a supportive and nurturing environment for all children 16

COMPETENCY 4.0 UNDERSTAND THAT CHILDREN, THROUGH PLAY, CONSTRUCT KNOWLEDGE BY EXPLORING AND INTERACTING WITH OBJECTS, MATERIALS, AND PEOPLE IN THEIR ENVIRONMENT AND THAT PLAY REFLECTS DEVELOPMENT 18

Skill 4.1 Ways in which children construct and expand concepts 18

Skill 4.2 Activities and resources that encourage children to explore, to manipulate, to understand relationships, and to use symbols 20

Skill 4.3 Problem-solving strategies 21

Skill 4.4 Strategies to help children reflect on their own thinking processes (metacognition) 23

TEACHER CERTIFICATION STUDY GUIDE

SUBAREA II   CURRICULUM DEVELOPMENT AND IMPLEMENTATION

COMPETENCY 5.0   UNDERSTAND HOW TO PLAN AND IMPLEMENT DEVELOPMENTALLY APPROPRIATE CURRICULUM AND INSTRUCTIONAL PRACTICES BASED ON KNOWLEDGE OF INDIVIDUAL CHILDREN, THE COMMUNITY, AND CURRICULUM GOALS AND CONTENT 25

Skill 5.1   Interrelationships among the content areas 25

Skill 5.2   Benefits and strategies of integrated learning across the curriculum 27

Skill 5.3   The rationale for developmentally appropriate methods that include play, small group projects, open-ended questioning, group discussion, problem solving, cooperative learning, and inquiry experiences to help young children develop intellectual curiosity, solve problems, and make decisions 28

COMPETENCY 6.0   UNDERSTAND HOW TO STRUCTURE A LEARNING CLIMATE AND SELECT STRATEGIES THAT ARE RESPONSIVE TO THE DIVERSE NEEDS AND BACKGROUNDS OF THE CHILDREN 33

Skill 6.1   Strategies for creating and adapting a classroom environment that provides for individual differences 33

Skill 6.2   The selection of appropriate activities, materials, and equipment 33

Skill 6.3   The development, implementation, and evaluation of appropriate lesson plans 37

Skill 6.4   Strategies for making learning and problem solving relevant to children's lives 39

COMPETENCY 7.0	UNDERSTAND HOW TO CREATE AN ENVIORNMENT THAT FOSTERS YOUNG CHILDREN'S SOCIAL AND EMOTIONAL DEVELOPMENT, INCLUDING SELF-ESTEEM, SELF-DISCIPLINE, AND COOPERATIVE BEHAVIORS 40
Skill 7.1	The relationship between children's social and emotional development and learning 40
Skill 7.2	Individual and group guidance and problem-solving techniques that develop positive and supportive relationships with children, encourage positive social interaction among children, promote positive strategies of conflict resolution, and develop personal self-control, self motivation, and self-esteem 42
Skill 7.3	Methods that promote independence and self-confidence 44
Skill 7.4	Strategies for helping children learn to deal effectively with their emotions 46

COMPETENCY 8.0	UNDERSTAND HOW TO CREATE A LANGUAGE-ENRICHED ENVIRONMENT THAT FOSTERS THE USE OF EXPRESSIVE AND RECEPTIVE LANGUAGE AND LITERACY 49
Skill 8.1	Indicators of language and literacy development 49
Skill 8.2	Factors that influence children's language development (e.g., being read to every day, given time to use language daily, family literacy) 51
Skill 8.3	The importance of acknowledging a child's language 52
Skill 8.4	Strategies for developing children's listening and speaking skills .. 53
Skill 8.5	The relationship between writing and the development of fine-motor control 54
Skill 8.6	Methods for promoting children's understanding of the diversity of communication 57

COMPETENCY 9.0 UNDERSTAND THE DEVELOPMENT OF YOUNG CHILDREN'S COGNITION IN MATHEMATICAL AND SCIENTIFIC CONCEPTS AND HOW TO HELP CHILDREN MAKE SENSE OF THEIR WORLD 58

Skill 9.1 Factors and practices that promote positive attitudes regarding math and science 58

Skill 9.2 The role of hands-on activities in building knowledge, language, and concepts 60

Skill 9.3 Strategies that promote the transfer of mathematical and scientific concepts and skills to everyday life 66

Skill 9.4 The use of everyday events to advance mathematics and science themes 68

Skill 9.5 The use of technology for children 70

COMPETENCY 10.1 UNDERSTAND HOW TO FOSTER PHYSICAL COMPETENCE (INCLUDING FINE-MOTOR, GROSS-MOTOR, AND PERCEPTUAL DEVELOPMENT) AND ROMOTE CHILDREN'S AWARENESS OF HEALTH, NUTRITION, AND SAFETY 72

Skill 10.1 The relationship between physical development and learning 72

Skill 10.2 Activities and resources that foster children's physical development 73

Skill 10.3 Behaviors and factors that affect individual, family, and community health and safety 75

Skill 10.4 Principles of nutrition 78

Skill 10.5 Influences of culture on practices relating to health, nutrition, and safety 80

Skill 10.6 Activities and resources that extend children's knowledge of ways to prevent accidents, injuries, and the spread of germs 81

Skill 10.7 Hazards and dangerous substances 84

Skill 10.8 Roles of people in the community who are responsible for health and safety 88

COMPETENCY 11.0 UNDERSTAND YOUNG CHILDREN'S CREATIVE DEVELOPMENT AND HOW TO PROMOTE SELF-EXPRESSION THROUGH THE CREATIVE ARTS AND ENHANCE CHILDREN'S UNDERSTANDING AND APPRECIATION OF THE ARTS 90

Skill 11.1 Indicators of creative development 90

Skill 11.2 The integration of the arts with other content areas to promote learning and to provide a way for children to demonstrate what they know (e.g., drawing a picture instead of explaining in words) 91

Skill 11.3 The role of creative arts in promoting self-expression and creative thinking and in developing a healthy self-concept 92

Skill 11.4 Activities and resources for promoting children's aesthetic appreciation of the arts (e.g., exposure to arts of various cultures) 93

Skill 11.5 Building knowledge about the arts and artists (e.g., creating one's own art, talking about elements of artistic works) 94

TEACHER CERTIFICATION STUDY GUIDE

SUBAREA III   **FAMILY AND COMMUNITY RELATIONSHIPS**

COMPETENCY 12.0 UNDERSTAND THE IMPORTANCE OF ESTABLISHING AND MAINTAINING POSITIVE, COLLABORATIVE RELATIONSHIPS WITH FAMILIES 98

Skill 12.1   The importance of respecting families' choices and goals for children, including strategies for communicating effectively with families about curriculum and children's progress 98

Skill 12.2   Ways to involve families in assessing and planning for individual children 99

Skill 12.3   Strategies for supporting families in making decisions related to child development and parenting 101

Skill 12.4   Ways of encouraging family involvement in the early childhood program 102

COMPETENCY 13.0 UNDERSTAND VARIATIONS IN FAMILY STRUCTURE AND SOCIAL CULTURAL BACKGROUNDS 104

Skill 13.1   The varying contexts and configurations of family 104

Skill 13.2   Strategies for creating a climate of respect and appreciation for both the diversity and the uniqueness of individuals, families, and community 105

COMPETENCY 14.0 UNDERSTAND HOW THE DYNAMICS, ROLES, AND RELATIONSHIPS WITHIN FAMILIES AND COMMUNITIES AFFECT CHILDREN 106

Skill 14.1   Ways in which physical and environmental factors (e.g., nutrition, health, economic issues, family issues) may affect children's success as learners 106

Skill 14.2   Strategies that build on positive factors and minimize the effects of environmental factors that may have a negative impact on children 108

COMPETENCY 15.0 UNDERSTAND THE IMPORTANCE OF COORDINATION, COOPERATION, AND PROGRAM SUPPORT TO MEET CHILDREN'S NEEDS AND TO ENSURE LEARNING 110

Skill 15.1 The identification of institutions, agencies, programs, and organizations that advocate for and serve children and families (e.g., Head Start, social services, teacher associations) 110

Skill 15.2 Practices that ensure a smooth transition for both children and families to public schools 112

Skill 15.3 The role of positive public relations 113

Skill 15.4 Sources of funding 113

Skill 15.5 Goals and benefits of collaborating with community institutions and businesses 115

Skill 15.6 Functions of an interagency council 116

SUBAREA IV — ASSESSMENT AND EVALUATION

COMPETENCY 16.0 UNDERSTAND INFORMAL ASSESSMENT STRATEGIES TO PLAN AND INDIVIDUALIZE CURRICULUM AND TEACHING PRACTICES 118

Skill 16.1 Ongoing observation, recording, and assessment of young children's development 118

Skill 16.2 The development and use of authentic, performance-based assessments 120

Skill 16.3 Ways to engage children in self-assessment 121

Skill 16.4 The importance of matching assessments to the diverse needs of children 123

Skill 16.5 The selection of appropriate assessments for a given purpose 123

Skill 16.6 The use of informal assessments for the purpose of planning appropriate programs, environments, and interactions and adapting for individual differences 124

COMPETENCY 17.0 UNDERSTAND FORMAL ASSESSMENT STRATEGIES TO PLAN AND INDIVIDUALIZE CURRICULUM AND TEACHING PRACTICES 126

Skill 17.1 The selection, evaluation, and interpretation of formal, standardized assessment instruments and information used in the assessment of children 126

Skill 17.2 The integration of authentic classroom assessment data with formal assessment information 128

Skill 17.3 The use of formal assessments for the purpose of planning appropriate programs, environments, and interactions and adapting for individual differences 130

COMPETENCY 18.0 UNDERSTAND THE USE OF FORMATIVE AND SUMMATIVE PROGRAM EVALUATION TO ENSURE COMPREHENSIVE QUALITY OF THE TOTAL ENVIRONMENT, REFLECTING THE DIVERSITY OF CHILDREN, FAMILIES, AND COMMUNITY 132

Skill 18.1 The role of ongoing evaluations in program accountability and in making adjustments to the early childhood education program (e.g., curriculum, staffing, environment) 132

Skill 18.2 The awareness of local, state, and national standards for various program models 134

COMPETENCY 19.0 UNDERSTAND THE COMMUNICATION OF ASSESSMENT INFORMATION 136

Skill 19.1 Ways to communicate (e.g., checklists, portfolios, anecdotal records, progress reports, surveys) and their strengths and weaknesses 136

Skill 19.2 An understanding of a family's role as an active participant in the development, implementation, and interpretation of assessments 137

Skill 19.3 The communication of assessment information to children, families, and others 137

TEACHER CERTIFICATION STUDY GUIDE

SUBAREA V   **PROFESSIONAL AND PROGRAM LEADERSHIP**

COMPETENCY 20.0 UNDERSTAND THE FRAMEWORK OF THE EARLY CHILDHOOD PROFESSION 140

Skill 20.1   The multiple historical, philosophical, and social foundations of the early childhood profession and how these foundations influence current thought and practice 140

Skill 20.2   The profession's code of ethical conduct 143

Skill 20.3   Current research, trends, and issues in early childhood 145

COMPETENCY 21.0 UNDERSTAND THE DEVELOPMENT AND ROLE OF AN ARTICULATED PHILOSOPHY IN AN EARLY CHILDHOOD EDUCATION PROGRAM 147

Skill 21.1   Purposes for developing an articulated philosophy (e.g., shaping the early childhood curriculum, accountability) 147

Skill 21.2   Sources of input in creating the philosophy 147

Skill 21.3   Factors that should be reflected in the philosophy (e.g., research; national, state, and local goals, standards, and guidelines 147

Skill 21.4   Recognition of the diverse needs of children and their families) .. 148

Skill 21.5   The dissemination and application of the philosophy 149

COMPETENCY 22.0 UNDERSTAND THE ASPECTS OF EFFECTIVE ADVOCACY TO IMPROVE THE QUALITY OF SERVICES FOR YOUNG CHILDREN AND THEIR FAMILIES 151

Skill 22.1   The conditions of children, families, and professionals 151

Skill 22.2   Legal issues 151

Skill 22.3   Legislation and public policies affecting children, families, programs for young children, and the early childhood profession 155

Skill 22.4   Methods for improving the quality of programs and services for young children 156

Skill 22.5   Ways of enhancing professional status and improving working conditions for early childhood educators 157

COMPETENCY 23.0 UNDERSTAND HOW TO WORK WITH AND SUPERVISE COLLEAGUES AND OTHERS IN AN EARLY CHILDHOOD PROGRAM............................. 159

Skill 23.1   Strategies for coordinating activities with members of the classroom team, families, and the community (e.g., social services departments, administrators, other school personnel)................. 159

Skill 23.2   Appropriate roles and responsibilities of various personnel (e.g., paraprofessionals, associate teachers, volunteers)..................... 160

Skill 23.3   Types and sources of professional development activities and organizations that help maintain and improve the effectiveness of the early childhood education program 161

COMPETENCY 24.0 UNDERSTAND THE BASIC PRINCIPLES OF ADMINISTRATION, ORGANIZATION, AND OPERATION OF EARLY CHILDHOOD PROGRAMS 163

Skill 24.1 Local, state, and national standards, rules, and regulations regarding early childhood programs and work environments (e.g., licensing, accreditation, health and safety requirements) ... 163

Skill 24.2 Communication skills and techniques 164

Skill 24.3 Funding streams and funded programs such as Head Start 164

Skill 24.4 The enrollment, qualification, and recruitment of children 164

Skill 24.5 The responsibility and procedures for recognizing, reporting, and making referrals of children and families to other resources (e.g., other early childhood programs, child abuse prevention and treatment agencies) 165

Skill 24.6 Principles of management 165

Pre Test 167

Pre Test Answer Key 190

Pre Test Rigor Table 191

Pre Test Rationales with Sample Questions 192

Post Test 232

Post Test Answer Key 256

Post Test Rigor Table 257

Post Test Rationales with Sample Questions 258

TEACHER CERTIFICATION STUDY GUIDE

Great Study and Testing Tips!

What to study in order to prepare for the subject assessments is the focus of this study guide but equally important is *how* you study.

You can increase your chances of truly mastering the information by taking some simple, but effective, steps.

Study Tips:

1. <u>Some foods aid the learning process</u>. Foods such as milk, nuts, seeds, rice, and oats help your study efforts by releasing natural memory enhancers called CCKs (*cholecystokinin*) composed of *tryptophan*, *choline*, and *phenylalanine*. All of these chemicals enhance the neurotransmitters associated with memory. Before studying, try a light, protein-rich meal of eggs, turkey, and fish. All of these foods release the memory-enhancing chemicals. The better the connections, the more you comprehend.

Likewise, before you take a test, stick to a light snack of energy boosting and relaxing foods. A glass of milk, a piece of fruit, or some peanuts all release various memory-boosting chemicals and help you to relax and focus on the subject at hand.

2. <u>Learn to take great notes</u>. A by-product of our modern culture is that we have grown accustomed to getting our information in short doses (i.e. TV news sound bites or *USA Today*-style newspaper articles.)

Consequently, we've subconsciously trained ourselves to assimilate information better in <u>neat little packages</u>. If your notes are scrawled all over the paper, it fragments the flow of the information. Strive for clarity. Newspapers use a standard format to achieve clarity. Your notes can be much clearer through use of proper formatting. A very effective format is called <u>*"Cornell Method."*</u>

> Take a sheet of loose-leaf lined notebook paper and draw a line all the way down the paper about 1-2" from the left-hand edge.
>
> Draw another line across the width of the paper about 1-2" up from the bottom. Repeat this process on the reverse side of the page.

Look at the highly effective result. You have ample room for notes, a left-hand margin for special emphasis items or inserting supplementary data from the textbook, a large area at the bottom for a brief summary, and a little rectangular space for just about anything you want.

3. **Get the concept then the details**. Too often we focus on the details and don't gather an understanding of the concept. However, if you simply memorize only dates, places, or names, you may well miss the whole point of the subject.

A key way to understand things is to put them in your own words. If you are working from a textbook, automatically summarize each paragraph in your mind. If you are outlining text, don't simply copy the author's words.

Rephrase them in your own words. You remember your own thoughts and words much better than someone else's, and subconsciously tend to associate the important details to the core concepts.

4. **Ask Why?** Pull apart written material paragraph by paragraph and don't forget the captions under the illustrations.

Example: If the heading is "Stream Erosion," flip it around to read, "Why do streams erode?" Then answer the questions.

If you train your mind to think in a series of questions and answers, not only will you learn more, but it also helps to lessen the test anxiety because you are used to answering questions.

5. **Read for reinforcement and future needs**. Even if you only have ten minutes, put your notes or a book in your hand. Your mind is similar to a computer; you have to input data in order to have it processed. *By reading, you are creating the neural connections for future retrieval.* The more times you read something, the more you reinforce the learning of ideas.

Even if you don't fully understand something on the first pass, *your mind stores much of the material for later recall.*

6. **Relax to learn so go into exile.** Our bodies respond to an inner clock called biorhythms. Burning the midnight oil works well for some people, but not everyone.

If possible, set aside a particular place to study that is free of distractions. Shut off the television, cell phone, and pager and exile your friends and family during your study period.

If you really are bothered by silence, try background music. Light classical music at a low volume has been shown to aid in concentration over other types. Music that evokes pleasant emotions without lyrics is highly suggested. Try just about anything by Mozart. It relaxes you.

7. Use arrows not highlighters. At best, it's difficult to read a page full of yellow, pink, blue, and green streaks. Try staring at a neon sign for a while and you'll soon see that the horde of colors obscure the message.

A quick note, a brief dash of color, an underline, and an arrow pointing to a particular passage is much clearer than a horde of highlighted words.

8. Budget your study time. Although you shouldn't ignore any of the material, *allocate your available study time in the same ratio that topics may appear on the test.*

TEACHER CERTIFICATION STUDY GUIDE

Testing Tips:

1. Get smart, play dumb. Don't read anything into the question. Don't make an assumption that the test writer is looking for something else than what is asked. Stick to the question as written and don't read extra things into it.

2. Read the question and all the choices *twice* before answering the question. You may miss something by not carefully reading, and then re-reading, both the question and the answers.

If you really don't have a clue as to the right answer, leave it blank on the first time through. Go on to the other questions, as they may provide a clue as to how to answer the skipped questions.

If later on, you still can't answer the skipped ones . . . **Guess.** The only penalty for guessing is that you *might* get it wrong. Only one thing is certain; if you don't put anything down, you will get it wrong!

3. Turn the question into a statement. Look at the way the questions are worded. The syntax of the question usually provides a clue. Does it seem more familiar as a statement rather than as a question? Does it sound strange?

By turning a question into a statement, you may be able to spot if an answer sounds right, and it may also trigger memories of material you have read.

4. Look for hidden clues. It's actually very difficult to compose multiple-foil (choice) questions without giving away part of the answer in the options presented.

In most multiple-choice questions you can often readily eliminate one or two of the potential answers. This leaves you with only two real possibilities, and automatically your odds go to fifty-fifty for very little work.

5. Trust your instincts. For every fact that you have read, you subconsciously retain something of that knowledge. On questions that you aren't really certain about, go with your basic instincts. **Your first impression on how to answer a question is usually correct.**

6. **Mark your answers directly on the test booklet.** Don't bother trying to fill in the optical scan sheet on the first pass through the test.

Just be very careful not to miss-mark your answers when you eventually transcribe them to the scan sheet.

7. **Watch the clock!** You have a set amount of time to answer the questions. Don't get bogged down trying to answer a single question at the expense of 10 questions you can more readily answer.

THIS PAGE BLANK

TEACHER CERTIFICATION STUDY GUIDE

DOMAIN I. CHILD DEVELOPMENT AND LEARNING

COMPETENCY 1.0   UNDERSTAND THE PROCESSES OF CHILD GROWTH AND DEVELOPMENT (AGES BIRTH–8) AND THE INTEGRATED NATURE OF DEVELOPMENT ACROSS ALL DOMAINS

Skill 1.1   Physical growth and development, social-emotional development, cognitive development, language development, and aesthetic development

The teacher of students in early childhood should have a broad knowledge and understanding of the phases of development that typically occur during this stage of life. The teacher must also be aware of how receptive children are to specific methods of instruction and learning during each period of development. A significant premise in the study of child development holds that all domains of development (physical, social, and academic) are integrated. Development in each dimension is influenced by the others, and developmental advances within the domains do not necessarily occur simultaneously or parallel to one another.

Physical Development

Children experience rapid growth from the time they are born until the age of 2. During this time, they learn how to sit up, crawl and walk as their bodies grow stronger and larger at a very fast pace. From the ages of 2 to 5 years, the physical development slows down, but children are still developing. At age 2, children can go up and down stairs and can run, gaining more agility, rather than just toddling around. At age 3, they can jump, run, climb and ride a tricycle. They can screw and unscrew lids, use silverware to feed themselves, use blocks to build simple structures, turn pages one at a time and draw strokes on paper.

By age 4, a child can probably ride a bike with training wheels, hop on one foot and throw a ball overhand. At this stage, the child can use scissors, draw circles and squares and write some upper case letters correctly. Most 5 years olds can skip and do somersaults. At this age, most children can dress and undress themselves, draw stick people and write some lower case as well as upper case letters.

Even though children are quite active when they enter school at age 5, they are still developing physically. At times, they may seem to be all hands and legs and may be prone to falling or tripping, especially on the playground. Between the ages of 5 and 8, they develop more control over their muscles and are able to write and draw with more skill. They seem to possess boundless energy and in class, especially physical education class, they want to be very active. It is important for the teacher to be aware of the physical stages of development and how changes to the child's physical attributes (which include internal developments, increased muscle capacity, improved coordination and other attributes as well as obvious growth) affect the child's ability to learn. Factors determined by the physical stage of development include: ability to sit and attend, the need for activity, the relationship between physical coordination and self-esteem, and the degree to which physical involvement in an activity (as opposed to being able to understand an abstract concept) affects learning and the child's sense of achievement.

Cognitive (Academic) Development

Children go through patterns of learning beginning with pre-operational thought processes and move to concrete operational thoughts. Eventually, they begin to acquire the intellectual ability to contemplate and solve problems independently, when they mature enough to manipulate objects symbolically. Students in early childhood can use symbols such as words and numbers to represent objects and relations, but they need concrete reference points. Successful acquisition of the skills taught in early childhood, through the fourth grade, will progressively prepare the student for more advanced problem solving and abstract thinking in the later grades. The content of curriculum for younger students must be relevant for their stage of development (accessible and comprised of acquirable skills), engaging, and meaningful to the students.

Social Development

Children progress through a variety of social stages beginning with an awareness of self and self-concern. They soon develop an awareness of peers but demonstrate a lack of concern for their presence. For a time, young children engage in "parallel" activities, playing alongside their peers without directly interacting with one another.

During the primary years, children develop an intense interest in peers. They establish productive, positive, social and working relationships with one another. This area of social growth will continue to increase in significance throughout the child's academic career. The foundation for the students' successful development in this area is established through the efforts of the classroom teacher to plan and develop positive peer group relationships and to provide opportunities and support for cooperative small group projects that not only develop cognitive ability but promote peer interaction. The ability to work and relate effectively with peers contributes greatly to the child's sense of competence. In order to develop this sense of competence, children need to be successful in acquiring the information base and social skill sets which promote cooperative effort to achieve academic and social objectives.

High expectations for student achievement, which are age-appropriate and focused, provide the foundation for a teacher's positive relationship with young students and are consistent with effective instructional strategies. It is equally important to determine what is appropriate for specific individuals in the classroom, and approach classroom groups and individual students with an understanding and respect for their emerging capabilities. Those who study childhood development recognize that young students grow and mature in common, recognizable patterns, but at different rates which cannot be effectively accelerated. This can result in variance in the academic performance of different children in the same classroom. With the establishment of inclusion as a standard in the classroom, it is necessary for all teachers to understand that variation in development among the student population is another aspect of diversity within the classroom. And this has implications for the ways in which instruction is planned and delivered and the ways in which students learn and are evaluated.

Language Development

In everyday language, we attach affective meanings to words unconsciously; we exercise more conscious control of informative connotations. In the process of language development, the student must come not only to grasp the definitions of words but also to become more conscious of the affective connotations and how his listeners process these connotations. Gaining this conscious control over language makes it possible to use language appropriately in various situations and to evaluate its uses in literature and other forms of communication.

The manipulation of language for a variety of purposes is the goal of language instruction. Advertisers and satirists are especially conscious of the effect word choice has on their audiences. By evoking the proper responses from readers/listeners, we can prompt them to take action.

The development of speaking and listening skills requires intensive attention to make sure that children acquire a good stock of words, learn to listen attentively, and to speak clearly and confidently. In many instances however, students with speech and listening disabilities will experience speaking and listening difficulties.

For more information on speech/language acquisition and delays, **SEE** Skill 8.1

Aesthetic Development

Aesthetic development refers to a sensory appreciation of things in the environment. Although it is closely associated with appreciation of art and music, young children can rarely judge whether art or music is good or bad, but they can tell you if they like or dislike something.

Aesthetic development also refers to the child's experience with music and the arts. By the time they come to school, children should be able to sing simple songs and recognize well-known children's stories. This development, however, does not occur in all homes.

Aesthetic development can be nurtured in the early childhood classroom by:
- Having children listen to music and stories for enjoyment
- Using personal movement to display feelings
- Performing simple plays and encouraging pretend play (drama)
- Creating images inspired by stories or personal experiences

Skill 1.2   Chronological age versus developmental age

Chronological age refers to the exact age of the child in years and months from the date of birth. This may be higher or lower than the developmental level of the child. Developmental level refers to the age at which children display traits, such as being able to socially interact with other children or be able to print or read. Some children may be right on target and others may lag behind in development, just as there are children who may be far ahead in their development and be able to do these things at an earlier age.

Students are tested before they enter school and during their school years to determine if there is a gap between chronological age and developmental level. Teachers then take the steps necessary to provide the supports the children need in order to narrow this gap. Some children may not take very long to catch up with their peers, but others may need extra help all the way through the school years. For children who are more advanced, supports should also be put in place to challenge them in ways that fit their developmental age. However, the chronological age of the child must be kept in mind when planning activities so as not to introduce topics to children beyond their years.

SEE Skill 1.1 for the various developmental levels.

Skill 1.3   Individual differences in development

Knowledge of age-appropriate expectations is fundamental to the teacher's positive relationship with students and effective instructional strategies. Equally important is the knowledge of what is individually appropriate for the specific children in a classroom. Developmentally oriented teachers approach classroom groups and individual students with a respect for their emerging capabilities. Developmentalists recognize that kids grow in common patterns, but at different rates which usually cannot be accelerated by adult pressure or input. Developmentally oriented teachers know that variance in the school performance of different children often results from differences in their general growth. With the establishment of inclusionary classes throughout the schools, it is vital for all teachers to know the characteristics of students' exceptionalities and their implications on learning.

The effective teacher takes care to select appropriate activities and classroom situations in which learning is optimized. The classroom teacher should manipulate instructional activities and classroom conditions in a manner that enhances group and individual learning opportunities. For example, the classroom teacher can organize group learning activities in which students are placed in a situation in which cooperation, sharing ideas, and discussion occurs. Cooperative learning activities can assist students in learning to collaborate and share personal and cultural ideas and values in a classroom learning environment.

If an educational program is child-centered, it will address the abilities and needs of the students because it will take its cues from students' interests, concerns, and questions. Making an educational program child-centered involves building on the natural curiosity children bring to school, and asking children what they want to learn.

Teachers help students to identify their own questions, puzzles, and goals, and then structure for them widening circles of experience and investigation of those topics. Teachers manage to infuse all the skills, knowledge, and concepts that society mandates into a child-driven curriculum. This does not mean passive teachers who respond only to students' explicit cues. Teachers also draw on their understanding of children's developmentally characteristic needs and enthusiasms to design experiences that lead children into areas they might not choose, but that they do enjoy and that engage them. Teachers also bring their own interests and enthusiasms into the classroom to share and to act as a motivational means of guiding children.

Skill 1.4 **The effect of development in one domain on development in other domains**

Child development does not occur in a vacuum. Each element of development impacts other elements of development. For example, as cognitive development progresses, social development often follows. The reason for this is that all areas of development are fairly inter-related. As babies, children develop at different rates. Some crawl, stand and walk quicker than others. When they come to school, some children can carry on a conversation or read a book, but they may have difficulty using scissors. As children develop physically, they develop the dexterity to demonstrate cognitive development, such as writing something on a piece of paper (in this case, this is cognitive development that only can be demonstrated by physical development), or, as they develop emotionally, they learn to be more sensitive to others and therefore enhance social development.

What does this mean for teachers? The concept of latent development is particularly important. While teachers may not see some aspects of development present in their students, other areas of development may give clues as to a child's current or near-future capabilities. For example, as students' linguistic development increases, observable ability may not be present (i.e., a student may know a word but cannot quite use it yet). As the student develops emotionally and socially, the ability to use more advanced words and sentence structures develops because the student will have a greater need to express him or herself.

In general, by understanding that developmental domains are not exclusive, teachers can identify current needs of students better, and they can plan for future instructional activities meant to assist students as they develop into adults.

TEACHER CERTIFICATION STUDY GUIDE

COMPETENCY 2.0   **UNDERSTAND HOW YOUNG CHILDREN DIFFER IN THEIR DEVELOPMENT AND APPLY THIS UNDERSTANDING TO SUPPORT THE DEVELOPMENT AND LEARNING OF INDIVIDUAL CHILDREN**

Skill 2.1   **Conditions that affect children's development and learning (e.g., risk factors, developmental variations, developmental patterns)**

In today's push toward academic achievement and standards, it is easy to forget the importance of the development of a child's emotional and physical growth and health. New teachers may be tempted to just teach faster or harder for fear that if they don't, their students will not learn. Yet, all teachers must remember that child development plays a huge part in the academic development of individuals.

While all children develop at different rates, and every child will have unique attributes, teachers have a responsibility to note concerns regarding the emotional or physical states of their students. Indeed, this is a legal responsibility of teachers, particularly where abuse is noted. Yet, other concerns may be justifiable for discussion with counselors or administrators, as well.

SEE also Skills 1.3 and 1.4

Risk Factors

When children are subjected to physical or emotional abuse, their development and learning suffers. If abuse is suspected, the best action is to immediately contact a superior at the school. The impact of abuse of a child's development in is often extensive. Abused children can be socially withdrawn, and typically, as one might suspect, their minds will not always be on their schoolwork. Significant emotional damage occurs as well, and teachers may notice very awkward social behavior around other children and adults. When reporting suspected abuse, teachers should remember that a student's privacy is extremely important.

Physical health can also effect learning and development. Prenatal or childhood exposure to drugs, alcohol, or nicotine can result in moderate to severe brain damage. More subtle impairment can also occur (trouble with breathing, attention deficit disorder, etc.). Because drugs, alcohol, and nicotine can impair brain development, children exposed to such things in the womb may need significant extra classroom support. Some of these children will also need to be referred to the Special Education teacher in order to be tested for learning disabilities.

Day-to-day issues, such as lack of sufficient sleep or nutrition, can harm children in a more temporal fashion. Symptoms of a lack of nutrition and sleep most notably include a lack of concentration, particularly in the classroom. Children who lack sufficient sleep or nutrition may also become agitated more easily than other children. While a child who has had sleep disruptions or insufficient nutrition can bounce back easily when these things are attended to, it is often the case that children living in environments where sleep and proper nutrition are not available will continue to struggle in school. Through federal and local funds, many schools are able to provide free or reduced-price breakfasts and lunches for children, however, consider that if this is a necessity, such children may not get a decent dinner, and during weekends and holidays, may struggle even more.

When a child has had little verbal interaction in the home, the symptoms can be rather similar to the symptoms of abuse or neglect. The child might have a "deer in the headlights" look and maintain a very socially awkward set of behaviors. In general, such a child will have a drastically reduced ability to express him or herself in words, and often, aggression can be a better tool for the child to get his or her thoughts across.

In early elementary school, children are particularly affected by emotional upsets in family structure, and they are susceptible to emotional harm when they are not cared for in an appropriate manner at home. When children are emotionally neglected or have recently endured family upsets, the level of attention toward school will be greatly reduced. They may also show signs of jealousy of other children, or they may feel a sense of anger toward other children, the teacher, or their parents. Aggression is a very common behavior of emotionally-neglected children.

Although cognitive ability is not lost due to such circumstances (abuse, neglect, emotional upset, lack of verbal interaction), the child will most likely not be able to provide as much intellectual energy as the child would if none of these things were present. But, also note that the classroom can be seen as a "safe" place by a child, so it is imperative that teachers be attentive to the needs and emotions of their students.

In summary, it is always a good idea for teachers to pay attention to the abnormalities in behavior of children, or even sudden drop-offs in achievement or attention, and notify superiors at the school with concerns.

Skill 2.2 Strategies to create and modify environments and experiences to meet the individual needs of all children, including those with disabilities, developmental delays, and special abilities

No two students are alike. It follows, then, that no students *learn* alike. To apply a one dimensional instructional approach and a strict tunnel vision perspective of testing is to impose learning limits on students. All students have the right to an education, but there cannot be a singular path to that education. A teacher must acknowledge the variety of learning styles and abilities among students within a class (and, indeed, the varieties from class to class) and apply multiple instructional and assessment processes to ensure that every child has appropriate opportunities to master the subject matter, demonstrate such mastery, and improve and enhance learning skills with each lesson.

Students' attitudes and perceptions about learning are the most powerful factors influencing academic focus and success. When instructional objectives center on students' interests and are relevant to their lives, effective learning occurs. Learners must believe that the tasks that they are asked to perform have some value and that they have the ability and resources to perform them. If a student thinks a task is unimportant, he/she will not put much effort into it. If a student thinks he lacks the ability or resources to successfully complete a task, even attempting the task becomes too great a risk. Not only must the teacher understand the students' abilities and interests, she must also help students develop positive attitudes and perceptions about tasks and learning.

Differentiated Instruction

The effective teacher will seek to connect all students to the subject matter through multiple techniques, with the goal that each student, through their own abilities, will relate to one or more techniques and excel in the learning process. Differentiated instruction encompasses several areas:

- Content: What is the teacher going to teach? Or, perhaps better put, what does the teacher want the students to learn? Differentiating content means that students will have access to content that piques their interest about a topic, with a complexity that provides an appropriate challenge to their intellectual development.
- Process: A classroom management technique where instructional organization and delivery is maximized for the diverse student group. These techniques should include dynamic, flexible grouping activities, where instruction and learning occurs both as whole-class, teacher-led activities, as well as peer learning and teaching (while teacher observes and coaches) within small groups or pairs.
- Product: The expectations and requirements placed on students to demonstrate their knowledge or understanding. The type of product expected from each student should reflect each student's own capabilities.

Teachers are learning the value of giving assignments that meet the individual abilities and needs of students. After instruction, discussion, questioning, and practice have been provided, rather than assigning one task to all students—teachers are asking students to generate tasks that will show their knowledge of the information presented. Students are given choices and thereby have the opportunity to demonstrate more effectively the skills, concepts, or topics that they as individuals have learned. It has been established that student choice increases student originality, intrinsic motivation, and higher mental processes.

Students Learning English

A diverse classroom should also address children who are learning English. Cognitive approaches to language learning focus on concepts. While words and grammar are important, when teachers use the cognitive approach, they focus on using language for conceptual purposes—rather than learning words and grammar for the sake of simply learning new words and grammatical structures.

Another very common motivational approach is Total Physical Response. This is a kinesthetic approach that combines language learning and physical movement. In essence, students learn new vocabulary and grammar by responding with physical motion to verbal commands. Some people say it is particularly effective because the physical actions create good brain connections with the words.

In general, the best methods do not treat students as if they have a language deficit. Rather, the best methods build upon what students already know, and they help to instill the target language as a communicative process rather than a list of vocabulary words that have to be memorized.

Students with Learning Challenges

Common learning disabilities include attention deficit hyperactivity disorder (where concentration can be very tough), auditory processing disorders (where listening comprehension is very difficult), visual processing disorders (where reading can be tough and visual memory may be impaired), dyslexia (where reading can be confusing), and many others. Physical disabilities include Down's Syndrome, where mental retardation may be a factor; cerebral palsy, where physical movement is impaired; and many others. Developmental disabilities might include the lack of ability to use fine motor skills.

IDEA 2004 defines *a child with a disability. . . as having mental retardation, a hearing impairment (including deafness), a speech or language impairment, a visual impairment (including blindness), a serious emotional disturbance (referred to in this part as emotional disturbance), an orthopedic impairment, autism, traumatic brain injury, an other health impairment, a specific learning disability, deaf-blindness, or multiple disabilities, and who, by reason thereof, needs special education and related services.*

Eligibility for special education services is based on a student having one of the above disabilities (or a combination thereof) and demonstration of educational need through professional evaluation. Special educators should be knowledgeable of the cause and severity of the disability and its manifestations in the specific student when planning an appropriate special education program. Because of the unique needs of the child, such programs are documented in the child's IEP – Individualized Education Program.

Seldom does a student with a disability fall into only one of the characteristics listed in IDEA 2004. For example, a student with a hearing impairment may also have a specific learning disability, or a student on the autism spectrum may also demonstrate language impairment. In fact, language impairment is inherent in autism. Sometimes the eligibility is defined as multiple disabilities (with one listed as a primary eligibility on the IEP and the others listed as secondary). Sometimes there are overlapping needs that are not necessarily listed as a secondary disability.

Most special needs students have an Individual Educational Plan or a 504 Plan. These documents clearly state the students' educational objectives and learning needs as well as persons responsible for meeting these objectives. A well-written Individual Educational Plan will contain evidence that the student is receiving resources from the school and the community that will assist in meeting the physical, social and academic needs of the student.

Students with disabilities (in all areas) may demonstrate difficulty in social skills. For a student with a hearing impairment, social skills may be difficult because of not hearing social language. However, the emotionally disturbed student may have difficulty because of a special type of psychological disturbance. An autistic student, as a third example, would be unaware of the social cues given with voice, facial expression, and body language. Each of these students would need social skill instruction but in a different way.

Students with disabilities (in all areas) may demonstrate difficulty in academic skills. A student with mental retardation will need special instruction across all areas of academics while a student with a learning disability may need assistance in only one or two subject areas.

Students with disabilities may demonstrate difficulty with independence or self-help skills. A student with a visual impairment may need specific mobility training while a student with a specific learning disability may need a checklist to help in managing materials and assignments.

Special education teachers should be aware that although students across disabilities may demonstrate difficulty in similar ways, the causes may be very different. For example, some disabilities are due to specific sensory impairments (hearing or vision), some due to cognitive ability (mental retardation), and some due to neurological impairment (autism or some learning disabilities). The reason for the difficulty should be a consideration when planning the program of special education intervention.

Additionally, special education teachers should be aware that each area of disability has a range of involvement. Some students may have minimal disability and require no services. Others may need only a few accommodations and have a 504 plan. Some may need an IEP that outlines a specific special education program which might be implemented in an inclusion/resource program, self-contained program, or in a residential setting.

A student with ADD may be able to participate in the regular education program with a 504 plan that outlines a checklist system to keep the student organized and additional communication between school and home. Other students with ADD may need instruction in a smaller group with fewer distractions and would be better served in a resource room.

The challenges of meeting the needs of all students in the classroom require that the teacher is a lifelong learner. Ongoing participation in professional staff development, attendance at local, state, and national conferences, and continuing education classes help teachers grow in many ways including an awareness of resources available for students.

Advanced Students

Students with disabilities are not the only ones who require adjusted instruction in a classroom. Oftentimes advanced/gifted students or the needs of students with exceptional talents are left unaddressed because the teacher assumes the students do not require additional instruction because they are so bright and handle assignments well. Not to say that the teacher purposely does this, but with the high demands teaching, it is often the case that teachers are so overtaxed that these students just are not as high on the instructional priority list as they should be. In other words, these students are not being encouraged to achieve to their fullest potential. Instead, these students often become bored with school as their coursework fails to challenge them. This can lead to the common problem of underachievement among talented learners.

Gifted students are typically most identifiable by the three following characteristics:

- They master concepts and assignments much more quickly than others, and therefore, are left with open time.
- They inquire about assignments, ideas and concepts at a higher level than other classmates; they may even seek further direction on assignments.
- They maintain interests in unique topics or in areas that are of interest to older students.

Depending on the student, free time can be spent in many ways including: being bored, being mischievous or reading or doing some other task. The effective teacher will ensure that these students have additional tasks to complete that perhaps compliment a current assignment. For example, suppose an advanced second-grade student completed his or her reading assignment. To modify this child's instruction, a teacher may propose one or more of the following directions (according to the student's interest):

- Research the author
- Connect the theme of this book to other books the child has read and complete a Venn diagram comparing and contrasting the books
- Design a poster that illustrates the book's theme
- Complete a computer presentation about the story
- Transform the story into a play
- Compose a musical piece that reflects the mood of a scene in the book
- Create a game based on the book for others to play
- Write a story following the same theme of the book
- Write another ending to the book
- Create a brochure that promotes the book

It is important to recognize advanced learners in more than just the traditional areas. Typically, students who excel in reading, writing and math are more easily recognized because of standardized testing results, as well as the fact that this is where most of early childhood education falls. However, students may show significant achievement in all areas including music, drama, art, social skills, science and other areas.

TEACHER CERTIFICATION STUDY GUIDE

COMPETENCY 3.0   **UNDERSTAND THE SIGNIFICANCE OF DIVERSITY FOR CHILD DEVELOPMENT AND LEARNING**

Skill 3.1   **Recognition that children are best understood in the contexts of family, culture, and society**

Effective teaching and learning for students begins with teachers who can demonstrate sensitivity for diversity in teaching and relationships within school communities. Teachers should also continuously make cultural connections that are relevant and empowering for all students and communicate academic and behavioral expectations.

Teachers must establish a classroom climate that is culturally respectful and engaging for students. In a culturally sensitive classroom, teachers maintain equity and fairness in student interactions and curriculum implementation. Assessments include cultural responses and perspectives that become further learning opportunities for students.

Other artifacts that could reflect teacher/student sensitivity to diversity might consist of the following:

- Student portfolios reflecting multicultural/multiethnic perspectives
- Journals and reflections from field trips/ guest speakers from diverse cultural backgrounds
- Printed materials and wall displays from multicultural perspectives
- Parent/guardian letters in a variety of languages reflecting cultural diversity
- Projects that include cultural history and diverse inclusions
- Disaggregated student data reflecting cultural groups
- Classroom climate of professionalism that fosters diversity and cultural inclusion

Skill 3.2   **The interrelationships among culture, language, and thought**

There are many uses for language, including communicating knowledge, reporting emotions, making requests, and others. Language is also important for building social cohesion and an ability to understand another person's culture. Our daily "small talk" enables strangers to become more comfortable with each other, and to find subjects they agree upon, (such as the weather or sports). With each new agreement, no matter how commonplace or obvious, the fear and suspicion of the stranger wears away, and the possibility of friendship enlarges.

Teachers must create personalized learning communities where every student is a valued member and contributor of the classroom experiences. In classrooms where socio-cultural attributes of the student population are incorporated into the fabric of the learning process, dynamic interrelationships are created that enhance the learning experience and the personalization of learning. When students are provided with numerous academic and social opportunities to share cultural incorporations into the learning, everyone in the classroom benefits from bonding through shared experiences and having an expanded viewpoint of a world experience and culture that vastly differs from their own.

Researchers continue to show that personalized learning environments increase the learning affect for students; decrease drop-out rates among marginalized students; and decrease unproductive student behavior which can result from constant cultural misunderstandings or miscues between students. Promoting diversity of learning and cultural competency in the classroom for students and teachers creates a world of multicultural opportunities and learning. When students are able to step outside their comfort zones and share the world of a homeless student or empathize with an English Language Learner (ELL) student who has just immigrated to the United States and is learning English for the first time, then students grow exponentially in social understanding and cultural connectedness.

Teachers should also continuously make cultural connections that are relevant and empowering for all students and communicate academic and behavioral expectations. Cultural sensitivity is communicated beyond the classroom with parents and community members to establish and maintain relationships.

Teachers must establish a classroom climate that is culturally respectful and engaging for students. In a culturally sensitive classroom, teachers maintain equity and fairness in student interactions and curriculum implementation. Assessments include cultural responses and perspectives that become further learning opportunities for students.

Skill 3.3   The function of home language in the development of young children

The language used in the home, whether it is English or another language, is important to the development of young children. When the child's mother tongue is a language other than English, this diversity must also be celebrated in the classroom. To reject the language is to reject the child. Being able to speak more than one language has a positive effect on the child's development. In the early childhood years, they gain a deeper understanding of language and how to use it effectively. When they have a chance to practice both languages, they can develop literacy in both.

Teachers should also be aware of how proficient the child is in their first language. When children are proficient in their home language as well as the second language, they are able to relate the stories of their parents and grandparents and this helps to infuse their cultural identity into the classroom. When they have a good grasp of the vocabulary and concepts of their first language, they are better able to grasp the vocabulary and concepts of the second language.

It is quite easy for children to lose their home language in the early years. Therefore, teachers should allow them to use their language along with the second language as much as possible. When students can do something in one language, it easily transfers to the second language and therefore the teacher knows that the child understands the concept. An example of this is telling time. When a child can tell the time in one language, he/she understands how to tell time. Teachers should get the message across to the students about how important it is in today's society to be able to speak more than one language. They should also encourage parents to communicate in both languages at home and not concentrate on the child learning and using the second language at home 100% of the time.

Skill 3.4   The importance of creating a supportive and nurturing environment for all children

The primary responsibility of the classroom teacher is to ensure that all aspects of the educational process, and all information necessary to master specified skills, are readily accessible by all students in the classroom. In the classroom, the teacher must actively promote inclusion and devise presentations which address commonalities among heterogeneous groups.

Initially, the teacher must take the time to know each student as an individual, and demonstrate a sincere interest in each student. Getting to know the student's background/cultural traditions helps to build a rapport with each student, as well as further educate the teacher about the world in which he or she teaches. For example, it is important to know the correct spelling and pronunciation of each student's name, and any preference in how the student would like to be addressed. Lesson plans should provide time for interaction in the classroom, when the teacher and the class can become familiar with each student's interests and experiences. This will help the teacher and the students avoid making assumptions based on any individual's background or appearance.

Encourage all students to respond to each other's questions and statements, in the classroom. Be prepared to respond, appropriately, should any issue or question regarding diversity arise during classroom discussions or activities. If necessary to promote or control discussion in the classroom, the teacher should provide the students with specific guidelines (which are easy to understand and to follow, at their level) defining the intended objectives and any restrictions. Inclusion means involving everyone in classroom discussions. The teacher should allow the students to volunteer, and then call on the more reluctant students to provide additional information or opinions. All opinions (which are not derogatory in case or by nature) are valid and should be reinforced as such by the teacher's approval.

When planning instruction for a diverse group (or teaching about diversity, for that matter) incorporate teaching through the use of perspective. There is always more than one way to "see" or approach a problem, an example, a process, fact or event, or any learning situation. Varying approaches for instruction helps to maintain the students' interest in the material and enables the teacher to address the diverse needs of individuals to comprehend the material.

SEE also Skill 3.2

TEACHER CERTIFICATION STUDY GUIDE

COMPETENCY 4.0 UNDERSTAND THAT CHILDREN, THROUGH PLAY, CONSTRUCT KNOWLEDGE BY EXPLORING AND INTERACTING WITH OBJECTS, MATERIALS, AND PEOPLE IN THEIR ENVIRONMENT AND THAT PLAY REFLECTS DEVELOPMENT

Skill 4.1 Ways in which children construct and expand concepts

There are several educational learning theories that can be applied to classroom practices. One classic learning theory is Piaget's stages of development which consist of four learning stages: sensory motor stage (from birth to age 2); pre-operation stages (ages 2 to 7 or early elementary); concrete operational (ages 7 to 11 or upper elementary); and formal operational (ages 7-15 or late elementary/high school). Piaget believed children passed through this series of stages to develop from the most basic forms of concrete thinking to sophisticated levels of abstract thinking.

Some of the most prominent learning theories in education today include brain-based learning and the Multiple Intelligence Theory. Supported by recent brain research, brain-based learning suggests that knowledge about the way the brain retains information enables educators to design the most effective learning environments. As a result, researchers have developed twelve principles that relate knowledge about the brain to teaching practices. These twelve principles are:

- The brain is a complex adaptive system
- The brain is social
- The search for meaning is innate
- We use patterns to learn more effectively
- Emotions are crucial to developing patterns
- Each brain perceives and creates parts and whole simultaneously
- Learning involves focused and peripheral attention
- Learning involves conscious and unconscious processes
- We have at least two ways of organizing memory
- Learning is developmental
- Complex learning is enhanced by challenge (and inhibited by threat)
- Every brain is unique

(Caine & Caine, 1994, Mind/Brain Learning Principles)

Educators can use these principles to help design methods and environments in their classrooms to maximize student learning.

The Multiple Intelligence Theory, developed by Howard Gardner, suggests that students learn in (at least) seven different ways. These include visually/spatially, musically, verbally, logically/mathematically, interpersonally, intrapersonally, and bodily/kinesthetically. Gardner later added an eighth intelligence. The naturalist intelligence refers to the ability to recognize and classify plants, minerals, and animals, including rocks and grass and all variety of flora and fauna. When teachers take individual differences among kids seriously, they are better able to plan lessons that interest children and to help them use their minds well.

The most current learning theory of constructivist learning allows students to construct learning opportunities. For constructivist teachers, the belief is that students create their own reality of knowledge and how to process and observe the world around them. Students are constantly constructing new ideas, which serve as frameworks for learning and teaching. Researchers have shown that the constructivist model is comprised of the four components:

1. Learner creates knowledge
2. Learner constructs and makes meaningful new knowledge to existing knowledge
3. Learner shapes and constructs knowledge by life experiences and social interactions
4. In constructivist learning communities, the student, teacher and classmates establish knowledge cooperatively on a daily basis.

Constructivist learning for students is dynamic and ongoing. For constructivist teachers, the classroom becomes a place where students are encouraged to interact with the instructional process by asking questions and posing new ideas to old theories. The use of cooperative learning that encourages students to work in supportive learning environments using their own ideas to stimulate questions and propose outcomes is a major aspect of a constructivist classroom.

The metacognition learning theory deals with "the study of how to help the learner gain understanding about how knowledge is constructed and about the conscious tools for constructing that knowledge" (Joyce and Weil 1996). The cognitive approach to learning involves the teacher's understanding that teaching the student to process his/her own learning and mastery of skill provides the greatest learning and retention opportunities in the classroom. Students are taught to develop concepts and teach themselves skills in problem solving and critical thinking. The student becomes an active participant in the learning process and the teacher facilitates that conceptual and cognitive learning process.

In 1956, Benjamin Bloom, an educational psychologist developed a detailed classification of critical thinking and learning skills/objectives into tiered levels. These hierarchal levels ordered thinking skills from the simplest (or lower-ordered) thinking skills to the highest (or higher-ordered) thinking skills. The goal of Bloom's taxonomy was to motivate teachers to teach at all levels of critical thinking and not just at the most common level – the lower-ordered thinking skills such as memorizing, restating, or defining.

For the six levels of Bloom's taxonomy, **SEE** Skill 4.3

Social and behavioral theories look at the social interactions of students in the classroom that instruct or impact learning opportunities in the classroom. The psychological approaches behind both theories are subject to individual variables that are learned and applied either proactively or negatively in the classroom. The stimulus of the classroom can promote conducive learning or evoke behavior that is counterproductive for both students and teachers. Students are social beings that normally gravitate to action in the classroom, so teachers must be cognizant in planning classroom environments that provide both focus and engagement in maximizing learning opportunities.

Designing classrooms that provide optimal academic and behavioral support for a diversity of students in the classroom can be daunting for teachers. The ultimate goal for both students and teachers is creating a safe learning environment where students can construct knowledge in an engaging and positive classroom climate of learning.

No one of these theories will work for every classroom, and a good approach is to incorporate a range of learning styles in a classroom. Still, under the guidance of any theory, good educators will differentiate their instructional practices to meet the needs of their students' abilities and interests using various instructional practices.

Skill 4.2 Activities and resources that encourage children to explore, to manipulate, to understand relationships, and to use symbols

Until pre-adolescence, students do not think in abstract forms. Sure, they are able to understand symbols, but deep symbolism is not yet comprehended. For example, language is a symbol, and they can understand that certain words symbolize things, actions, emotions, etc. But they do not yet have the ability to see how symbolism works in a story as well as an adolescent would.

When we say that young children are concrete thinkers, we mean that they are driven by senses. In other words, they are very literal thinkers. If they can see something, hear something, or feel something, they are more likely to believe it—and learn it.

Therefore, the more teachers can utilize this concrete thinking, the better their students will master grade-level standards at this age. Let's take the example of math. Ever wonder why young children always count with their fingers? This is because, even though they might be able to do it in their heads, seeing it (and feeling it, as they move their fingers) makes it more "real" to them. So, instead of teaching math through words and numbers on a chalkboard, teachers can be more effective at teaching math through manipulatives.

By simply putting objects on a table, having students count the objects, taking away a certain number and having them re-count the left-over objects, students are more likely to understand the CONCEPT of subtraction.

Many reading teachers have learned that students can comprehend stories better if they get a chance to dramatize the story. In other words, they "act out" a story, and thereby learn what the words mean more clearly than they could have if they just read it and talked about it.

The whole concept of science laboratory learning in elementary school is founded on the idea that students will be more successful learning concepts if they use their hands, eyes, ears, noses, etc., in the learning process. Many concepts that would otherwise be very difficult for students to learn can be attained very quickly in a laboratory setting.

Skill 4.3   Problem-solving strategies

Students use basic skills to understand things that are read such as a reading passage or a math word problem or directions for a project. However, students apply additional thinking skills to fully comprehend how what was read could be applied to their own life or how to make comparatives or choices based on the factual information given.

These higher-order thinking skills are called critical thinking skills as students "think about thinking." Teachers can help students use these skills in everyday activities:
- Comparing shopping ads or catalogue deals
- Finding the main idea from readings
- Applying what's been learned to new situations
- Gathering information/data from a diversity of sources to plan a project
- Following a sequence of directions
- Looking for cause and effect relationships
- Comparing and contrasting information in synthesizing information

As discussed in Skill 4.1, Benjamin Blooms outlined six levels of thinking. The six levels of Bloom's taxonomy and the skills each entails, from simplest to most complex, are as follows:

- **Knowledge:** This level is the most basic level of learning where students learn terminology and specific facts; tasks at this level ask students to define, label, recall, memorize, and list
- **Understanding/Comprehension:** This level of learning requires students grasp the meaning of a concept; tasks at this level ask students to classify, explain, identify, locate, and review
- **Application:** This level of learning requires students to take previous learning and utilize it in a new way; tasks at this level ask students to demonstrate, illustrate, distinguish, solve, write, choose, and dramatize
- **Analysis:** This level of learning involves the breakdown of material to its component parts and requires students to utilize those parts; tasks at this level ask students to calculate, categorize, compare, contrast, criticize, distinguish, examine, and experiment
- **Synthesis:** This level of learning requires students to take the analyzed parts from the previous level and converge them into creative new wholes; tasks at this level ask students to collect, compose, design, manage, plan, organize, and formulate
- **Evaluation:** This is the highest level of learning on the taxonomy, and according to research, is the level that is least often achieved. This level of learning requires students to judge the value of material based on experience, prior knowledge, opinions, and/or the resulting product; tasks at this level ask students to assess, appraise, predict, rate, support, evaluate, judge, and argue

Since most teachers want their educational objectives to use higher level thinking skills, teachers need to direct students to these higher levels on the taxonomy. Questioning is an effective tool to build up students to these higher levels.

Low order questions are useful to begin the process. They insure the student is focused on the required information and understands what needs to be included in the thinking process. For example, if the objective is for students to be able to read and understand the story "Goldilocks and the Three Bears," the teacher may wish to start with low order questions (i.e., "What are some things Goldilocks did while in the bears home?" [Knowledge] or "Why didn't Goldilocks like the Papa Bear's chair?" [Analysis]).

Through a series of questions, the teacher can move the students up the taxonomy and control the thinking process of the class. (For example, "If Goldilocks had come to your house, what are some things she may have used?" [Application], "How might the story differ if Goldilocks had visited the three fishes?" [Synthesis], or "Do you think Goldilocks was good or bad? Why?" [Evaluation]).

The effective teacher uses advanced communication skills such as clarification, reflection, perception, and summarization as a means to facilitate communication. Teachers who couple diversity in instructional practices with engaging and challenging curriculum and the latest advances in technology can create the ultimate learning environment for creative thinking and continuous learning for students. Teachers who are innovative and creative in instructional practices are able to model and foster creative thinking in their students. Encouraging students to maintain journals and portfolios of their valued work from projects and assignments will allow students to make conscious choices on including a diversity of their creative endeavors in a filing format that can be treasured throughout the educational journey.

A classroom atmosphere that frowns on closed-mindedness and rewards openness to new and different approaches and ideas is powerful in shaping students' attitudes. Many of them will come from homes that display narrow-minded thinking and frequent criticism of differences, so there will be obstacles. However, the classroom can be powerful in the development of children's future attitudes and philosophies; and even though some students seem intractable, it's important to keep in mind that the experience of participating in a free and open classroom will have effect in the long run.

Skill 4.4 Strategies to help children reflect on their own thinking processes (metacognition)

For each unit that will be used, the teacher should consider the component parts and ask the question, "What response do I want from the students at this point? Contemplation? Questions? Discussion or other activity? Writing or testing?" Based on his or her answer, the teacher should be able to approximate the effort involved and plan adequate time, accordingly. The same process would be used when the teacher designs and develops her or his own units or adopts them from another source.

The needs of the students for personal review and reflection, or self-assessment, or to internalize ideas, information or skills, or to achieve a sense of completion, should be recognized as valid, identified in the particular, and allocated appropriate time.

Purposes for allocating such time to students would include:

- After difficult or complex tasks or skills have been introduced
- After difficult or complex tasks or skills have been utilized
- After technically difficult or complex instructional materials have been introduced
- After technically difficult or complex instructional materials have been utilized
- After independent research has been conducted by students
- After student reports or presentations to the class
- After returning graded examinations, assignments or other evaluations to students
- After planned classroom activities and discussions
- After presentation or instruction on life skills, social skills, at-risk behaviors, etc.

For all students, even those in early childhood classes a learning log is helpful in having the students think about what they learned. At the end of a class or at the end of the day, the students have to write about one thing they learned and whether or not they think there is something else they would like to know.

Before beginning a new unit, many teachers use a K-W-L chart. Although this is to assess prior knowledge and set the tone for the unit, when the unit is finished the students also have to tell what they learned.

When students complete a task, whether it is a worksheet, a piece of writing or artwork or a group project, they can also complete a sheet that tells about their learning. They can choose smiley faces or sad faces to tell whether or not they did their best work, whether they understood the concept and tell what they would like to work on next.

TEACHER CERTIFICATION STUDY GUIDE

DOMAIN II.   **CURRICULUM DEVELOPMENT AND IMPLEMENTATION**

COMPETENCY 5.0   **UNDERSTAND HOW TO PLAN AND IMPLEMENT DEVELOPMENTALLY APPROPRIATE CURRICULUM AND INSTRUCTIONAL PRACTICES BASED ON KNOWLEDGE OF INDIVIDUAL CHILDREN, THE COMMUNITY, AND CURRICULUM GOALS AND CONTENT**

Skill 5.1   Interrelationships among the content areas

Teaching students how subjects connect and are interrelated, and bridging the gaps between various subjects by integration of learning, helps students in numerous ways. When the content of the curriculum is divided into separate subjects for science, social studies, art, music, reading, spelling, handwriting, etc., knowledge becomes fragmented. These various subject matter areas can often be combined into themes or units. Integration of content also provides a clearer understanding of real life situations. In reality, students will not have a separate math, reading, and science time at the grocery store or other venues. Instead they will be expected to incorporate all of their information together into one process to complete the task.

Educational research has shown a strong correlation between the need for interdisciplinary instruction and cognitive learning application. Understanding how students process information and create learning was the goal of earlier educators who looked at how the brain connected information pieces into meaning and found that learning takes place along intricate neural pathways that formulate processing and meaning from data input into the brain. The implications for student learning are vast in that teachers can work with students to break down subject content area into bits of information that can be memorized and applied to a former learning experience and then processed into integral resources of information.

Students can have discussions and debates about a subject in the current news that correlates with a Social Studies theme. Students can orally present their reactions to observations about a Science experiment. Teachers may even have students orally explain how they found the answers to certain Math problems. Giving speeches and sharing about personal experiences can also be related to themes and units.

When a class prepares food before/after completing a Math lesson on fractions, students apply mathematical concepts and skills as they measure different ingredients. Other mixing activities which involve measuring math skills involve: making play dough, making slime, and creating the perfect bubble blowing mixture. Cooking and mixture activities also have a direct connection to the sciences and allow the teacher to combine subject areas into one lesson.

Other methods to incorporate math activities into more regular parts of students' lives and other subject areas include:

- Charting/graphing the weather on a regular basis
- Predicting temperatures based on a pattern or other information
- Helping students keep track of the score of a sporting event using tally marks
- Finding the age of other family members or characters in stories
- Building race cars or straw structures to represent buildings from stories or having your own race, similar to a NASCAR event
- Redesigning the layout of the classroom/cafeteria
- Playing card, dice, and board games with the students (the popular games like Pokemon involve a lot of math if played correctly)
- Timing activities or determining how long until a special event will occur

Math, science and technology have common themes in how they are applied and understood. All three use models, diagrams, and graphs to simplify a concept for analysis and interpretation. Patterns observed in these systems lead to predictions. Another common theme among these three systems is equilibrium. Equilibrium is a state in which forces are balanced, resulting in stability. Static equilibrium is stability due to a lack of changes and dynamic equilibrium is stability due to a balance between opposite forces. Scale is a ratio of size. For example, a map may have a scale of true miles per every inch drawn on the map. A model drawn to scale is a representation of something that is larger or smaller than its actual size. There is also the very literal interpretation of scale. In this context the scale would be used to measure mass, and would often be called a balance.

The knowledge and use of basic mathematical concepts and skills is a necessary aspect of scientific study. Science depends on data and the manipulation of data requires knowledge of mathematics. As children grow and increase their math competency, an understanding of basic statistics, graphs, charts, and algebra will be expected. For now, studying and creating patterns, identifying the tens, hundreds, and thousands places, basic math, and an introduction to graphing would be appropriate.

The fundamental relationship between the natural and social sciences is the use of the scientific method and the rigorous standards of proof that both disciplines require. This emphasis on organization and evidence separates the sciences from the arts and humanities. Natural science, particularly biology, is closely related to social science, the study of human behavior. Biological and environmental factors often dictate human behavior and accurate assessment of behavior requires a sound understanding of biological factors.

For information on how physical education relates, **SEE** Skill 10.1

The arts provide essential opportunities to explore connections among all disciplines. Content areas are unique, but they share common themes and terms and ideas. Skills developed in the arts enhance learning across content areas. Conversely, increased knowledge in curriculum content areas enhance the depth of knowledge and experience in the arts.

Charles Fowler effectively argues in his book, *Strong Arts, Strong Schools: the Promising Potential and Shortsighted Disregard of the Arts in American Schooling,* that the best schools have the best arts programs. He explains that we need to utilize every possible way to represent and interpret our world, and that means combining content areas, not isolating them. Science, Math, Literature, History or the Arts by themselves only convey a part of the subject. Charles Fowler believes that integrating these programs to provide students with a more complete picture is crucial. He uses the Grand Canyon as an example. A teacher can discuss mathematically the dimensions of the Grand Canyon or the science behind how it was formed, but this lesson is taken a step further by providing examples of artistic renderings of the Grand Canyon or asking students to write a poem describing the canyon. This integration provides a more three dimensional understanding of the subject.

Using African cultural history as another example, a teacher begins with a short history lesson on select African cultures. Geography may also come into play in the lesson, as the teacher chooses a specific region, such as Senegal-Gambia in West Africa, to describe to the children what an area of Africa looks like. This may be expanded to a music lesson on African musical styles and how they influenced Western music, such as gospel, jazz, spirituals, hip hop and rap. The teacher can introduce various African instruments, and discuss what the instruments are made of and how they are played. Students will learn several drum techniques and experiment with creating their own unique drum beats. Again, at the end of this lesson students have experienced Africa through an integrated teaching approach, and they come away with a more complete understanding.

The effective teacher will seek to connect all students to the subject matter through multiple techniques, with the goal that each student, through their own abilities, will relate to one or more techniques and excel in the learning process.

Skill 5.2 Benefits and strategies of integrated learning across the curriculum

The integrated curriculum is a method that teaches students to break down barriers between subjects. Lessons are planned around broad themes that students can identify with, such as "The Environment." Major concepts are pulled from this broad concept, and teachers then plan activities that teach these concepts.

Characteristics of an integrated curriculum

- A combination of subjects
- An emphasis on projects
- Sources that go beyond textbooks
- Relationships among concepts
- Thematic units as organizing principles
- Flexible schedules
- Flexible student groupings.

Integrated curriculum is an education that is organized in such a way that it cuts across subject-matter lines, bringing together various aspects of the curriculum into meaningful association to focus upon broad areas of study. It views learning and teaching in a holistic way and reflects the real world, which is interactive. (Humphreys, Post, and Ellis)

Interdisciplinary and thematic instruction, by definition and design, provide for teaching from perspective. One example of an effective, readily available instructional unit is displayed, below.

Discovering Your World by Anita Yeoman
This integrated unit introduces students to various countries as they plan a trip around the world. The unit is very flexible and can be adapted for any middle-level grade and time period. It consists of detailed suggestions for planning a "journey" according to the needs of each class. Worksheets for planning an itinerary, making passports and calculating distances are included, together with peer and self evaluation sheets and tracking sheets. Students will utilize research skills as they learn about language, history, geography and culture of the countries they "visit" on their world trip.

By being exposed to an integrated approach, students have the benefit of developing and using cross-disciplinary approaches to solving real-life problems. Students are exposed to balanced teaching, a flexible curriculum and a chance to learn how to work collaboratively.

Skill 5.3 **The rationale for developmentally appropriate methods that include play, small group projects, open-ended questioning, group discussion, problem solving, cooperative learning, and inquiry experiences to help young children develop intellectual curiosity, solve problems, and make decisions**

Anyone who has been in a classroom for young children knows that students do not sit still and focus on one thing for too long. Some people joke that the age of a person equals the amount of time the person is willing to sit and listen for any one time. So, a kindergartener, under this premise, would only be able to sit and concentrate on one thing for 5 to 6 minutes.

The bottom line is this: young children do not concentrate for long periods of time, and good teachers know how to capitalize on the need of children to move and change topics. Generally, young children should be changing academic activities every 15-20 minutes. This means that if a teacher wants to fill a block of two hours for literacy learning in the morning, the teacher should have about 6-8 activities planned.

Here's an example:
1. The teacher has students write something to access background knowledge. In kindergarten, this might include just a picture.
2. The teacher might spend a few minutes asking students what they wrote about in a large group.
3. The teacher might introduce a new book by doing a "book walk"—looking at the title, the pictures, etc.
4. The teacher reads a book aloud as students follow along.
5. Students do a pair-share activity where they turn to their neighbors to discuss a question.
6. Students return to desks to do a comprehension activity on their own.
7. The teacher facilitates a whole class discussion of what students wrote.
8. Students go to centers to practice specific skills as the teacher works with small groups of students.
9. The teacher conducts a vocabulary activity with the whole class.

This list could go on and on. Hopefully, you'll see that the activity changes rapidly, but the same skills are being taught in different ways. Teachers who understand and plan for the students' developmental needs are more likely to keep their students' attention, engage their students more, and have more well-behaved students. When children get bored, many will become disruptive. The key is to keep them interested in what they are learning.

Teachers can also enhance student motivation by planning and directing interactive, "hands-on" learning experiences. Research substantiates that cooperative group projects decrease student behavior problems and increase student on-task behavior. Students who are directly involved with learning activities are more motivated to complete a task to the best of their ability.

The role of play

Too often, recess and play is considered peripheral or unimportant to a child's development. It is sometimes seen as a way to allow kids to release physical energy or simply a "tradition" of childhood. The truth is, though, that play is very important to human development.

For children (who will soon be active citizens of our democracy, parents, spouses, friends, colleagues, and neighbors), play is an activity that helps teach basic values such as sharing and cooperation. It also teaches that taking care of oneself (as opposed to constantly working) is good for human beings and further creates a more enjoyable society.

The stages of play development move from solitary (particularly in infancy stages) to cooperative (in early childhood), but even in early childhood, children should be able to play on their own and entertain themselves from time to time. Children who do not know what to do with themselves when they are bored should be encouraged to think about particular activities that might be of interest.

But it is also extremely important that children play with peers. While the emerging stages of cooperative play may be awkward (as children will at first not want to share toys, for example), with some guidance and experience, children will learn how to be good peers and friends.

Play—both cooperative and solitary—helps to develop very important attributes in children. For example, children learn and develop personal interests and practice particular skills. The play that children engage in may even develop future professional interests.

Finally, playing with objects helps to develop motor skills. The objects that children play with should be varied and age appropriate. For example, playing with a doll can actually help to develop hand-eye coordination. Sports, for both boys and girls, can be equally valuable. Parents and teachers, though, need to remember that sports at young ages should only be for the purpose of development of interests and motor skills—not competition. Many children will learn that they do not enjoy sports, and parents and teachers should be respectful of these decisions.

In general, play is an appropriate place of children to learn many things about themselves, their world, and their interests. Children should be encouraged to participate in different types of play, and they should be watched over as they encounter new types of play.

Varying Instructional Strategies

Children learn at different paces due to reasons including prior experiences, personal situations, abilities, interests, and more. Today, teachers are using flexible grouping strategies to address the different learning needs of various students, and the ways they are organizing their classrooms are beginning to change.

Depending on the lesson objectives and classroom participants, teachers are starting to consider the dynamics of a group when planning instruction. Grouping flexibly also allows for various levels of differentiating learning when it is needed. Below are some of the most common organization methods for grouping students flexibly.

Teacher-led groups
- Whole class instruction such as lecture or mini-lessons
- Small group instruction such as guided reading
- Teacher-directed activities such as workshops

Student Groups
- Collaborative groups such as circle sharing
- Performance-base groups such as group study or interviews
- Student dyads (pair work) such as "think, pair, share"

For more info on flexible groups:
http://www.eduplace.com/science/profdev/articles/valentino.html

Learning activities selected for younger students (below age eight) should focus on short time frames in highly simplified form. The nature of the activity and the content in which the activity is presented affects the approach that the students will take in processing the information. Younger children tend to process information at a slower rate than older children (age eight and older).

Younger students do not respond well to instruction that is singularly formatted (e.g., lectures, audio/video presentations, etc.), which expend the entire class period. Young children need variety to avoid boredom and remain interested and motivated, but they also require a mix of physical and mental activities broken by restful periods where their minds and bodies can adjust and prepare for further activities. As a teacher would not lecture to an early elementary class for an entire hour, she or he would also not expect them to play a game requiring physical exertion for an hour or more. In planning each module of instruction, the teacher must anticipate the physical and intellectual demands necessary for the students to meet the lesson objectives and incorporate limitations which will provide variety in activities and avoid stressing the students' capacity to attend, retain, remain interested and acquire skills.

Guidelines for allocating time by activity type and varying activities within the lesson module may be provided to the teacher within the school system and are usually available at the departmental level. But even guidelines may need to be tempered by common sense and specific classroom experience to ensure that young students are not stressed by demands beyond their current developmental levels and yet are working, learning and achieving to their full potential.

Allowing for the differing needs of younger students does not mean abandoning classroom discipline and organized instruction. At this level, students need the reassurance of structure, organization and discipline. While early childhood and elementary students are generally more easily controlled—often appearing better behaved and more responsive to authority—than older students, they still have a tendency to socialize and play just for the sake of play. This can quickly allow the classroom situation to deteriorate, replacing the learning environment with chaos. When the teacher is implementing a well-structured plan, with measurable milestones and specific objectives, he/she will quickly identify and redirect conversation and activity that is not relevant or supportive of the instructional objectives. If the appropriate attitudes and responses to structure and discipline are internalized at an early age, they will serve the student throughout his/her educational experience and provide a solid foundation upon which the individual can develop the self-discipline necessary in later life. The teacher who can instill these values in a young student will have earned the gratitude and respect of all the teachers who instruct this student in the future.

TEACHER CERTIFICATION STUDY GUIDE

COMPETENCY 6.0   **UNDERSTAND HOW TO STRUCTURE A LEARNING CLIMATE AND SELECT STRATEGIES THAT ARE RESPONSIVE TO THE DIVERSE NEEDS AND BACKGROUNDS OF ALL CHILDREN**

Skill 6.1   **Strategies for creating and adapting a classroom environment that provides for individual differences**

SEE Skills 2.1, 2.2 and 3.4.

Skill 6.2   **The selection of appropriate activities, materials, and equipment**

A well organized classroom often begins with the room's physical arrangement — the arrangement of desks, the attractiveness of bulletin boards, and the storage of supplies and materials. By identifying various ways of organizing learning space teachers can create a caring and child-centered environment.

Furthermore, today's educator must address the needs of diverse learners within a single classroom. The teacher is able to attain materials that may be necessary for the majority of the regular education students and some of the special needs children and, more and more frequently, one individual student. The "effective" teacher knows that there are currently hundreds of adaptive materials that could be used to help these students increase achievement and develop skills.

Although most school centers cannot supply all the materials that special needs students require, each district more than likely has a resource center where teachers can check out special equipment. Most communities support agencies which offer assistance in providing the necessities of special needs people including students. Teachers must know how to obtain a wide range of materials including school supplies, medical care, clothing, food, adaptive computers and books (such as Braille), eye glasses, hearing aids, wheelchairs, counseling, transportation, etc.

In considering suitable learning materials for the classroom, the teacher must have a thorough understanding of the state-mandated competency-based curriculum. According to state requirements, certain objectives must be met in each subject taught at every designated level of instruction. It is necessary that the teacher become well acquainted with the curriculum for which he/she is assigned.

In choosing materials, teachers should also keep in mind that not only do students learn at different rates, but they bring a variety of cognitive styles to the learning process. Prior experiences influence the individual's cognitive style, or method of accepting, processing, and retaining information. According to Marshall Rosenberg, students can be categorized as:

    a) rigid-inhibited

    b) undisciplined

    c) acceptance-anxious

    d) creative

"The creative learner is an independent thinker, one who maximizes his/her abilities, can work by his/herself, enjoys learning, and is self-critical." This last category constitutes the ideal, but teachers should make every effort to use materials that will stimulate and hold the attention of learners of all types.

Keeping in mind what is understood about the students' abilities and interests, the teacher should design a course of study that presents units of instruction in an orderly sequence. The instruction should be planned so as to advance all students toward the next level of instruction, although exit behaviors need not be identical due to the inevitability of individual differences.

Textbooks

Most teachers chose to use textbooks, which are suitable to the age and developmental level of specific student populations. Textbooks reflect the values and assumptions of the society that produces them, while they also represent the knowledge and skills considered to be essential in becoming an educated adult. Finally, textbooks are useful to the school bureaucracy and the community, for they make public and accessible the private world of the classroom. The teacher must also be aware that it is unlawful to require students to study from textbooks or materials other than those approved by the state Department of Education.

From time to time, controversy has arisen about the possible weakness of textbooks—the preponderance of pictures and illustrations, the avoidance of controversy in social studies textbooks, the lack of emphasis on problem-solving in science books, and so on. In the 1980's, certain books were criticized for their attention to the "liberal" or "secular" values, and the creationism/evolution argument has re-surfaced again and again. Finally, recent decades have witnessed a movement to grant more attention to women, African-Americans, and other groups whose contributions to our developing culture may have been overlooked in earlier textbooks. Individual teachers would be well advised to keep themselves informed of current trends or developments, so as to make better informed choices for their students and deal with the possibility of parental concern.

Focusing on the needs evident in almost any classroom population, the teacher will want to use textbooks that include some of the activities and selections to challenge the most advanced students as well as those who have difficulty in mastering the material at a moderate pace. Some of the exercises may be eliminated altogether for faster learners, while students who have difficulty may need to have material arranged into brief steps or sections. For almost any class, some experience in co-operative learning may be advisable. Thus, the faster learners will reinforce what they have already mastered, while those of lesser ability at the tasks in question can ask about their individual problems or areas of concern. Most textbook exercises intended for independent work can be used in cooperative learning, though in most cases, teachers will encourage better participation if the cooperating group is asked to hand in a single paper or project to represent their combined efforts, rather than individual papers or projects.

Technological Materials

Aside from textbooks, there is a wide variety of materials available to today's teachers. Textbook publishers often provide films, recordings, and software to accompany the text, as well as maps, graphics, and colorful posters to help students visualize what is being taught.

Microcomputers are now commonplace, as well as laser discs and DVD players to bring alive the content of a reference book in text, motion, and sound. Hand-held calculators eliminate the need for drill and practice in number facts, while they also support a problem solving and process to mathematics.

Digital cameras are inexpensive enough to enable students to photograph and display their own work, as well as keep a record of their achievements in teacher files or student portfolios.

Studies have shown that students learn best when what is taught in lecture and textbook reading is presented more than once in various formats. In some instances, students themselves may be asked to reinforce what they have learned by completing some original production—for example, by drawing pictures to explain some scientific process, by writing a monologue or dialogue to express what some historical figure might have said on some occasion, by devising a board game to challenge the players' mathematical skills, or by acting out (and perhaps filming) episodes from a classroom reading selection. Students usually enjoy having their work displayed or presented to an audience of peers. Thus, their productions may supplement and personalize the learning experiences that the teacher has planned for them.

Factoring In Student Readiness

When choosing appropriate materials for the classroom, the teacher must first determine the abilities of the incoming students assigned to his/her class or supervision. It is essential to be aware of their entry behavior—that is, their current level of achievement in the relevant areas. The next step is to take a broad overview of students who are expected to learn before they are passed on to the next grade or level of instruction. Finally, the teacher must design a course of study that will enable students to reach the necessary level of achievement, as displayed in their final assessments, or exit behaviors. Textbooks and learning materials must be chosen to fit into this context.

To determine the abilities of incoming students, it may be helpful to consult their prior academic records. Letter grades assigned at previous levels of instruction as well as scores on standardized tests may be taken into account. In addition, the teacher may choose to administer pre-tests at the beginning of the school year, and perhaps also at the initial stage of each new unit of instruction. The textbooks available for classroom use may provide suitable pre-tests, tests of student progress, and post-tests.

In selecting tests and other assessment tools, the teacher should keep in mind that different kinds of tests measure different aspects of student development. The tests included in most textbooks chosen for the classroom, and in the teacher's book that accompanies them are usually achievement tests. Few of these are the type of tests intended to measure the students' inherent ability or aptitude. Teachers will find it difficult to raise students' scores on ability tests, but students' scores on achievement tests may be expected to improve with proper instruction and application in the area being studied.

In addition to administering tests, the teacher may assess the readiness of students for a particular level of instruction by having them demonstrate their ability to perform some relevant task. In a class that emphasizes written composition, for example, students may be asked to submit writing samples. These may be used not only to assure the placement of the students into the proper level, but as a diagnostic tool to help them understand what aspects of their composition skills may need improvement. In the like manner, students in a speech class may be asked to make an impromptu oral presentation before beginning a new level or specific level of instruction. Others may be asked to demonstrate their psychomotor skills in a physical education class, display their computational skills in a mathematics class, and so on. Whatever the chosen task, the teacher will need to select or devise an appropriate assessment scale and interpret the results with care.

Teachers may also gauge student readiness by simply asking them about their previous experience or knowledge of the subject or task at hand. While their comments may not be completely reliable indicators of what they know or understand, such discussions have the advantage of providing an idea of the students' interest in what is being taught. Teachers can have little impact unless they are able to demonstrate how the material being introduced is relevant to the students' lives.

Skill 6.3 The development, implementation, and evaluation of appropriate lesson plans

Lesson plans are important in guiding instruction in the classroom. Incorporating the nuts and bolts of a teaching unit, the lesson plan outlines the steps of teacher implementation and the assessment of teacher instructional capacity and student learning capacity. Teachers are able to objectify and quantify learning goals and targets by using effective performance-based assessments for identifying when a student has learned the material presented. All components of a lesson plan including the unit description, learning targets, learning experiences, explanation of learning rationale and assessments must be present to provide both quantifiable and qualitative data to ascertain whether student learning has taken place and whether effective teaching has occurred for the students. National and state learning standards must be taken into account because not only will the teacher and the students be measured by the students' scores at the end of the year, the school will also.

A typical format would include the following items below:

1. Written instructional lesson plan - guidelines for what is being taught and how the students will be able to access the information. Subsequent evaluations and assessments will determine whether students have learned or correctly processed the subject content being taught.
2. Unit Description - provides description of the learning and classroom environment.
    a. Classroom characteristics - describes the physical arrangements of the classroom, along with the student grouping patterns for the lesson being taught. Classroom rules and consequences should be clearly posted and visible.
    b. Student characteristics - demographics of the classroom that include student number, gender, cultural and ethnic backgrounds, along with Special Education students with IEPs (Individualized Education Plans).
3. Learning Goals/Targets/Objectives - What are the expectations of the lessons? Are the learning goals appropriate to the state learning standards and District academic goals? Are the targets appropriate for the grade level, subject content area and inclusive of a multicultural perspective and global viewpoint?

4. Learning Experiences for students - How will student learning be supported using the learning goals?
    a. What prior knowledge or experiences will the students bring to the lesson? How will you check and verify that student knowledge?
    b. How will you engage all students in the classroom?
    c. How will the lesson plan be modified for students with IEPs and how will Special Education students be evaluated for learning the modified lesson targets?
    d. How will the multicultural aspect be incorporated into the lesson plan?
    e. What interdisciplinary links and connections will be used to incorporate other subject areas?
    f. What types of assessments/evaluations will be used to test student understanding and processing of the lesson plan?
    g. How will students be cooperatively grouped to engage in the lesson?
    h. What internet links are provided in the lesson plan?
5. Rationales for Learning Experiences - provide data on how the lesson plan addresses student learning goals and objectives. Address whether the lesson provides accommodations for students with IEPs and provides support for marginalized students in the classroom.
6. Assessments - constructing pre and post assessments that evaluate student learning as it correlates to the learning goals and objectives. Do the assessments include a cultural integration that address the cultural needs and inclusion of students?

The teacher must be very knowledgeable about the writing of behavioral objectives that fall within the guidelines of the state and local expectations, and objectives must be measurable so that when the unit or semester is complete, the teacher can know for sure whether the objectives were accomplished.

When given objectives by the school or county, teachers may wish to adapt them so that they can meet the needs of their student population. For example, if a high level advanced class is given the objective, *"State five causes of World War II,"* a teacher may wish to adapt the objective to a higher level. *"State five causes of World War II and explain how they contributed to the start of the war."* Subsequently objectives can be modified for a lower level as well. *"From a list of causes, pick three that specifically caused World War II."*

Skill 6.4 Strategies for making learning and problem solving relevant to children's lives

Although problem solving is usually associated with Mathematics and Science, it should be an integral part of the school day in early childhood classes. Children also have to be able to relate the problem to their own lives so they can see the relevance of finding a solution and be able to apply this in other settings. In Math, the problems children have to solve should be related to their everyday lives, as should the experiments that the teacher and students perform in the classroom. These are usually relatively easy because the curriculum is designed to have age-appropriate activities. However, the teacher may have to change the wording of some of these to make the problem clearer for the student.

In learning to perform addition and subtraction skills, the use of manipulatives helps the students see the problem in action. Consider the following problem:

Susie had 3 red crayons and you gave her 2 blue crayons. How many crayons does she have now?

If the students use red and blue crayons, they can see the problem and obtain the answer by counting the total number of crayons.

In Language Arts, problem-solving skills are developed when the teacher asks students to predict what might happen in a story being read to the class. As the teacher charts responses and then goes back to see which responses were correct or close to what happened, the children can see the relevance of this activity and be able to refine their thinking. Since most of the content of early childhood curriculum is written within the context of a story, teachers can ask the students such questions as:
- Why do you think that happened?
- What would you have done differently? Why?
- Have you ever been in a situation like that? What did you do?

Opportunities to practice problem solving skills occur in the early childhood classroom when children do not agree about something, do not want to share or are being mean to other children in the class. This is real-life problem solving as the teacher discusses the problem with the children, discusses the actions and asks them to think about what happened. Through discussion, the teacher can lead the children to solving the problem by helping them arrive at the right conclusion. In this way, children have a model to go by when the problem arises in the future. Rules for working in groups need to be established beforehand, but by engaging the students in setting these rules, the teacher is also teaching them how to function in society. When students determine the rules for working together or general classroom rules, the teacher should ask them **why** they think that rule should be included. This strategy helps students apply safety rules in everyday situations

COMPETENCY 7.0 UNDERSTAND HOW TO CREATE AN ENVIRONMENT THAT FOSTERS YOUNG CHILDREN'S SOCIAL AND EMOTIONAL DEVELOPMENT, INCLUDING SELF-ESTEEM, SELF-DISCIPLINE, AND COOPERATIVE BEHAVIORS

Skill 7.1 The relationship between children's social and emotional development and learning

Students at this level are continually undergoing physical and emotional changes and development. Everything occurring to them is new, unfamiliar and sometimes discomforting. A student undergoing such a change may suddenly exhibit the disorientation and uneasiness more often seen in a child on his/her first day of school. As a result, a student may feel socially awkward, and this may be reflected in schoolwork and especially in classroom participation. The teacher must be sensitive to the issues of a developing child and aware of the impact this may have on student learning, classroom decorum and the cohesion among classmates, which the teacher is trying to foster.

The teacher must be prepared to adapt and control the classroom environment to the degree possible, to ensure a safe and productive learning environment is established and maintained. However, some situations are more readily anticipated and incorporated than controlled or changed. Behavior modification, in the classroom, can often mean simply channeling existing energies and interests (of the students) into acceptable activities which provide a meaningful, educational experience as a positive outcome.

It is always beneficial for the teacher to remain current with the studies and findings published in numerous journals related to child and educational psychology and physical and intellectual development in early childhood. For classroom use, there are numerous resources (instructional videos, printed materials, instructional games) which provide for controlled interaction among the students and between teacher and students, and address issues of concern for young students. They are usually age and/or grade specific, activity-driven, and employ multimedia. Examples of pertinent topics, with stated educational goals, available for instructional use would include, "Listening to Others," "Caring," "Bullying," "Working Out Conflicts," "Controlling Anger," "Caring," "Fairness," "Saying No," "Dealing with Feelings," "Being Friends," "Appreciating Yourself," and "Dealing with Disappointment."

Successful social skills allow students to have more effective and positive interactions with their peers, therefore enhancing their emotional development. Teaching social skills can be rather difficult because social competence requires a repertoire of skills in a number of areas. The socially competent person must be able to get along with family and friends, function in a work environment, take care of personal needs, solve problems in daily living, and identify sources of help. A class of students may display several deficits in a few areas or a few deficits in many areas. Therefore, the teacher must begin with an assessment of the skill deficits and prioritize the ones to teach first.

Type of Assessment	Description
Direct Observation	Observe student in various settings with a checklist
Role Play	Teacher observes students in structured scenarios
Teacher Ratings	Teacher rates student with a checklist or formal assessment instrument
Sociometric Measures: Peer Nomination	Student names specific classmates who meet a stated criterion (i.e., playmate). Score is the number of times a child is nominated.
Peer Rating	Students rank all their classmates on a Likert-type scale (e.g., 1-3 or 1-5 scale) on stated criterion. Individual score is the average of the total ratings of their classmates.
Paired-Comparison	Student is presented with paired classmate combinations and asked to choose who is most or least liked in the pair.
Context Observation	Student is observed to determine if the skill deficit is present in one setting, but not others
Comparison with other student	Student's social skill behavior is compared to two other students in the same situation to determine if there is a deficit, or if the behavior is not really a problem.

Social skills instruction can also include teaching for conversation skills, assertiveness, play and peer interaction, problem solving and coping skills, self-help, task-related behaviors, self-concept related skills (i.e., expressing feelings, accepting consequences), and job related skills.

SEE also the "Role of Play" section of Skill 5.3.

For lesson plans on specific social skills, including surveys, checklists and progress reports ideas, you may access the Social Skills Instruction Guide developed by the Special School District of St. Louis County (1992) at http://www.ssd.k12.mo.us/Staff/instructional_tools/assets/SOCIAL_SKILLS.pdf

The **Center on the Social and Emotional Foundations for Early Learning** is a national center focused on strengthening the capacity of child care and Head Start programs to improve the social and emotional outcomes of young children. The Center develops and disseminates evidence-based, user-friendly information to help early childhood educators meet the needs of the growing number of children with challenging behaviors and mental health challenges in child care and Head Start programs. (http://www.vanderbilt.edu/csefel/)

Skill 7.2 **Individual and group guidance and problem-solving techniques that develop positive and supportive relationships with children, encourage positive social interaction among children, promote positive strategies of conflict resolution, and develop personal self-control, self motivation, and self-esteem**

One of the primary tasks of early childhood is to develop self discipline. Teachers often find themselves correcting their students for interrupting, being wild, not following instructions or for not controlling their hands or mouths. These all require self discipline or self-control. Young children are by nature impulsive.

Helping children learn to engage in self-talk increases their self-control. For example, if a child gets hit, he or she needs to stop, think and evaluate before hitting back. The student might say to him or herself:

- If I hit him, he'll hit me and we'll get into a fight.
- I might get hurt or I might hurt him.
- I might be sent to the office.
- My parents may have to come to school.
- I'm not going to let him get me in trouble.
- I don't know what his problem is, but I'm going to stay away from him.
- I'll choose to do the smart thing and walk away.

Other coping skills include taking deep breaths, counting slowly, drawing a picture or writing down feelings, talking to someone, or asking for help.

Children who lack self-control are often unable to empathize with another child's feelings or point of view. They may misinterpret ambiguous social situations as being hostile. When they feel upset they may provoke others rather than think of positive alternatives like playing with someone else or choosing another activity. These children often do not understand that their anger is a secondary emotion that results from feeling misunderstood, hurt, rejected, afraid, embarrassed, or frustrated. In addition, they may have the distorted view that their aggressive behavior makes them seem tough and admired, while peers often consider them mean. An educator's responsibility is to help dispel their illusions and teach self-control by example and other methods.

Remember that teaching children self-control is an ongoing process. Be attentive to small accomplishments. Comment and encourage peers to notice when a child demonstrates self-control. If educators continually look for opportunities to help students gain control of themselves and stop inappropriate behaviors, they will be contributing to children's future success and to a positive school climate.

A classroom is a community of learning, and when students learn to respect themselves and the members around them, learning is maximized. A positive environment, where open, discussion-oriented, non-threatening communication among all students can occur, is a critical factor in creating an effective learning culture. The teacher must take the lead and model appropriate actions and speech, and intervene quickly when a student makes a misstep and offends (often inadvertently) another.

Teachers should create a classroom climate that encourages extensive participation from the students. Collaborations and discussions are enhanced when students like and respect each other, and therefore, each student's learning can benefit. To create this environment, teachers must first model how to welcome and consider all points of view for the students. The teacher should then positively affirm and reinforce students for offering their ideas in front of the other students. Even if somewhat amiss, the teacher should receive the idea while perhaps offering a modification or corrected statement (for more factual pieces of information). The idea is for students to feel confident and safe in being able to express their thoughts or ideas. Only then will students be able to engage in independent discussions that consider and respect everyone's statements.

SEE Skill 7.3 for more information about self-concept

Skill 7.3 Methods that promote independence and self-confidence

Students generally do not realize their own abilities and frequently lack self-confidence. Teachers can instill positive self-concepts in children and thereby enhance their innate abilities by providing certain types of feedback. Such feedback includes attributing students' successes to their effort and specifying what the student did that produced the success. Qualitative comments influence attitudes more than quantitative feedback such as grades.

Appealing to Student Interests

Teachers must avoid teaching tasks that fit their own interests and goals and design activities that address the students' concerns. In order to do this, it is necessary to find out about students and to have a sense of their interests and goals. Teachers can do this by conducting student surveys or simply by questioning and listening to students. Once this information is obtained the teacher can link students' interests with classroom tasks.

Teachers are learning the value of giving assignments that meet the individual abilities and needs of students. After instruction, discussion, questioning, and practice have been provided, rather than assigning one task to all students—teachers are asking students to generate tasks that will show their knowledge of the information presented. Students are given choices and thereby have the opportunity to demonstrate more effectively the skills, concepts, or topics that they as individuals have learned. It has been established that student choice increases student originality, intrinsic motivation, and higher mental processes.

Enhancing Self-Concept

As in all aspects of education, each student must have an equal opportunity to succeed. A positive self-concept for a child or adolescent is a very important element in terms of the students' ability to learn and to be an integral member of society. If students think poorly of themselves or have sustained feelings of inferiority, they probably will not be able to optimize their potentials for learning. It is therefore part of the teacher's task to ensure that each student develops a positive self-concept.

A positive self-concept does not imply feelings of superiority, perfection, or competence/efficacy. Instead, a positive self-concept involves self-acceptance as a person, liking oneself, and having a proper respect for oneself. The teacher who encourages these factors has contributed to the development of a positive self-concept in students.

Teachers may take a number of approaches to enhancement of self-concept among students. An approach aimed directly at the enhancement of self concept is "Invitational Education." According to this approach, teachers and their behaviors may be inviting or they may be disinviting. Inviting behaviors enhance self-concept among students, while disinviting behaviors diminish self-concept.

Disinviting behaviors include those that demean students, as well as those that may be chauvinistic, sexist, condescending, thoughtless, or insensitive to student feelings. Inviting behaviors are the opposite of these, and characterize teachers who act with consistency and sensitivity. Inviting teacher behaviors reflect an attitude of "doing with" rather than "doing to." Students are "invited" or "disinvited" depending on the teacher behaviors.

Invitational teachers exhibit the following skills (Biehler and Snowman, 394):
    a) reaching each student (e.g., learning names, having one-to-one contact)
    b) listening with care (e.g., picking up subtle cues)
    c) being real with students (e.g., providing only realistic praise, "coming on straight")
    d) being real with oneself (e.g., honestly appraising your own feelings and disappointments)
    e) inviting good discipline (e.g., showing students you have respect in personal ways)
    f) handling rejection (e.g., not taking lack of student response in personal ways)
    g) inviting oneself (e.g., thinking positively about oneself)

For more information on "Invitational Education" go to the website for the **International Alliance for Invitational Education**,
http://www.invitationaleducation.net/

Increasing Motivation

Motivation is essential to student learning in education. Instructors should recognize and understand the important elements of student motivation. Important theories and concepts in student motivation include attribution theory, social learning theory, learned helplessness, and self-efficacy.

Attribution theory describes how people make causal explanations and how they answer questions beginning with 'Why?' For instance, a student's aggressively competitive behavior may reflect her personality, or it may be a response to situational pressures. Attribution theory describes the processes of explaining events and the behavioral and emotional consequences of those explanations. Attribution theory also claims that student's perception of their educational experience affects their motivation more than the experience itself.

Social learning theory focuses on the learning that occurs within a social context. Social learning theory asserts that people can learn by observing the behavior of others and the outcomes of those behaviors. It further states that learning can occur without a permanent change in behavior. Instructors should also be note that cognition plays an important role in learning. Awareness and expectations of future rewards or punishments can have a major effect on the behaviors that people exhibit. Thus, socialization and reward/punishment can motivate students to learn.

Learned helplessness occurs in situations where continued failure may inhibit somebody from trying again and can also lead to many forms of depression. Thus, it is very important how instructors respond to children's failures and successes. If a student feels as though he cannot control his environment, this lack of control will impair learning in certain situations. That is, learned helplessness often occurs in environments where people experience events in which they have, or feel as though they have, no control over what happens to them.

Self-efficacy describes a person's belief about his/her capability to produce designated levels of performance that exercise influence over events that affect their lives. Self-efficacy beliefs determine how people feel, think, motivate themselves, and behave. A strong sense of efficacy enhances human accomplishment and personal well-being in many ways. People with high assurance in their capabilities view difficult tasks as challenges rather than threats. A student with high self-efficacy will be highly motivated to participate in classroom activities. To build efficacy, the instructor must not only raise the student's belief in his/her capabilities, but also structure situations that breed success and limit repeated failure. Students with high self-efficacy measure success in terms of self-improvement rather than by triumphs over others.

Skill 7.4   Strategies for helping children learn to deal effectively with their emotions

Young children are continually developing physically, emotionally and intellectually. Even among peers in a classroom setting there can be diverse levels of development. The classroom teacher must plan according to the norm, allowing for exceptions, which ensure the inclusion of all students in the education process. Regardless of the particular level of development attained by any individual student or the class in general, no student can be entirely successful when stress becomes a factor. Just as we would not ask a child to perform a physical task, which might be difficult even for an adult, we should not create emotional or intellectual stress in the child by making demands which exceed the student's developing attention span.

Building resilience in children is the best way to help them deal effectively with their emotions. Resilience refers to the ability to persevere and adapt when things don't go the way they were planned. First of all, the teacher has to be aware of any situations in the child's life that may precipitate outbursts in the classroom or contribute to the teacher's understanding of why the child behaves in a certain way. For example:

- Are the parents divorced?
- Has there been a death in the family or the birth of a baby?
- Is there suspected abuse in the home?
- Does the child relate well to other siblings?
- Is this an only child?

Students that are prone to emotional outbursts should be instructed to become aware of themselves and what they can do. Then the teacher can help them become aware of their feelings in various situations and work to develop ways the child can cope in these situations. It may mean putting the child on a behavior contract where the child receives an award for behaving in an appropriate manner, such as being allowed extra free time in the classroom.

Children in early childhood education classes are often not aware of their emotions and how to act appropriately. Teachers can have them draw posters or pictures of things that make then feel a certain way, such as things that make them happy, sad, angry, etc. This will help the child recognize these emotions. Through discussions with the whole class, small groups or with an individual, the teacher can help the child recognize how they react to these situations and in so doing both the teacher and the child can recognize the triggers. Role play is another strategy that works well with children to help them learn appropriate ways of dealing with emotions.

It is important for children to have positive self-esteem in order to cope with their emotions. An "All about Me' book can help the children identify their likes and dislikes. They can identify things they do well and describe an activity that might help them do well in areas they see as one in which they have a deficit. A show and tell presentation in which the child shows the rest of the class what they can do well is a good way of helping them develop positive self-esteem.

Teachers can present the students with "what if" situations in which the child uses problem-solving skills to determine what they would do in different situations. For children who are still developing emotionally, they can benefit from this strategy because they learn from the other students in the class by watching what they do.

School-wide and classroom expectations should be presented to the students, even in Kindergarten. This gives the students a sense of responsibility in that they feel they have a job to do in the classroom and school.

There are many books and stories about children dealing with their emotions. Teachers can choose a story to read to the class and employ the strategy of predicting and confirming so that all students have an awareness of different ways of dealing with emotions.

SEE also Skill 7.2 for ideas on developing students' self-control

COMPETENCY 8.0 UNDERSTAND HOW TO CREATE A LANGUAGE-ENRICHED ENVIRONMENT THAT FOSTERS THE USE OF EXPRESSIVE AND RECEPTIVE LANGUAGE AND LITERACY

Skill 8.1 Indicators of language and literacy development

There is wide agreement that there are generally five stages of second language development. The first stage is "pre-production." While these students may actually understand what someone says to them (for the most part), they have a much harder time talking back in the target language. Teachers must realize that if students cannot "produce" the target language, it does not mean that they aren't learning. Most likely, they are. They are taking it in, and their brains are trying to figure out what to do with all the new language.

The second phase is early production. This is where the student can actually start to produce the target language. It is quite limited, and teachers most likely should not expect students to produce eloquent speeches during this time.

The third phase is emergent speech or speech emergence. Longer, more complex sentences are used, particularly in speech—and in social situations. But remember that students aren't fully fluent in this stage, and they cannot handle complex academic language tasks.

The fourth phase is intermediate fluency. This is where more complex language is produced. Grammatical errors are common.

The fifth stage is advanced fluency. While students may appear to be completely fluent, they will still need academic and language support from teachers.

Speech Intelligibility

Speech intelligibility guidelines provide a tracking of a child's oral speech development. General researchers have shown that the following guidelines are recognizable age/language acquisition:

- Children at 2 years old should have speech patterns that are about 70% intelligible.
- Children at 3 years old should have an increased 10% speech pattern that is about 80% intelligible.
- Children at 4 years old should have a 20% speech pattern that is about 90% intelligible.
- Children at 5 years old should have a speech pattern that is 100% intelligible.
- Children >5 years old will develop speech patterns that continue at 100% intelligibility with increased vocabulary databases.

Given the speech intelligibility guidelines, parents, adult caregivers and teachers are able to track what is normal development versus language developmental delays or differences. If a child is not developing intelligible and recognizable speech patterns at age appropriate development levels, intervention and additional in depth evaluations will provide the proper tools to address and correct language delays that could have long range impacts on a child's final development of speech pattern intelligibility of language.

Teachers and parents who have concerns about a child's language development should be proactive in addressing language delays. Contacting speech pathologists, auditory specialists to test for hearing disorders, pediatricians to test for motor functioning delays, and utilizing other assessment resources for evaluation are effective steps for those concerned about a child's language delays or differences. Early intervention is the key to addressing children's language delays or differences.

SEE Skill 1.1 under *Language Development*

Literacy Development

The term literacy relates to both reading and writing and suggests the simultaneous development and mutually reinforcing effects of these two aspects of communication. Literacy development is seen as emerging from children's oral language development and their initial, often unconventional attempts at reading (usually based on pictures) and writing (at first, scribbling) -- hence the term emergent literacy. Within an emergent literacy framework, children's early unconventional attempts at reading and writing are respected as legitimate beginnings of literacy.

All children who enter kindergarten have some foundation of oral language skills that can serve as a foundation for their reading and writing. Oral language skills can be expanded and further developed through listening activities, especially the reading aloud of stories, and eventually through reading experiences. There is a strong, significant relationship between listening comprehension and reading comprehension. Listening to stories is an excellent vehicle for expanding oral language patterns, for extending thinking skills, and for building vocabulary.

To grow as readers and writers, young children must develop other understandings about language, often referred to as metalinguistic awareness. They must, for example, develop a concept of what a word is, both printed and spoken, and know how it is different from numbers, letters, sounds, and sentences. They must learn that print is read from left to right and from top to bottom.

In effect, written language is a code that stands for oral language. Beginning readers must become familiar with the printed code in order to equate it with oral language. Young children can understand and enjoy a book if someone reads the text to them; however, in order to understand and enjoy the book on their own, they must learn to recognize printed words as the equivalent of what was read to them. To gain this ability to appreciate written text independently, a child must develop word identification, or decoding, skills.

For an extensive summary of the best available research and professional expertise to help teachers provide high-quality literacy instruction for students from kindergarten through Grade 8, go to http://www.eduplace.com/rdg/res/literacy/ (Issues in Literacy Development, by John J. Pikulski and J. David Cooper)

Skill 8.2 Factors that influence children's language development (e.g., being read to every day, given time to use language daily, family literacy)

The majority of young children's language development begins during their second year. By the age of two, most children are likely to speak at least 50 words and can combine them to make short phrases. During the preschool years, a child's sentence patterns become increasingly complex and vocabulary increases to include relational terms that express concepts of size, location, quantity and time. When a young child reaches the age of four to six, they have acquired the basic grammar of the sentence.

Even when young children spend most of their waking hours in child care, and later school; parents still remain the most influential adults in their lives. The child's primary caregivers, whether they are the parents, grandparents or foster parents, structure the child's experiences and shape the environments as their early language development unfolds. Parents who read books, play music and talk to their newborn babies are helping them to develop a basic understanding of language - its rhythms, tones and moods. As young children grow, parents should continue to look for opportunities to engage their kids in conversation. When talking with children, adults and parents try to pose questions that encourage them to formulate questions.

A child's early verbal environment influences language learning throughout their entire life. From ages one to three, children from highly verbal families often hear nearly three times as many words per week as children from low verbal families. When talking with children it is important to use descriptive language in order to expand their vocabularies. Adults and parents can describe a vase of flowers as: "small, bright yellow flowers" giving children a descriptive and informative picture of what is in the vase on the table.

Another good idea for increasing language developing is to use a variety of words, rather than the same few repeatedly. Rather than always saying "big," adults could use the words: large, huge, gigantic, or enormous.

Children learn a lot from being around other students and adults. Not only is interaction beneficial from a social standpoint, but it can also help to enhance a child's language development. Children should be encouraged to be active in various social activities. These varying environments are advantageous as each situation will likely require different listening and speaking skills which will allow the children to develop their language skills. For example, attending a story-time session at the library will help enhance a child's listening skills as well as possibly increasing their vocabularies and attention spans, while playing with peers at the park encourages the art of back-and-forth conversation.

Strategies to encourage family literacy

- Talk with your child frequently
- Read a variety of books
- Help your child focus on sound patterns of words such as those found in rhyming games
- Have your child retell stories and talk about events of the day
- Talk with your child during daily activities; give directions for your child to follow (e.g., making cookies)
- Encourage your child to form opinions about what he or she hears or reads and relate what is read to experiences
- Help your child make connections between what is read and heard at school, at home, and in other daily activities

Increasing the opportunities children experience with the social world around them can provide an early foundation for solid and strong language development.

Skill 8.3   The importance of acknowledging a child's language

Teachers and caregivers of children developing oral language proficiency can provide effective instructional, cultural, linguistic and language development tools that enhance and increase language acquisition. Teachers and parents must remember that language development in children develops in an efficient manner, so the focus should be on allowing the child to create his/her own language scenarios in constructing language repertoires.

The promotion of language development should include repetition and language engagement. The act of simulating the sounds and words in their environment provides the child with language enhancement and acquisition. Children can be presented with a question that helps them process object and meaning association such as when pointing to the color blue in the sky "What color is that?" or to the sky, "What is that?"

Children's toys, games and books can be used to further language development. Providing language simulation activities that model for children how to ask questions or put words into sentences is an effective instructional strategy that can provide children with proper guidance through the maze of language acquisition and oral communication.

Providing children with instructional language cues can facilitate learning and language development. Using strategic tools such as rephrasing sentences into questions such as "dada goed" into "Is daddy going?" can provide children with sentence formats and other ways of looking at oral meaning. When children are given labels for objects, they can use word association in developing language acquisition. Personalizing interactions with children during the formative years of oral and language development can become effective tools and strategies to create life long learners.

Skill 8.4 Strategies for developing children's listening and speaking skills

Teachers should remain focused on oral language skills throughout the day, even while teaching other subjects. The following activities encourage students to develop oral language skills in the early stages of oral language development:

Encourage meaningful conversation
Let student "read" a favorite book to you. Ask them why it is their favorite book. Ask questions prompting a purposeful discussion that allows the student to develop and demonstrate their speaking skills.

Allow dramatic playtime
Make sure children have time for "pretend play" to develop. Provide props that associate play to favorite books.

Let children share personal stories.
Support their efforts to communicate complex thoughts by waiting patiently, suggesting words as needed, and encouraging their efforts to vocalize new words, while they compare their own experiences with other students.

Sing Alphabet Songs
Sing the alphabet song in order to teach students to enjoy and identify the different musical sounds of the alphabet.

Teach the art of questioning
Read a book to the students. Allow them to ask curiosity questions (who, what, why, when and where). This encourages the students to develop higher cognitive skills through questions.

Read rhyming books
By listening to a favorite book of rhymes, students can identify the rhyming words and sound them out.

Play listening games
Let students pretend they are talking on the phone to each other. Have them repeat the conversation. This encourages students to hear the words and then repeat them.

Encourage sharing of information
By encouraging each student to share information about an idea, the student is able to vocalize their words and thoughts in a logical sequence

Skill 8.5   The relationship between writing and the development of fine-motor control

Learning to write is generally a sequential process. Research confirms that children develop spelling strategies in predictable stages. There is a continuous growth in writing, but the children vary in the development of these stages. A child's writing may show evidence of more than one stage. Children may even skip levels on their way to developing writing competency.

Children progress as writers from one phase to the next, with one set of skills building on the skills acquired earlier. Writing, however, combines many skills, and relies on development in many areas not specific to writing. A child's fine motor control and vocabulary, for example, must improve in order for writing to progress normally.

Writing is a process that flows gradually. As you give your students time to explore and experiment with writing, you will begin to see evidence of growth. Since writing is a process and stages are connected, students may show evidence of more than one stage in a single piece of writing.

In order for a child to write correctly, **fine motor skills** must be developed. Before being required to manipulate a pencil, children should have dexterity and strength in their fingers, which helps them to gain more control of small muscles.

The activities below will build strength in fingers and hands, aiding in the development of a child's writing skills.

Tearing
Tear newspaper into strips and then crumple them into balls. Use the balls to stuff a Halloween pumpkin or other art creation.

Cutting
Cut pictures from magazines
Cut a fringe on the edge of a piece of construction paper.

Puzzles
Have children put together a puzzle with large puzzles pieces. This will help to develop proper eye-hand coordination.

Clay
Manipulating play dough into balls strengthens a child's grasp. Let the children explain what they created from their play dough objects.

Finger Painting
Many times when a child has not developed fine motor skills yet, it helps to trace the pattern with his finger before he tries it with a pencil. Have the child trace a pattern in sand, cornmeal, finger paint, etc.

Drawing
Draw at an easel with a large crayon. Encourage children to practice their name or letters of the alphabet

Learning to Write

The most important factors of learning to write are the grip on the writing instrument, the position of the arm and wrist, and the position of the writing paper.

The Primary Grip
Beginning writers with undeveloped fine motor skills should be taught the primary grip. First, have the child join the tips of the thumb and middle finger. Then place the pen in the space between them. Finally, have the child lay the index finger on top of the pen. This way, the index finger pushes against the thumb and middle finger. As children grow, the proportions of their hands change. This allows them to hold the pen differently and write faster.

Paper Position
Right-handed children should place the paper directly in front of them and hold it in place with the left hand. The light should come from the left. Otherwise, the child's' hand will cast a shadow just where they need to see what they are writing. With the paper slightly to the right of the writer, their line of vision is clear. Teachers should check to see if the students are the children sitting upright. Make sure they are not gripping the pen too hard, and the paper in the right position.

Beginning Strokes
A teacher may need to teach a student the direction of the pencil strokes. A good word to practice with is their first name. Identify one letter at a time. Show the beginning point right on the top line and the ending point on the bottom line. Slowly write their name on one line, one letter at a time, so the child can clearly see it. Have the child write directly under your sample, not to the side. Write your sample in straight, easy to copy letters.

Problems to look for:

Gripping the pencil too tightly
A common problem for all young children learning to write is gripping the pencil too tightly, which makes writing tiresome. Usually the student learns to relax their grip as writing skill develops, but teachers can remind students to hold the instrument gently.

Holding the pencil incorrectly
If the child tends to hold the pencil too close to the point, make a mark on the pencil at the correct spot, to remind the student where to grip the pencil.

Left-handed writers

In languages that are written left-to-right; like the English language, it is more difficult to write with the left hand. A right-hander writes away from their body and pulls the pencil, while a left-hander must write toward their body and push the pencil. Left-handed students should place their paper at an angle and to the left.

Skill 8.6 Methods for promoting children's understanding of the diversity of communication

When communicating with others, the communication style should be adjusted for various audiences. While audiences should not be stereotyped, certain methods of communication are more appropriate with certain people than with others. Age is an easy one to consider: Adults know that when they talk to children, they should come across as pleasant and non-threatening, and they should use vocabulary that is simple for children to understand. On the other hand, teenagers realize that they should not speak to their grandmothers they way the speak with their peers. When dealing with communications between cultures and genders, people must be sensitive, considerate, and appropriate.

How do teachers help students understand these "unspoken" rules of communication when these rules are not easy to communicate in regular classroom lessons? Teachers must model these behaviors, and they must have high expectations for students (clearly communicated, of course) inside and outside the classroom walls.

Teachers must also consider these aspects as they deal with colleagues, parents, community members, and even students. They must realize that all communication should be tailored so that it conveys appropriate messages and tones to listeners.

Informal and formal language is a distinction made on the basis of the occasion as well as the audience. At a "formal" occasion, for example, a meeting of executives or of government officials, even conversational exchanges are likely to be more formal. A cocktail party or a golf game is an example of where language is likely to be informal. Formal language uses fewer or no contractions, less slang, longer sentences, and more organization in longer segments.

Speeches delivered to executives, college professors, government officials, etc., are likely to be formal. Speeches made to fellow employees are likely to be informal. Sermons tend to be formal; Bible lessons will tend to be informal.

Different from the basic writing forms of discourse is the art of debating, discussion, and conversation. The ability to use language and logic to convince the audience to accept your reasoning and to side with you is an art. This form of writing/speaking is extremely structured, logically sequenced, with supporting reasons and evidence. At its best, it is the highest form of propaganda. Position statements, evidence, reason, evaluation and refutation are integral parts of this type of communication.

TEACHER CERTIFICATION STUDY GUIDE

COMPETENCY 9.0   **UNDERSTAND THE DEVELOPMENT OF YOUNG CHILDREN'S COGNITION IN MATHEMATICAL AND SCIENTIFIC CONCEPTS AND HOW TO HELP CHILDREN MAKE SENSE OF THEIR WORLD**

Skill 9.1   **Includes factors and practices that promote positive attitudes regarding math and science**

Math

When presented with a challenging activity, students who have been encouraged to face it with a positive attitude will be more likely to overcome the challenge presented. It is for this reason that teachers need to take time to build positive interests and attitudes related to math for all of their students. Research has proven that setting high expectations with appropriate teaching and encouragement is one of the best strategies for developing higher-level thinking and math skills.

In order for this to occur, the teacher must provide an appropriate learning environment where children feel safe to take risks and are encouraged to do so. Helping students to feel welcome within the classroom and providing a comfortable, orderly classroom will go a long way in providing the most appropriate learning environment for students. These classroom management issues may seem redundant but set the foundation for all learning experiences, not simply math.

Within the math program, it is necessary for children to understand the value and purpose of tasks presented in a clear and explicit manner. Considering student interests, how the tasks are relevant to their lives, and providing open-ended learning activities help students to connect in a meaningful manner to the subject. Tapping into the natural curiosity of the students and expanding it to include their interests encourages students to develop a better sense of their surroundings.

Throughout all of these processes, the teacher must display a positive attitude about math. Statements that are derogatory about the subject should be eliminated. The cliché of enthusiasm being contagious is very true. The more excited and positive a teacher is about the subject, the more likely the students will be to view math as a positive part of their lives. As students struggle, it can be important for the teacher to provide the necessary scaffolding to limit frustrations or negative feelings related to the subject.

In the end, connecting math to real-life events that are interesting and meaningful to the students is the key to developing this positive attitude. The students who play Little League may complete some activities based on baseball cards. Pokemon games or other high interest activities can be incorporated into the math class periodically to boost learning and interest. Cooking with students near holidays or as a special event can help students to understand better the value of the more difficult concepts of fractions. Using play and games are excellent motivators that also can be used to build math skills in a positive manner for students.

Basic money skills and snack-time math can be used to develop the idea of the value of math in real life with Pre-K and kindergarten students. In kindergarten, students learn to recognize a penny, nickel, dime, quarter, and one-dollar bill. In 1st grade, they learn how different combinations of coins have equivalent values, for example, that 10 pennies are the same as 1 dime and 10 dimes are the same as 1 dollar. Teaching children that money has value can start with a simple exercise of counting pennies to understand their monetary value. From here, students can advance to counting nickels, dimes, and so on. The next step might be to have students combine different coins and compute the value of the combination. As students advance in their understanding of the value of money, shopping math can be introduced where students see that money has value in exchange for goods. They can also learn to make change and count change.

Science

Science should also be exciting. Teacher behaviors that motivate students include:

- Maintaining success expectations through teaching, goal setting, establishing connections between effort and outcome, and self-appraisal and reinforcement
- Having a supply of intrinsic incentives such as rewards for appropriate competition between students that connects with the value of the academic activities
- Focusing on students' intrinsic motivation through adapting the tasks to students' interests, providing opportunities for active response, including a variety of tasks, providing rapid feedback, incorporating games into the lesson, and allowing students the opportunity to make choices, create, and interact with peers
- Stimulating students' learning by modeling positive expectations and attributions. Project enthusiasm and personalize abstract concepts. The teacher should also model problem-solving and task-related thinking so students can see how the process is done.

If you'd like to learn more about how to promote positive attitudes about math and science, you may enjoy reading this article on Educationworld.com by educator Sheila Tobias: http://www.education-world.com/a_curr/profdev026.shtml

She is the author of the long-selling 1978 book *Overcoming Math Anxiety* (revised in 1994), which was followed in 1987 by *Succeed with Math: Every Student's Guide to Conquering Math Anxiety*.

Skill 9.2 The role of hands-on activities in building knowledge, language, and concepts

Learning can be broadly divided into two types—active and passive. Active learning, as the name indicates, involves a learning atmosphere full of action, whereas in passive learning, students are taught in a non-stimulating and inactive environment. Active learning involves and draws students into it, thereby interesting them to the point of participating and purposely engaging in learning.

It is crucial that students are actively engaged, not entertained. They should be taught the answers for "How" and "Why" questions and encouraged to be inquisitive and interested.

Active learning is conceptualized as follows:

A Model of Active Learning

Experience of	Dialogue with
Doing	Self
Observing	Others

This model suggests that all learning activities involve some kind of experience or some kind of dialogue. The two main kinds of dialogue are "Dialogue with self" and "Dialogue with others." The two main kinds of experience are "Observing" and "Doing."

Dialogue with self: This is what happens when learners think reflectively about a topic. They ask themselves a number of things about the topic.

Dialogue with others: When the students are listening to a book being read by another student or when the teacher is teaching, a partial dialogue takes place because the dialogue is only one-sided. When they are listening to an adult and when there is an exchange of ideas back and forth, it is said to be a dialogue with others.

Observing: This is a most important skill in science. This occurs when a learner is carefully watching or observing someone else doing an activity or experiment. This is a good experience, although it is not quite the same as doing it for themselves.

Doing: This refers to any activity where a learner actually does something, giving the learner a firsthand experience that is very valuable.

The scientific attitude is to be curious, open to new ideas, and skeptical. In science, there is always new research, new discoveries, and new theories proposed. Sometimes, old theories are disproved. To view these changes rationally, one must have openness, curiosity, and skepticism. (Skepticism is a Greek word, meaning a method of obtaining knowledge through systematic doubt and continual testing. A scientific skeptic is one who refuses to accept certain types of claims without subjecting them to a systematic investigation.)

The students may not have these attitudes inherently, but it is the responsibility of teachers to encourage, nurture, and practice these attitudes so that their students will have good role models.

The use of supplementary materials in the classroom can greatly enhance the learning experience by stimulating student interest and satisfying different learning styles. Manipulatives, models, and technology are examples of tools available to teachers.

Manipulatives are materials that students can physically handle and move. Manipulatives allow students to understand mathematic concepts by allowing them to see concrete examples of abstract processes. Manipulatives are attractive to students because they appeal to the students' visual and tactile senses. Available for all levels of math, manipulatives are useful tools for reinforcing operations and concepts. They are not, however, a substitute for the development of sound computational skills.

Models are another means of representing mathematical and scientific concepts by relating the concepts to real-world situations. Teachers must choose wisely when devising and selecting models because, to be effective, models must be applied properly. For example, a building with floors above and below ground is a good model for introducing the concept of negative numbers. It would be difficult, however, to use the building model in teaching subtraction of negative numbers.

Example:
Use tiles to demonstrate both geometric ideas and number theory.
Give each group of students 12 tiles and instruct them to build rectangles.
Students draw their rectangles on paper.

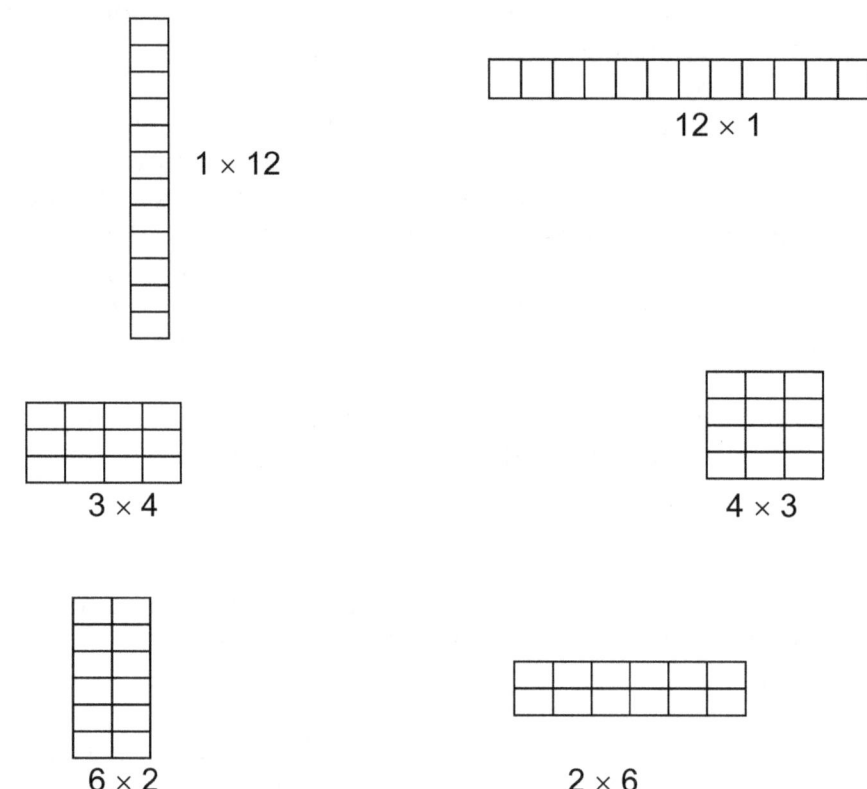

Visual aids such as math fact posters and number lines can be beneficial in helping primary age students learn basic math concepts. A number line may be introduced to help students understand addition and subtraction. Suppose we want to show 6 + 3 on a number line.

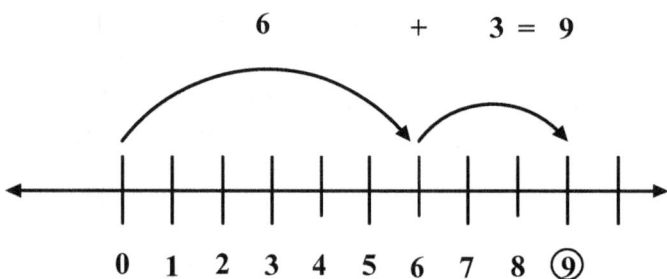

Addition can be thought of as starting from zero and counting 6 units to the right on the line (in the positive direction) and then counting 3 more units to the right. The number line shows that this is the same as counting 9 units to the right.

In the same way, a number line may be used to represent subtraction. Suppose we have 6 − 3 or rather 6 + (−3).

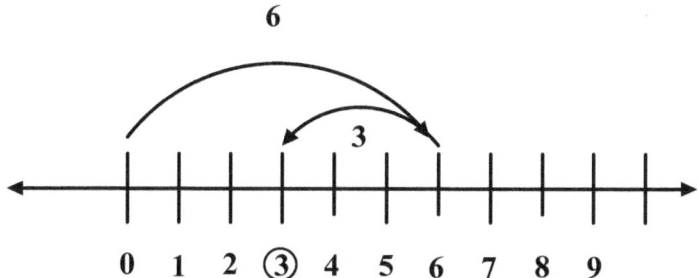

If 3 is shown by counting 3 positions to the right, then −3 can be shown as 3 positions to the left. We start from zero and count 6 positions to the right and then count 3 positions to the left. This illustrates how 6 + (−3) = 3.

Teaching young children mathematics requires a progression from the tangible to the abstract. As new concepts are introduced, it is important for the teacher to utilize concrete objects. This allows students to manipulate, touch, and explore the learning in a real way. This exploration provides the students the opportunity to be actively engaged in the learning. In this way, students can construct their own foundations, questions, and concepts related to numbers.

A popular activity that illustrates the base ten number system is to count the days towards the 100th day of school. Students use straws (or small sticks) to represent each day. The students add a straw to their collection each day, and when they have ten, they bundle them with a rubber band. By the time they reach the 100th day, they have 9 bundles of 10, and when they add the last straw, they will have 10 bundles of 10. The students then bundle the 10 bundles of 10 into 1 bundle of 100.

Unifix cubes are another excellent manipulative for teaching the base ten number system. They can be easily used as base ten blocks for exploring ones and tens. Each color can act as a group of ten when connected.

Providing the students with concrete and meaningful learning experiences is more involved than simply passing out blocks or beans to help introduce a concept. It involves utilizing and developing the language of subject. Inquiry–based learning provides the students the opportunity to not only explore the materials and concepts, but to begin to organize the information in order to be able to communicate their ideas of mathematics.

Without this concrete level of exploration, students may be able to memorize rote processes for solving problems (algorithms), but they may lack the foundational understanding necessary to make mathematical connections to everyday situations and experiences. Some students will be unable to see the broader generalizations found throughout math unless they have the time and exposure to the concepts through concrete learning experiences.

Mathematics has its own language, which requires practice and development. Often students who are struggling with the concepts presented lack the appropriate vocabulary and exposure to mathematical language to be successful. It is important to promote the development of this vocabulary, as you would do with reading vocabulary or in other subjects.

Children at this age should be able to begin to use simple quantity words such as *more, fewer, same, enough, some, many,* and *lots of* and apply these words to daily situations. "May I have one more cookie?" "She has fewer blocks than I do." "I have some toys."

Students will learn the language associated with operations:

Addition:
How many are there in all?
What does that add up to?
How many are there all together?
If we put this together with that, how many will there be?
What is the total?

Subtraction:
How many fewer?
How many less?
How many more than …?
How many less than …?
How many more are needed?
How many are left over?

Multiplication:
How many in all?
How many all together?
What is the total?

Division:
How many in each set?
How many sets?
How many times does this number go into this number?

Successful math teachers introduce their students to multiple problem-solving strategies and create a classroom environment where free thought and experimentation are encouraged. Teachers can promote problem solving by allowing multiple attempts at problems, giving credit for reworking test or homework problems, and encouraging the sharing of ideas through class discussion. Once the students are successful at completing problem solving activities at the concrete level, students should be exposed to the semi-concrete (use of pictures and symbols) level and finally to the abstract level (use of symbols or letters to represent numbers or concepts). Teachers should be familiar with several specific problem-solving skills.

The **guess-and-check** strategy calls for students to make an initial guess at the solution, check the answer, and use the outcome to guide the next guess. With each successive guess, the student should get closer to the correct answer. Constructing a table from the guesses can help organize the data.

Example: There are 100 coins in a jar, and 10 are dimes. The rest are pennies and nickels. There are twice as many pennies as nickels. How many pennies and nickels are in the jar?

There are 90 total nickels and pennies in the jar (100 coins – 10 dimes).

There are twice as many pennies as nickels. Make guesses that fulfill the criteria and adjust based on the answer found. Continue until you find the correct answer: 60 pennies and 30 nickels.

Number of Pennies	Number of Nickels	Total Number of Pennies and Nickels
40	20	60
80	40	120
70	35	105
60	30	90

When solving a problem where the final result and the steps to reach the result are given, students must **work backwards** to determine what the starting point must have been.

Example:
John subtracted 7 from his age, and divided the result by 3. The result was 4. What is John's age?

Work backward by reversing the operations:
$4 \times 3 = 12$
$12 + 7 = 19$
John is 19 years old.

Estimation and testing for **reasonableness** are related skills students should employ prior to and after solving a problem. These skills are particularly important when students use calculators to find answers.

Example:
Find the sum of 4387 + 7226 + 5893.

    4400 + 7200 + 5900 = 17500   Estimation.
    4387 + 7226 + 5893 = 17506   Actual sum.

By comparing the estimate to the actual sum, students can determine that their answer is reasonable.

Throughout the process, students should be encouraged to develop methods for recording their information using pictures, symbols, numbers, or other more appropriate ideas. Venn diagrams are excellent for comparing mathematical concepts. Learning to use pictures and numbers together to represent an idea provides students with a means to communicate to each other the concepts they are learning. Teachers can build the vocabulary and thinking skills of their students by using these pictures or student–created models and providing the students with the correct mathematical name or label for the idea. Together, these student–created and teacher-labeled representations can provide students with not only a communication tool, but also a concrete method for explaining conjectures to each other.

Skill 9.3   Strategies that promote the transfer of mathematical and scientific concepts and skills to everyday life

One of the most important concepts of any lesson is to help the students realize the importance of the skills being learned to their everyday lives outside of the school setting. This is equally true within the field of math. As students identify and realize the importance of the skills being learned to their lives at home, they will become more involved in the learning, as it has new and better value for them. For very young children, this may require specific and explicit explanations or connections.

If learning is connected to everyday life, students are motivated because they can easily see its relevance. If they are taught about something remote, they will not be able to relate, and the results are decreased interest, decreased motivation to study, and a general decrease in learning.

Mathematics

One of the easiest ways to incorporate real life mathematical activities is to bring real life activities into the classroom. Working as a class to prepare food where the students need to measure different ingredients before/after completing lessons on fractions is an excellent way for the students to understand the importance of the learning. Other mixing activities that involve measuring math skills include making play dough, making slime, and creating the perfect bubble blowing mixture. Cooking and mixture activities also have a direct connection to the sciences and allow the teacher to combine subject areas into one lesson.

Other methods to incorporate math activities into more regular parts of students' lives and other subject areas include:

- Charting/graphing the weather on a regular basis
- Predicting temperatures based on a pattern or other information
- Helping students keep track of the score of a sporting event or a game using tally marks
- Finding the age of other family members or characters in stories
- Building race cars or straw structures to represent buildings from stories or having your own race, similar to a NASCAR event
- Redesigning the layout of the classroom/cafeteria
- Playing card, dice, and board games with the students (popular games like Pokemon involve a lot of math if played correctly)
- Having students count the squares on a board game
- Figuring out who is older when given the single-digit ages of two children
- Timing activities or determining how long until a special event will occur
- Handing out treats—does the student have enough for everyone? How many are left once the treats are handed out?
- Compare classmates—Who is taller? Who is shorter?

Science

The science concept being taught should have some practical relevance to the students' lives. Science should be placed in context for ease of understanding and application.

Because biology is the study of living things, we can easily apply the knowledge of biology to daily life and personal decision-making. For example, biology greatly influences the health decisions humans make every day. What foods to eat, when and how to exercise, and how often to bathe are just three of the many decisions we make every day that are based on our knowledge of biology. Young children are also naturally curious about the world around them, and teachers can use this curiosity to teach many scientific concepts.

Skill 9.4   The use of everyday events to advance mathematics and science themes

Mathematics and science can be seen/utilized everyday. Children do not always translate these instances into a lesson, and that is okay. Let them have fun. Some great examples include weather, life cycles, and purchases made at a store. The following list includes ideas for classroom activities surrounding science and math.

Mathematics

Math is easily incorporated into the classroom through workbooks and activities. Patterns are an important concept in math. Children as young as preschoolers can recognize and create patterns according to color. Classification is also relevant. Children can reach into a large bucket of assorted items and categorize them according to color, shape, animal, beginning letter or sound, etc. Identifying particular coins and their value can be a challenging concept. Children need help recognizing, for example, that five nickels are equivalent to a quarter. One way to aid in this area is to use blocks instead. Single blocks are equal to one unit. Ten single blocks can be exchanged for a larger, rectangular unit. Ten of these can be exchanged for a 100's unit. While the exchange of monetary units and making change for a dollar can be challenging, children are familiar with the process of buying something and readily engage in games with play money.

For very young children, almost any mathematical question posed is a problem to be solved. Too often, the term problem solving is misrepresented as word problems. In fact, problem solving skills are used any time a problem is presented to a child where they are unaware of the answer. From the very beginning, children need to experience a variety of mathematical situations across all subject areas. Exposing children to a variety of contexts in which to solve problems allows them to develop their own constructs upon which they can build new learning.

Problem solving is not about one strategy or one right way, but rather it is about allowing students of varying mathematical skills and abilities to look at the same situation presented and find a way to solve it. In a group of five, it may be reasonable to expect five different methods to reach the solution. Providing students with the means to investigate a problem allows them to be flexible in their approach. Often times, teachers limit the abilities of their students to solve problems by restricting them to one mode of reaching a solution. Parents can also be guilty of this as well. For example, the kindergartener who is presented with a problem where there are three pies and twelve people to feed may easily use pieces of real pie to work out an appropriate solution. However, the parent or teacher who indicates you must use the division algorithm to solve the problem may automatically set this same student up for failure.

Problem solving needs to be incorporated in a real way for students to understand, appreciate, and value the process. Using daily activities or problems can help make problem solving a regular part of a child's day. As situations arise, in any subject area, it is important for the teacher to incorporate problem-solving activities. Having the students help with lunch count, attendance, counting the number of days left in the school year, calculating the time left until recess, or other daily types of activities are examples of ways to include realistic problem solving in the classroom. In science, children can graph the daily temperatures and make predictions for the future temperatures. In social studies, they can gather, tabulate, and calculate the data related to the topic presented (how many classmates agree that drugs are bad for your body). In language arts, children can solve problems found in all types of children's literature. Charting favorite books, calculating ages of characters in stories, and drawing maps of the setting(s) of books are some beginning examples of ways to connect the two subjects.

It is important for the teacher to be a role model. Thinking aloud as you come across a problem in the course of the day will help the students begin to realize the necessity and real-world implications of solving problems. Encouraging students to be reflective will also help in building the necessary mathematical language. In addition, students can begin to share their ideas and methods with each other, which is an excellent strategy for learning about problem solving.

Science

The quintessential science experiment for a chemical reaction is the volcano experiment. The addition of vinegar to baking soda in a contained area will cause a chemical reaction similar to an erupting volcano. Children love this as it gives them a visual representation of the abstract idea of a chemical reaction.

An idea for changes of state (these represent a physical change not a chemical change) would be the freezing and melting of water/ice. If you do this on a large enough scale, you can literally go back and forth between states every few days without too much loss of water (due to evaporation).

While not an experiment, it sets a good example to keep a recycling bin in your classroom for recyclable materials (where recycling capabilities exist). It is never too early to teach a child to respect the Earth.

Because **growth** is such a central concept in science, there are many appropriate experiments. Some familiar ideas include the peeling apart of a seed or bean to study its various parts. Leftover seeds not dissected can be planted. Students enjoy seeing their seeds grow. However, if you set a few aside and change the conditions, you can examine experimental variables (lack of sunlight, drought conditions, etc.). Continuing on the idea of growth, children can create a growth chart of themselves.

Hatching and/or housing animals in your classroom teaches children valuable lessons about respect for the Earth and its inhabitants. If you choose to hatch an organism (popular choices are tadpoles and butterflies), students can be introduced to the concept of life cycle. The duration of each stage in the life cycle can be tracked, tallied, and displayed in a graph format. Housing animals teaches children about responsibility and humane treatment. Animals should always be fed, watered, and cleaned appropriately and cared for adequately over school vacations. Be particularly careful about the temperature of the classroom.

Discuss weather every day. Introduce the idea of temperature by reading a thermometer together and discussing whether it is sunny, cloudy, rainy, snowy, etc. If there is a rainbow or thunderstorm outside (or was recently) discuss that phenomenon. If desired, the class could chart how many days are sunny versus how many are inclement.

Disclaimer: Experiments involving young children should never include toxic or harmful materials. The ideas listed above are generally considered safe. With that said, use appropriate discretion when conducting experiments and never leave your students alone.

Skill 9.5 The use of technology for children

There are many forms of technology available to math teachers. For example, students can test their understanding of math concepts by working on skill-specific computer programs and websites. Math games on the computer or the smart board can supplement and reinforce the learning from the teacher. Graphing calculators can help students visualize the graphs of functions. Teachers can also enhance their lectures and classroom presentations by creating multimedia presentations.

Calculators are an important tool. They should be encouraged in the classroom and at home. They do not replace the basic knowledge that should be taught early in a child's schooling, but they can relieve the tedium of mathematical computations later on, allowing students to explore more challenging mathematical directions. Even so, at times, it may be appropriate to have students complete the calculations themselves and then check it with a calculator. Some special needs students rely on calculators to complete computation, and all students are allowed to use calculators on certain standardized tests. An important thing to remember is that students will be able to use calculators more intelligently if they are taught how. Students always need to check their work by estimating. The goal of mathematics is to prepare the child to survive in the real world and technology is a reality in today's society.

There are many fun, educational, and age–appropriate computer games for children. Through these games, children can explore language, math, and science without feeling lectured. There is usually the added benefit of a motivational reward within the game, as well as the privilege to play. Computer games should be used as a supplement to, not a replacement for, interactive activities with their peers and teacher engagement.

COMPETENCY 10.0 UNDERSTAND HOW TO FOSTER PHYSICAL COMPETENCE (INCLUDING FINE-MOTOR, GROSS-MOTOR, AND PERCEPTUAL DEVELOPMENT) AND PROMOTE CHILDREN'S AWARENESS OF HEALTH, NUTRITION, AND SAFETY

Skill 10.1   The relationship between physical development and learning

Physical education is a key component of an interdisciplinary learning approach because not only does it draw from, but also it contributes to many other curriculum areas. Instructors can relate concepts from the physical sciences, mathematics, natural sciences, social sciences, and kinesiology to physical education activities.

Physical science is a term for the branches of science that study non-living systems. However, the term "physical" creates an unintended, arbitrary distinction, since many branches of physical science also study biological phenomena. Topics in physical science such as movement of an object through space and the effect of gravity on moving objects are of great relevance to physical education. Physical sciences allow us to determine the limits of physical activities.

Mathematics is the search for fundamental truths in pattern, quantity, and change. Examples of mathematical applications in sport include measuring speed, momentum, and height of objects; measuring distances and weights; scorekeeping; and statistical computations.

Natural science is the study of living things. Content areas in the natural sciences of great importance to physical education include physiology, nutrition, anatomy, and biochemistry. For example, a key component of physical education is an understanding of proper nutrition and the affect of food on the body.

The social sciences are a group of academic disciplines that study the human aspects of the world. Social scientists engage in research and theorize about both aggregate and individual behaviors. For example, a basic understanding of psychology is essential to the discussion of human patterns of nutrition and attitudes toward exercise and fitness. In addition, sport psychology is a specialized social science that explores the mental aspects of athletic performance.

Finally, kinesiology encompasses human anatomy, physiology, neuroscience, biochemistry, biomechanics, exercise psychology, and sociology of sport. Kinesiologists also study the relationship between the quality of movement and overall human health. Kinesiology is an important part of physical therapy, occupational therapy, chiropractics, osteopathy, exercise physiology, kinesiotherapy, massage therapy, ergonomics, physical education, and athletic coaching. The purpose of these applications may be therapeutic, preventive, or high-performance. The application of kinesiology can also incorporate knowledge from other academic disciplines such as psychology, sociology, cultural studies, ecology, evolutionary biology, and anthropology. The study of kinesiology is often part of the physical education curriculum and illustrates the truly interdisciplinary nature of physical education.

To read more about physical development and learning, go to http://www.wholefamily.com/aboutyourkids/child/normal/physical_development.html for an article entitled, *Is My Child Normal? Early Childhood Physical Development.* The article contains a checklist for physical development by age level, developed by Ziva Schapiro, OTR.

Skill 10.2 Activities and resources that foster children's physical development

Locomotor skills move an individual from one point to another. Locomotor skills acquisition usually follows sequential development: crawl, creep, walk, run, jump, hop, gallop, slide, leap, skip, step-hop.

- **Activities to develop walking skills** include walking slower and faster in place; walking forward, backward, and sideways with slower and faster paces in straight, curving, and zigzag pathways with various lengths of steps; pausing between steps; and changing the height of the body.

- **Activities to develop running skills** include having students pretend they are playing basketball, trying to score a touchdown, trying to catch a bus, finishing a lengthy race, or running on a hot surface.

- **Activities to develop jumping skills** include alternating jumping with feet together and feet apart, taking off and landing on the balls of the feet, clicking the heels together while airborne, and landing with a foot forward and a foot backward.

- **Activities to develop galloping skills** include having students play a game of Fox and Hound, with the lead foot representing the fox and the back foot the hound trying to catch the fox (alternate the lead foot).

- **Activities to develop sliding skills** include having students hold hands in a circle and sliding in one direction, then sliding in the other direction.

- **Activities to develop hopping skills** include having students hop all the way around a hoop and hopping in and out of a hoop reversing direction. Students can also place ropes in straight lines and hop side-to-side over the rope from one end to the other and change (reverse) the direction.

- **Activities to develop skipping skills** include having students combine walking and hopping activities leading up to skipping.

- **Activities to develop step-hopping skills** include having students practice stepping and hopping activities while clapping hands to an uneven beat.

Nonlocomotor skills are stability skills where the movement requires little or no movement of one's base of support and does not result in change of position. Nonlocomotor skills acquisition usually follows sequential development: stretch, bend, sit, shake, turn, rock and sway, swing, twist, dodge, and fall.

- **Activities to develop stretching** include lying on the back and stomach and stretching as far as possible; stretching as though one is reaching for a star, picking fruit off a tree, climbing a ladder, shooting a basketball, or placing an item on a high self; waking and yawning.

- **Activities to develop bending** include touching knees and toes then straightening the entire body and straightening the body halfway; bending as though picking up a coin, tying shoes, picking flowers/vegetables, and petting animals of different sizes.

- **Activities to develop sitting** include practicing sitting from standing, kneeling, and lying positions without the use of hands.

- **Activities to develop falling skills** include first collapsing in one's own space and then pretending to fall like bowling pins, raindrops, snowflakes, a rag doll, or Humpty Dumpty.

Manipulative skills use body parts to propel or receive an object, controlling objects primarily with the hands and feet. Two types of manipulative skills are receptive (catch + trap) and propulsive (throw, strike, kick). Manipulative skills acquisition usually follows sequential development: striking, throwing, kicking, ball rolling, volleying, bouncing, catching, and trapping.

- **Activities to develop striking** begin with the striking of stationary objects by a participant in a stationary position. Next, the person remains still while trying to strike a moving object. Then, both the object and the participant are in motion as the participant attempts to strike the moving object.

- **Activities to develop throwing** include throwing yarn/foam balls against a wall, then at a big target, and finally at targets decreasing in size.

- **Activities to develop kicking** include alternating feet to kick balloons/beach balls, then kicking them under and over ropes. Change the type of ball as proficiency develops.

- **Activities to develop ball rolling** include rolling different size balls to a wall, then to targets decreasing in size.

- **Activities to develop volleying** include using a large balloon and, first, hitting it with both hands, then one hand (alternating hands), and then using different parts of the body. Change the object as students progress (balloon, to beach ball, to foam ball, etc.)

- **Activities to develop bouncing** include starting with large balls and, first, using both hands to bounce and then using one hand (alternate hands).

- **Activities to develop catching** include using various objects (balloons, beanbags, balls, etc.) to catch and, first, catching the object the participant has thrown him/herself, then catching objects someone else threw, and finally increasing the distance between the catcher and the thrower.

- **Activities to develop trapping** include trapping slow and fast rolling balls; trapping balls (or other objects such as beanbags) that are lightly thrown at waist, chest, and stomach levels; trapping different size balls.

Skill 10.3 Behaviors and factors that affect individual, family, and community health and safety

Many factors and behaviors affect individual, family, and community health and safety. While very young children are not ready to appreciate the intricacies of health and safety, early childhood educators play an important role in introducing children to the basics of lifetime health and safety. Important factors to address include diet, exercise and activity level, environment, and interpersonal relationships.

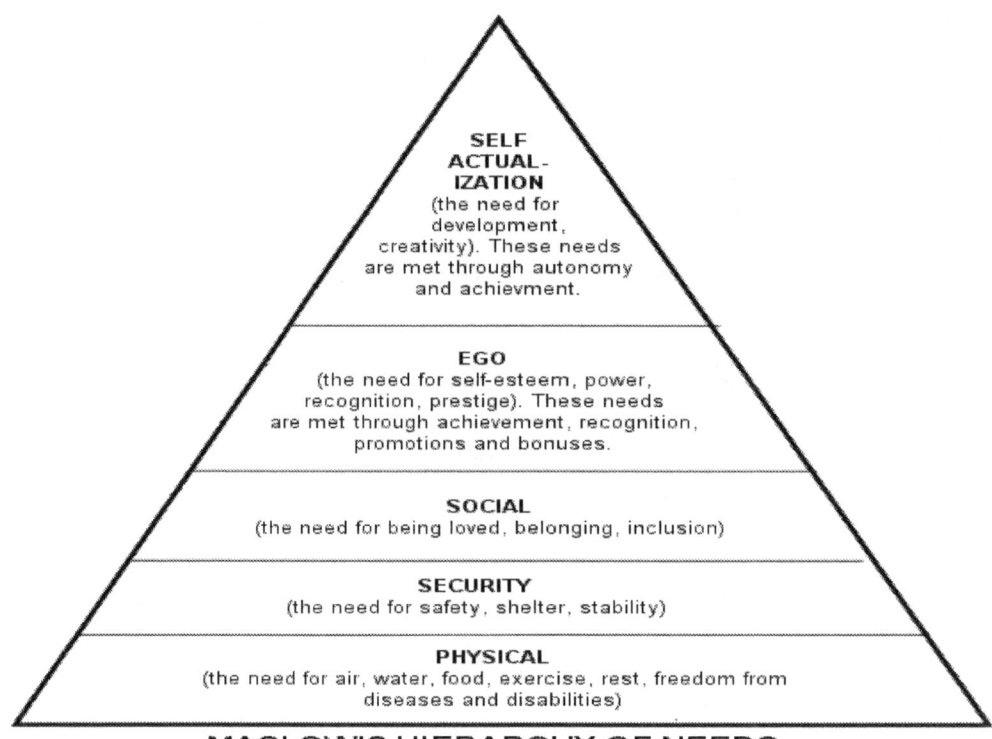

MASLOW'S HIERARCHY OF NEEDS

Drawing upon Maslow's Hierarchy of Needs, it is recognized that the fundamentals of safety, food and shelter must be maintained in order for a child to grow and mature in an appropriate manner. Indeed, children – especially young children – are almost completely dependent upon others for their safety, nutritional needs, and all other aspects of life. Unfortunately, as a society there are innumerable pressures that impact the lives of students often with negative consequences. For example, poverty may place a child at risk of injury at home due to lack of adult supervision. Other students may struggle with inadequate nutrition due to parents working multiple jobs and a heavy reliance on fast food products. Many families lack medical insurance and still other students may be the victim of abuse or neglect.

Take for example the following statistics related to nutrition as taken from the book *Fast Food Nation* by Eric Schlosser:

- Americans now spend more money on fast food than on higher education, personal computers, computer software, or new cars. They spend more on fast food than on movies, books, magazines, newspapers, videos, and recorded music -- Combined!
- In 1968, McDonald's operated about one thousand restaurants. Today, it has about twenty-eight thousand restaurants worldwide and opens almost two thousand new ones each year. An estimated one out of every eight workers in the United States has at some point been employed by McDonald's.

- McDonald's operates more playgrounds than any other private entity in the United States. It is one of the nation's largest distributors of toys. A survey of American schoolchildren found that 96 percent could identify Ronald McDonald. The only fictional character with a higher degree of recognition was Santa Claus.
- The typical American now consumes approximately three hamburgers and four orders of French fries every week.

Maintaining a healthy diet is an integral part of a lifetime health and wellness plan. Young children should learn the basic distinctions between healthy and less healthy foods. For example, educators should encourage children to eat fruits and vegetables and limit their consumption of sweets and fast food while also discussing the benefits of the choosing the healthier options. Older students may benefit from keeping a "diet diary" where they record all food and beverage intake over a three day period and then analyze for nutrition, fat intake and long term results!

Exercise and physical activity is another key aspect of a lifetime health and wellness plan. Physical educators at the early childhood level can lay the foundation for participation in and enjoyment of a variety of physical activities. Instructors should emphasize the importance of exercise and encourage each student to find physical activities they enjoy. In addition, to help promote family health, instructors should encourage students to ask their parent and other family members to join them in regular exercise at home.

Environmental factors such as air quality, sanitation, vaccination rates, and neighborhood dynamics also impact health and safety. While largely out of the teacher's control, these factors are important to consider when assessing a child's health and safety. For example, children who live in areas with poor air quality or poor sanitation may be more susceptible to illness. In addition, children who live in impoverished neighborhoods with high crime rates have increased safety concerns. Instructors can work with children to help them understand their environments and develop strategies to best promote health and safety.

Finally, low vaccination rates and inadequate preventative medical care can negatively affect individual, family, and community health. A concerted effort of collaboration between teachers and the school health nurse, social worker and community resources may often assist students and their families in obtaining much needed medical, social and other resources.

Most schools maintain a list of social service agencies and resources in each community. It is often kept in the office but is available upon request. If your school does not have one then the local library will. These are invaluable resources for teachers and schools; in fact, many social service agencies are available for free screening programs, presentations and much more. By working together, teachers are often able to improve the lives of their students and families.

Interpersonal relationships are another source of health and safety concerns. Domestic violence is a serious problem that can directly and indirectly harm children. Early childhood educators should teach their students that they should report harmful behavior because such behaviors are unacceptable. Teachers must take care to introduce such delicate topics in a way that is appropriate for young children and avoid using too much detail. Finally, teachers are typically considered "Mandatory Reporters" which legally requires a teacher to report any suspected abuse or neglect.

Abuse and neglect are epidemic in this society. An estimated 906,000 children are victims of abuse and neglect every year. The rate of victimization is 12.3 children per 1,000 children. Children ages 0-3 are the most likely to experience abuse. They are victimized at a rate of 16.4 per 1,000. To make matters worse, 1,500 children die every year from child abuse and neglect. That is just over four fatalities every single day! 79% of the children killed are younger than 4 years old. These statistics are so startling that it is typically not a question of "if" a teacher will need to make a report but rather "when".

To report child abuse or for more information on how to prevent child abuse contact your local Child Protective Services Agency or Childhelp:
Childhelp® USA National Child Abuse Hotline
1-800-4-A-CHILD®
(1-800-422-4453)
TDD: 1-800-2-A-CHILD

Skill 10.4   Principles of nutrition

Proper nutrition positively influences the quality of a child's physical activity level, their cognitive abilities, such as classroom concentration, as well as their emotional and mental growth. Adequate and proper nutrition is vital to encourage and support all aspects of children's development. Obesity, chronic diseases, high blood pressure, type 2 diabetes and even heart disease are just a few of the negative consequences that can result from poor nutrition in children. Additionally, obese children are at greater risk of becoming obese adults.

Daily calorie intact is determined by children's age, size and their activity level. Meals should mainly include whole grains, low-fat or nonfat dairy products, vegetables, fruits and lean meats. It is also recommended introducing fish into children's diets along with reductions in the intake of beverages high in sugar and highly salted foods.

The components of nutrition are **carbohydrates, proteins, fats, vitamins, minerals, and water.**

Carbohydrates – the main source of energy (glucose) in the human diet. The two types of carbohydrates are simple and complex. Complex carbohydrates have greater nutritional value because they take longer to digest, contain dietary fiber, and do not excessively elevate blood sugar levels. Common sources of carbohydrates are fruits, vegetables, grains, dairy products, and legumes.

Proteins – are necessary for growth, development, and cellular function. The body breaks down consumed protein into component amino acids for future use. Major sources of protein are meat, poultry, fish, legumes, eggs, dairy products, grains, and legumes.

Fats – a concentrated energy source and important component of the human body. The different types of fats are saturated, monounsaturated, and polyunsaturated. Polyunsaturated fats are the healthiest because they may lower cholesterol levels, while saturated fats increase cholesterol levels. Common sources of saturated fats include dairy products, meat, coconut oil, and palm oil. Common sources of unsaturated fats include nuts, most vegetable oils, and fish.

Vitamins and minerals – organic substances that the body requires in small quantities for proper functioning. People acquire vitamins and minerals in their diets and in supplements. Important vitamins include A, B, C, D, E, and K. Important minerals include calcium, phosphorus, magnesium, potassium, sodium, chlorine, and sulfur.

Water – makes up 55 – 75% of the human body. Water is essential for most bodily functions and is attained through foods and liquids.

For information about the new food pyramid for children, go to http://www.mypyramid.gov/kids/index.html. This website contains posters, a coloring page, and a computer game designed specifically for children aged 6 to 11.

Skill 10.5   Influences of culture on practices relating to health, nutrition, and safety

Many factors influence children's health, nutrition and safety. Dealing with factors that are out of the teacher's control requires both structure and flexibility. When necessary, the teacher should make adjustments among the students and/or the activity. For example, when teaching how to throw a softball, don't hesitate to pair girls with boys if their maturity and strength levels are similar. If the distance is too far for some pairs, move them closer. If some pairs are more advanced, challenge them by increasing the partner's distance while continuing to work on accuracy and speed. Add a personal challenge to see how many times they can toss without dropping the ball. Finally, having more advanced students teach their peers that aren't as competent will benefit all students.

Psychological – Psychological influences on motor development and fitness include a student's mental well-being, perceptions of fitness activities, and level of comfort in a fitness-training environment (both alone and within a group). Students experiencing psychological difficulties, such as depression, will tend to be apathetic and lack both the energy and inclination to participate in fitness activities. As a result, their motor development and fitness levels will suffer. Factors like the student's confidence level and comfort within a group environment, related to both the student's level of popularity within the group and the student's own personal insecurities, are also significant. It is noteworthy, though, that in the case of psychological influences on motor development and fitness levels, there is a more reciprocal relationship than with other influences. While a student's psychology may negatively affect their fitness levels, proper fitness training has the potential to positively affect the student psychologically, thereby reversing a negative cycle.

Cultural – Culture is a significant and sometimes overlooked influence on a student's motor development and fitness, especially in the case of students belonging to minority groups. Students may not feel motivated to participate in certain physical activities, either because they are not associated with the student's sense of identity or because the student's culture discourages these activities. For example, students from cultures with strict dress codes may not be comfortable with swimming activities. On the same note, students (especially older children) may be uncomfortable with physical activities in inter-gender situations. Educators must keep such cultural considerations in mind when planning physical education curricula.

Economic – The economic situation of students can affect their motor development and fitness because a lack of resources can detract from the ability of parents to provide access to extra-curricular activities that promote development, proper fitness training equipment (ranging from complex exercise machines to team sport uniforms to something as simple as a basketball hoop), and even adequate nutrition.

Familial – Familial factors that can influence motor development and fitness relate to the student's home climate concerning physical activity. A student's own feelings toward physical activity often reflect the degree to which caregivers and role models (like older siblings) are athletically inclined and have a positive attitude towards physical activity. It isn't necessary for the parents to be athletically inclined, so much as it is important for them to encourage their child to explore fitness activities that could suit them.

Environmental and Health – Genetic make-up (i.e. age, gender, ethnicity) has a big influence on growth and development. Various physical and environmental factors directly affect one's personal health and fitness. Poor habits, living conditions, and afflictions such as disease or disability can impact a person in a negative manner. A healthy lifestyle with adequate conditions and minimal physical or mental stresses will enable a person to develop towards a positive, healthy existence. A highly agreed upon motor development theory is the relationship between one's own heredity and environmental factors.

Instructors should place students in rich learning situations, regardless of previous experience or personal factors, which provide plenty of positive opportunities to participate in physical activity. For example, prior to playing a game of softball, have students practice throwing by tossing the ball to themselves, progress to the underhand toss, and later to the overhand toss.

Skill 10.6 Activities and resources that extend children's knowledge of ways to prevent accidents, injuries, and the spread of germs

Young children are at increased risk for contracting infectious diseases because they:
- are grouped together, and are exposed to many new germs
- have immune systems that are not fully developed to fight germs
- do not have complete control of body fluids that contain germs
- have personal habits that spread germs, including thumb sucking, rubbing eyes, and putting things in their mouths

Hand Washing plays a major role in preventing the spread of diseases. Washing your hands regularly with soap and water can protect you from many illnesses caused by viruses and bacteria. Washing removes germs you pick up when you touch people, animals, or surfaces. If not removed, these germs may get into your eyes, nose, or mouth and cause illness. Using finger puppets to help children visualize the invisible germs can be effective, as well as modeling and practice. Teachers should also remind children frequently about washing hands. For a lesson plan about hand washing, see http://www.health.state.mn.us/handhygiene/toolkit/curricula/curriculumyoung.pdf. For a free poster that demonstrates the steps to effective hand washing, go to http://www.health.state.mn.us/handhygiene/wash/fsgermbuster.html.

Physical education classes, whether conducted outdoors, in a gymnasium or classroom setting have inherent hazards which require close supervision. For example, when a group of children engage in physical activity and motion, the potential for injury is greatly increased. Teachers must monitor all activity to assure safe conduct, modify potentially risky behavior and redirect students to appropriate playtime. In addition, teachers must ensure equipment, playing fields, and courts are in proper condition and free from all hazards.

Physical Injuries on the Playground

Playground related injuries are a leading cause of hospital emergency room visits for children under the age of fourteen. According to research conducted by the U.S. Consumer Product Safety Commission in 2001, over 200,000 children annually are treated in the ER for playground related injuries with roughly 45% representing serious injuries including fractures, internal injuries, concussions, dislocations, and amputations (Tinsworth, 2001). Of these, the majority of injuries occur at schools and daycare centers (Phelan, 2001). Specific areas of concern for the supervising instructor include maintenance concerns such as trash which could cause a cut or puncture wound, rusty play equipment, damaged fall surfaces, wet conditions and under or unsupervised play activity leading to "rough housing" or "risk taking".

Younger children of elementary school age are at even greater risk of injury or harm due to playground injuries with first graders representing the highest percentage of all school related playground injuries; in some cases as high as 23%. Nearly 90% of playground injuries occur during recess or lunch.

Clearly, given the frequency and severity of playground related injuries in the school setting there are several protocols each and every school should have in place.
1. CPR and First Aid Training: All teachers should be certified in CPR for both adult and children in order to properly respond to potential injuries while emergency assistance is en route. As indicated from the data above; fractures, potential head injuries, lacerations and a host of other injuries may result in the need for emergency medical assistance.
2. Maintain an up-to-date fully stocked First Aid Kit that is portable and easily accessible! The First Aid Kit should be immediately available and on location even when outdoors.
3. Daily Maintenance and Inspection: Do not rely solely upon the maintenance staff to inspect playground equipment, surfaces and surrounding area. Instead, before allowing students access to equipment, a routine examination of the surrounding area should be conducted by staff. Pay close attention to objects that may have fallen in the sand or grass, loose or broken objects, surface quality and the operation of equipment itself. Report any problems and remove students from the immediate area until corrected.

4. Weather and environment: Wet, slippery equipment increases the risk of an accident and should be avoided. Students should never be allowed outside during a thunderstorm or when lightning is approaching. Likewise, days presenting poor air quality can also pose a special risk for students with asthma or other respiratory issues. Insets are another common problem with potentially deadly results for any student who is allergic so be sure to take the threat of bee stings, wasps or even fire ants very seriously. Develop an alternative plan of activity for those days when weather, insects or air quality doesn't permit safe play for all students.
5. Train and educate students about the proper use of equipment at the beginning of the school year. Research has found nearly 1/3 of playground related injuries occur during September and October when children return to school. Colorful posters, signs and other visual reminders should be posted in the gymnasium and play areas to remind students of proper conduct and safety.
6. Establish and enforce rules: Students should not be allowed to do "flips," climb outside of equipment, or use equipment in any manner outside of that prescribed by the manufacturer.
7. Develop an emergency response procedure should a student be injured. In addition to CPR and a well stocked First Aid Kit, emergency phone numbers, school nurse and other reporting procedures should be practiced in advance to assure a timely and appropriate response to an injury.

Child abuse is a serious problem that can have lasting harmful effects on a child's life. The goal for prevention is simple—to stop child abuse and neglect from happening in the first place. Child abuse can be best prevented by supporting families through providing skills and resources. One key way to prevent child maltreatment is for parents to develop nurturing parenting skills and build positive relationships with their children.

The most common form of injury for young children is accidents. In this vein, teachers can only follow district and school procedures, use common sense and report and accidents that may happen through the filing of an accident report and notification to the parent(s)/guardian.

Teacher's need to continually know where all there students are at all times, never leave the classroom unattended and always follow the applicable school and district-wide standards in regard to safety precautions.

Skill 10.7 Hazards and dangerous substances

There are numerous environmental, chemical and other hazards and dangerous substances that children may encounter in the school setting. In fact, by their very nature children are more susceptible to environmental hazards than adults for a variety of reasons including:

1. Children are still developing
2. Children eat, drink, and breathe more proportionate to their body size – creating a greater risk of toxicity and detrimental impact in a shorter period of time compared to adults.
3. Their behavior can expose them more to chemicals, organisms and other hazards: children frequently put objects in their mouths, touch unfamiliar items and engage in less than optimum hygiene particularly at an early age.
4. Students are not always aware of their own medical issues: particularly young students who may not have encountered a situation to evoke an allergic, asthmatic or other response to chemical or environmental stimuli.

Dealing with Dangerous Substances

Students may also encounter dangerous substances either at school or in the home including many commonly encountered chemicals, cleaners and other substances that adults routinely take for granted. The first step in dealing with a dangerous substance is to recognize it as a potentially harmful substance; a practice that is often easier said than done. Recognizing a potentially harmful substance requires teachers to use a different frame of reference.

First, it's important to understand what types of chemicals and substances can be dangerous and in what circumstances. Below are a few of the more commonly encountered situations that every teacher should be aware of but keep in mind, there are literally hundreds of others! Remain alert and vigilant to the specific setting and student population: Remember, prevention is the best policy!

Quantity: Nearly any substance can be dangerous if taken to the extreme. For example, although generally safe, children's vitamins have been known to cause serious injury or even death when taken in quantity – otherwise known as an overdose. Children are more prone to an overdose due to their small size and lack of full development. Nearly any type of medication including over-the-counter medications can be toxic to children in much smaller dosage levels than that of an adult.

Individual Allergies and Sensitivities: Some substances are perfectly safe even for the majority of children but deadly for students who have individual allergies. A common example is a peanut allergy but almost any substance can be a potential allergen. Anaphylaxis is a deadly allergic response where the airway may shut down and lead to anaphylactic shock: A serious situation where blood pressure rapidly drops and respiratory and cardiac arrest take place. Even trace amounts of an allergen may trigger this deadly response so it is imperative for a teacher to be aware of all student allergies. Common allergic triggers include peanuts and shellfish or their derivatives. Many of these derivatives come in products ranging from cosmetics to cookies so it is important that students be advised against sharing personal products, food or medications of any type – no matter how innocent and harmless they may appear!

Known Chemicals and Substances: As an adult you may not recognize the temptation that a bright colored fluid such as Anti-Freeze holds for a child but depending upon the student age range, there are literally hundreds of chemicals and substances of frightening toxicity encountered daily. Children, especially young children, tend to explore with their hands and even mouths; potentially exposing themselves to accidental poisoning via ingestion or absorption, serious chemical burns and a host of other adverse consequences. Other known chemicals such as fertilizers and pesticides may be inadvertently absorbed by students through their natural tendency to play by rolling in the grass, wresting or playing. Other less recognized, but just as potentially serious substances, include cleaning products, dry erase board cleaner, chalk, art supplies and even large amounts of anti-microbial soap! Remember, by their nature children are curious and may experiment with products that are harmful when absorbed or ingested!

Given the prevalence of potentially harmful substances, prevention is the best policy. Here are the steps you need to know in order to create a safe environment for all students.

1. Educate students on good and bad substances. Be sure to make it age appropriate and instruct students to avoid bad substances or any unknown substances. As a rule, teachers should instruct students to refrain from touching or ingesting any substance with which they are unfamiliar and report it to the teacher or other adult. In addition, students should learn never to drink from unmarked containers and never share food, drinks or any type of medication, make-up or personal belonging with others.
2. Clearly mark hazardous materials and then store in a secured cabinet, room or other area. Even if bottles or containers are clearly marked they should still be securely stored away and vice versa; even if containers are stored away they should still be clearly marked in the event they are inadvertently in the vicinity of children. Common classroom hazards include cleaning supplies which have actually been known to cause illness, injury and even death.

3. Take nothing for granted! Young children learn by doing and very young children come to class with a wide variety of experiences. Take time to teach children the proper way to use soap, art supplies and commonly encountered classroom substances. Glue, paste, paint, play dough and much more may seem like fun experiments to children. Educate them on the proper use of each and then make sure everything is stored away when finished using. Always supervise children! Remember, even though many are listed as "non-toxic" that does not mean they should be ingested!
4. Establish a place for everything and everyone! Remember, children should be taught not to share food, combs, hats, cosmetics, medications or any other product. Make sure students understand this policy in accordance with their age and grade level!
5. Maintain Material Safety Data Sheets (MSDS) in the office and classroom for any and all chemicals found in the school setting including the gymnasium, laboratories and field! This includes pesticides and other chemicals used on turf and grounds maintenance! For a list of common used pesticides in schools visit: http://www.beyondpesticides.org/schools/publications/48%20School%20Pesticides.pdf
6. Establish a chemical and substance control policy at each school including recognition, reporting and response!
7. Maintain emergency contact numbers, CPR and 1st Aid in the event of an emergency.

How to Recognize the Effects of Hazardous Substances

Symptoms of an overdose or accidental poisoning can vary widely but may include:
- Abnormal Breathing (very fast or very slow)
- Slurred Speech (or the inability to speak)
- Lack of Coordination
- Confusion
- Fast or Slow Pulse
- High or Low Body Temperature
- Very Large or Very Small Pupils
- Heavy Sweating
- Drowsiness
- Delusions or Hallucinations
- Unconsciousness

Allergy and Anaphylaxis

Not everyone realizes they have an allergy even to foods, chemical or medications they have taken in the past. Some allergic reactions seem mild but can become more serious after repeated exposure so children are particularly vulnerable to discovering a "new" allergy! Symptoms of an allergic reaction range from mild to life threatening as in the case of Anaphylaxis. Anaphylaxis is a medical emergency that requires immediate medical assistance!

Symptoms of an Anaphylaxis include:
- Hives (a type of reddish looking rash)
- Difficulty Breathing
- Difficulty Swallowing
- Abdominal Cramps, Nausea, Vomiting, or Diarrhea
- Rapid Heart Rate
- Drop in Blood Pressure
- Sudden Weakness
- Anxiety or an Overwhelming Sense of Doom
- Collapse
- Loss of Consciousness

What to Do in an Emergency

Call local 911 for Emergency Assistance
1-800-222-1222 for Poison Control

If in Doubt – Seek Help!

Don't delay. Remain calm and seek medical help. Some substance or medication emergencies like anaphylactic reactions or accidental poisonings might initially appear mild before growing more serious. Don't make the mistake of waiting. Once symptoms worsen they can be much harder to treat and every minute counts!

If known, bring the medication, chemical or substance with you or give it to the paramedics when they arrive. If you don't know what caused the problem then bring everything the person was recently exposed to if possible. This will help medical professionals understand what might be wrong and how to treat it while also preventing possible administration of other drugs that might interfere with their standard medications.

Finally, follow standard CPR procedures until help arrives. Most important, don't delay in getting help as soon as possible and remember: If In Doubt – Seek Help!

While hazards and dangerous substances are ever present, taking the necessary precautions and acting proactively to eliminate hazardous situations can prevent the majority of injuries and accidents.

Skill 10.8   Roles of people in the community who are responsible for health and safety

While the health, safety and well-being of children is primarily the responsibility of the home, ultimately the responsibility for the physical health and safety of children should be shared by the whole community and its institutions. School and community health promotion efforts acknowledge that the shared responsibility for student health should lie not only with the home, but also, public and private health care systems, law enforcement and justice systems, environmental agencies, civic groups and the media.

Community efforts to promote the health and safety of children should include youth organizations, social and civic organizations, child-care centers; businesses, public health agencies; city planners and private developers; safety organizations; and schools. Many of these organizations are currently involved in efforts to improve the health and safety of children and youth through initiatives that are focused on reducing underage tobacco and alcohol consumption, preventing sexually transmitted diseases, increasing health awareness, and preventing automobile injuries.

Local governments, private developers, and community groups should expand opportunities for physical activity for children, including recreational facilities, parks, playgrounds, sidewalks, bike paths, routes for walking or bicycling to school, and safer streets and neighborhoods.

School officials can also implement a Health curriculum that is comprehensive for all students from preschool through 12th grade, sequentially developed, age and culturally appropriate that reflects current health issues of the community, and taught by educators qualified to present health instruction. The curriculum and instruction program should include the following content areas: accident prevention and safety, community health, disease control and prevention, environmental health, family life education, mental and emotional health, nutrition, personal health, self-esteem building, substance abuse prevention, and violence prevention.

The Michigan State Board of Education Policy on Comprehensive School Health Education can be found online at:
http://www.michigan.gov/documents/Health_Education_Policy_final_94135_7.pdf

Over the past, public officials throughout the United States have faced increasing problems in keeping their communities safe. Disorder, crime, drugs, and guns have become daily reminders of the threats to children to living in safety and security. Tragedies such as the shootings at Columbine High School in Colorado have demonstrated that crime and violence are not limited to inner cities and large urban areas

Therefore, parents, schools, and communities are encouraged to work together in partnership to provide effective, comprehensive health programs and policies. The belief that the community lies at the heart of public health, and that interventions work best when they are rooted in the values, knowledge, and interests of the community itself.

Agencies involved in the promotion of the health and safety of children
- Bureau of Child and Adolescent Health
- The Division of Environmental Disease Prevention; analysis of lead content
- Bureau of Community Sanitation and Food Protection
- Bureau of Occupational Health; coordinates with programs such as the Supplemental Nutrition Program for Women, Infants and Children (WIC), and the Early Intervention Program
- Child Protective Services; responsible for investigating allegations of child abuse or neglect
- Pediatrician; provides expertise in health and medical matters concerning children

For a listing of health care programs available for children in Michigan, go to the website of the Michigan Department of Community Health at
http://www.michigan.gov/mdch/0,1607,7-132-2943_4860-35199--,00.html

COMPETENCY 11.0 UNDERSTAND YOUNG CHILDREN'S CREATIVE DEVELOPMENT AND HOW TO PROMOTE SELF-EXPRESSION THROUGH THE CREATIVE ARTS AND ENHANCE CHILDREN'S UNDERSTANDING AND APPRECIATION OF THE ARTS

Skill 11.1 Indicators of creative development

Visual Arts

Some of the areas that should be mastered by students and can be modeled by the teacher include the following:
- Experimentation through works of art using a variety of mediums, drawing, painting, sculpture, ceramics, printmaking and video
- Producing a collection of art works (portfolio) and using a variety of mediums, topics, themes and subject matter
- Create and evaluate different art works and which types of mediums chosen
- Reflection on individual work and the work of others

Some examples should include:
- Mixing paint in ranges of shades and tints
- Using the computer to design an idea for sculpting
- Developing a portfolio of works that display at least two mediums
- Researching a design such as a building or a landmark and design a new piece based on the research
- Painting a picture using tempera or watercolor recalling a specific experience or memory

Music

The ability to repeat melodies and rhythms of varying lengths and read musical notation are early signs of creative development. Older students expand their skills by learning to play an instrument or singing. The motor skills and listening techniques required to play an instrument or to learn a vocal piece of music are important indicators of creative development.

The use of music vocabulary taught in the classroom and the ability to describe music using this vocabulary is another barometer of creative development in music. Students show musical development by using words such as legato, staccato, forte and piano to describe music. They can also classify a musical work, such as a symphony, and name typical instruments used in performing that work, such as the violin, viola, cello, and bass. These are all signs that students are developing their knowledge and skills in the arts.

Movement

Students should be able to judge the effectiveness of a dance composition based on the intent, structure, meaning and purpose. Dance is a way of expressing everything from feelings of mood to appreciation of cultures and historical time periods. Students express empathy for others as they take on various roles within the dance. Participation in dances helps students develop self confidence, body awareness, and communication skills and provides experiences in areas otherwise left undiscovered.

Drama

In drama, creative development is gauged by the degree to which a student is able to use the five senses in improvisation exercises and dramatic performances, as well as their ability to answer the five essential questions of Who, What, Where, When, and Why.

Students' abilities to demonstrate various aspects of a dramatic production, such as acting, directing, set design, scriptwriting, and audience participation are additional indicators of creative development. It is important for the student to understand that drama is not only a game of make-believe, but that there are many pieces that go into a theatrical production.

Skill 11.2   The integration of the arts with other content areas to promote learning and to provide a way for children to demonstrate what they know (e.g., drawing a picture instead of explaining in words)

The Michigan Department of Education website (http://www.michigan.gov/mde) emphasizes that the Office of School Improvement will work with partners throughout the state to ensure all schools are providing students with ongoing sequential education in the arts. Research shows that the arts not only enrich the lives of children but also improve their performance in the academic arena. The MDE website highlights that education in the arts has a way of "leveling the playing field" for disadvantaged children.

Lynn Hallie Najem provides further evidence of the importance of integrating the arts into standard curriculum in her research article, "Sure It's Fun, But Why Bother With It During the School Day? The Benefits of Using Drama with Primary Students" A copy of this article may be found on the following website: http://www.madison.k12.wi.us/ . In her research, she found that integrating the arts into primary school curriculum had a very positive effect on the self-esteem of students and opened them up to learning in all subject areas.

SEE also Skill 5.1, Interrelationships among the content areas, for more information and examples

Skill 11.3 The role of creative arts in promoting self-expression and creative thinking and in developing a healthy self-concept

The benefits of engaging our children in the arts whether it is visual arts, theatre arts, music or dance, are well known. Art activities help kids develop their own self esteem, self reliance. And when children are discovering the world through art, they also enjoy self discovery. It's universally true that everyone is different. When learning the visual arts of drawing, painting, and animating, children and develop faith in themselves, through self expression, because each work is unique.

Visual Arts

When children are given the opportunity for creative, open-ended play, the imagination is stimulated and they learn to think in new ways. New ideas form because in creative play they are free to see things in different ways. They begin to rearrange things and think outside of the box they normally live in. They fantasize and dream about things, and do whatever feels fun or interesting. They exercise their curiosity as well as their visual muscles.

Music

Students can explore creating moods with music, analyzing stories and creating musical compositions that reflect or enhance it. Their daily routines can include exploration, interpretation, and understanding of musical sound. Immersing them in musical conversations as we sing, speak rhythmically, and walk in-step stimulates their awareness of the beauty and structure of musical sound.

In some schools, computer-assisted programs provide students with opportunities to evaluate music. Programs are designed to present two performances of one or more musical pieces so they can work with the teacher to compare and contrast the pieces. The Internet allows students to collect musical information for evaluation and provide information about studied or performed compositions. Knowledge of these resources and tools enable teachers to provide the richest education in music.

Movement

Begin with primitive patterns of **rhythm**. Rhythm is the basis of dance. A child can sit in a chair and clap or tap their hands on their legs to express thoughts of rhythm. With older children, imagery enables a dancer to visualize and internalize the particular qualities of a specific movement.

Because the younger child is more unsteady the initial level emphasis is not on gracefulness but rather to develop **body awareness**. The uniqueness of dance is that it is self-expression that can be guided through instruction. The student is taught the elements that are available such as **time and space.** Therefore, the student is incorporating **listening skills** to develop a sense of tempo.

Creative dance is the one that is most natural to a young child. Creative dance depicts feelings through movement. It is the initial reaction to sound and movement. The older elementary student will incorporate mood and expressiveness. Stories can be told to release the dancer into imagination.

Drama
In theatre, students should learn to use all of their five senses to observe their environment and recreate experiences through drama and other theatre skills. Using role play and prior knowledge of experiences, students should develop the ability to react to a feeling or a situation to expand their ability to develop character. Using sight, smell, taste, touch, hearing and memory recall, students should be able to retell stories, myths, and fables. Experience using costumes and props for performances should be provided. Students can relate to familiar jobs that are relevant to their everyday experiences and should be provided experiences to "act out" some of the following: firefighters, police officers, teachers, doctors, nurses, postal employees, clerks, and other service related professions that students may have witnessed.

SEE also Skill 7.3

Skill 11.4 Activities and resources for promoting children's aesthetic appreciation of the arts (e.g., exposure to arts of various cultures)

A live performance or first hand view of the arts is invaluable when it comes to promoting children's aesthetic appreciation of the arts. The best resources for teachers are local performing arts venues, art museums, symphonies, operas and dance companies. All of these venues have outreach programs geared toward elementary school students. In fact, many of the venues provide programs where artists visit the school and offer hands on lessons for kids, as well as a live performance. Kindling an appreciation of the arts in students is a priority for most arts organizations, as these students will become their future patrons.

Two excellent online resources for arts appreciation are:
- http://www.metmuseum.org/ - The **Explore and Learn** section of the Metropolitan Museum of Art online has a vast collection of images, video and printed material. The **Timeline of Art History** allows students to explore history through images at the Museum of Art.

- http://artsedge.kennedy-center.org/ - **Arts Edge** on the Kennedy Center website provides a wealth of information for teachers. The **Look. Listen. Learn** section highlights various arts forms through audio, video, images, printed material and interactive exercises.

Skill 11.5 Building knowledge about the arts and artists (e.g., creating one's own art, talking about elements of artistic works).

Visual Arts

Students are expected to fine tune observation skills and be able to identify and recreate the experiences that teachers provide for them as learning tools. For example, students may walk as a group on a nature hike taking in the surrounding elements and then begin to discuss the repetition found in the leaves of trees, or the bricks of the sidewalk, or the size and shapes of the buildings and how they may relate. They may also use such an experience to describe lines, colors, shapes, forms and textures. Beginning elements of perspective are noticed at an early age. The questions of why buildings look smaller when they are at a far distance and bigger when they are closer are sure to spark the imagination of early childhood students. Students can then take their inquiry to higher level of learning with some hands-on activities such as building three dimensional buildings and construction using paper and geometric shapes. Eventually students should acquire higher level thinking skills such as analysis, in which they will begin to question artists, art work, and analyze many different aspects of visual art.

Movement

Dance is an artistic form of self expression that uses the various elements of dance, such as use of space, time, levels, and force, to form a composition.

The primary grades have a gross understanding of their motor movements whereas older children are more apt to have a refined concept of their bodies. Individual movements are developed by the instructor when attention is given to various aspects such as:

- the range of movement or gestures through space
- the direction of the action or imaginary lines the body flows through space
- the timing of when movements form the dramatic effects
- the awareness of the planes formed by any two areas such as height and width or width and depth
- levels that are introduced so that the composition incorporates sitting, standing, and kneeling, etc.
- the elevation or the degree of lift as in leaping and the movements that are done under that allusion of suspension
- the force and energy of dance that reflects the music, such as adagio (slow music) or allegro (quickening steps).

Students should be able to judge the effectiveness of a dance composition based on the intent, structure, meaning and purpose. Dance is a way of expressing everything from feelings of mood to appreciation of cultures and historical time periods. Students express empathy for others as they take on various roles within the dance. The application and participation in dances helps students develop self confidence, body awareness, and communication skills and provide experiences in areas otherwise left undiscovered. Dance is a way of expressing the connections and relationships between the dancers and appreciation of dance as creative expression.

Music

Some of the most basic music techniques include learning about rhythm, tempo, melody, and harmony. **Rhythm** refers to the pattern of regular or irregular pulses in music that result from the melodic beats of the music. When rhythm is measured and divided into parts of equal time value, it is called **meter**. Simple techniques to teach and practice rhythm include clapping hands and tapping feet to the beat of the music. Teachers can also incorporate the use of percussion instruments to examine rhythmic patters which also increases students' awareness of rhythm. As a result of exercises such as these, students learn the basics of conducting music and through conducting, students learn to appreciate and develop musical awareness. Understanding rhythm also introduces students to the concept of **tempo**, or the speed of a given musical piece. Practicing with well-known songs with a strong musical beat such as "Happy Birthday" helps students become aware of patterns and speed.

The **melody** of a musical piece refers to the pattern of single tones in a composition that is distinguished from rhythm and harmony. The melody of a musical piece is often considered the "horizontal" aspect of the piece that flows from start to finish. **Harmony** refers to the combination of single tones at one time in a musical piece, or the full sound of different notes at the same time. To practice these concepts, students can compose their own ascending and descending melodies on staff paper. Students should be able to sing the melodies by reading the notation.

Drama

It is vital that teachers be trained in critical areas that focus on important principles of theatre education. The basic course of study should include state mandated topics in arts education, instructional materials, products in arts, both affective and cognitive processes of art, world and traditional cultures, and the most recent teaching tools, media and technology.

Areas that should be included are as follows:

Acting - Acting requires the student to demonstrate the ability to effectively communicate using skillful speaking, movement, rhythm, and sensory awareness.

Directing - Direction requires the management skills to produce and perform an onstage activity. This requires guiding and inspiring students as well as script and stage supervision.

Designing - Designing involves creating and initiating the onsite management of the art of acting.

Scriptwriting - Scriptwriting demands that a leader be able to produce original material and staging an entire production through the writing and designing a story that has performance value.

Each of the above mentioned skills should be incorporated in daily activities with young children. It is important that children are exposed to character development through stories, role-play, and modeling through various teacher guided experiences. Some of the experiences that are age appropriate for early childhood level include puppet theatre, paper dolls, character sketches, storytelling, and re-telling of stories in a student's own words.

DOMAIN III. FAMILY AND COMMUNITY RELATIONSHIPS

COMPETENCY 12.0 UNDERSTAND THE IMPORTANCE OF ESTABLISHING AND MAINTAINING POSITIVE, COLLABORATIVE RELATIONSHIPS WITH FAMILIES

Skill 12.1 The importance of respecting families' choices and goals for children, including strategies for communicating effectively with families about curriculum and children's progress

Respecting Families

There will be times when parents/caregivers will not agree with the teacher's decisions regarding their children. Teachers should treat all the family members with respect and patience. Parents are often fearful about coming to the school to talk with the teacher, because of their own negative experiences with schools. Therefore, they need to be welcomed in the classroom and made to feel as if they do have something to offer to the teacher and the student.

Some families may have higher goals for the child than the child is capable of achieving. The teacher has to be cognizant of the family's goals and be able to discuss the child's progress with them. On the other hand, when a teacher determines that a child needs further testing for a possible learning disability, it will require tactful conversations with the parents in order to get the required signatures and permission for this testing.

Families may also make choices for the children based on cultural factors, such as not allowing their children to participate in school activities, such as Christmas concerts, class parties or listening to certain types of music. Teachers should demonstrate respect of other cultures by providing or allowing alternate activities for these students.

When parents ask questions about the curriculum, the teacher needs to demonstrate knowledge of the curriculum design and the rationale so as to inform the parents about the program of study the child is following.

Teachers must be willing to meet with parents after school or in the evening because of the parents' work schedules. This simple matter of being able to meet the parents will go a long way towards helping them become partners in the child's education.

SEE also Skill 12.2

Skill 12.2 Ways to involve families in assessing and planning for individual children

The support of the parent is an invaluable aid in the educational process. It is in the best interests of child, parent, and teacher for there to be cooperation and mutual support between parent and teacher. One of the teacher's professional responsibilities is to establish and maintain effective communication with parents. A few basic techniques to pursue are oral communication (phone calls), written communication in the form of general information classroom newsletters, notes to the parent of a particular child, and parent-teacher conferences.

Teachers should share items of interest, including but not limited to, classroom rules and policies, class schedules and routines, homework expectations, communication procedures, conferences plans, and other similar information. Much of this can be done in a newsletter format sent home early in the school year. It is imperative that all such written communications be error free. It is a good idea to have another teacher read your letter before you send it out. Good writing and clear communication are learned skills and require time and effort to develop.

When you find it necessary to communicate (whether by phone, letter, or in person) with a parent regarding a concern about a student, allow yourself a "cooling off" period before making contact with the parent. It is important that you remain professional and objective. Your purpose for contacting the parent is to elicit support and additional information that may have a bearing on the student's behavior or performance. Be careful that you do not demean the child and do not appear antagonistic or confrontational. Be aware that the parent is likely to be quite uncomfortable with the bad news and will respond best if you take a cooperative, problem solving approach to the issue. It is also a nice courtesy to notify parents of positive occurrences with their children. The teacher's communication with parents should not be limited to negative items.

Parent Conferences

The parent-teacher conference is generally for one of three purposes. First, the teacher may wish to share information with the parents concerning the performance and behavior of the child. Second, the teacher may be interested in obtaining information from the parents about the child. Such information may help answer questions or concerns that the teacher has. A third purpose may be to request parent support or involvement in specific activities or requirements. In many situations, more than one of the purposes may be involved.

Planning the conference

When a conference is scheduled, whether at the request of the teacher or parent, the teacher should allow sufficient time to prepare thoroughly. Collect all relevant information, samples of student work, records of behavior, and other items needed to help the parent understand the circumstances. It is also a good idea to compile a list of questions or concerns you wish to address. Arrange the time and location of the conference to provide privacy and to avoid interruptions.

Conducting the conference

Begin the conference by putting the parents as ease. Take the time to establish a comfortable mood, but do not waste time with unnecessary small talk. Begin your discussion with positive comments about the student. Identify strengths and desirable attributes, but do not exaggerate.

As you address issues or areas of concern, be sure to focus on observable behaviors and concrete results or information. Do not make judgmental statements about parent or child. Share specific work samples, anecdotal records of behavior, etc., which demonstrate clearly the concerns you have. Be a good listener and hear the parent's comments and explanations. Such background information can be invaluable in understanding the needs and motivations of the child.

Finally, end the conference with an agreed plan of action between parents and teacher (and, when appropriate, the child). Bring the conference to a close politely but firmly and thank the parents for their involvement.

After the conference

A day or two after the conference, it is a good idea to send a follow-up note to the parents. In this note, briefly and concisely reiterate the plan or steps agreed to in the conference. Be polite and professional; avoid the temptation to be too informal or chatty. If the issue is a long term one such as the behavior or on-going work performance of the student, make periodic follow-up contacts to keep the parents informed of the progress.

Interpreting and communicating assessment results

When children are tested for developmental or cognitive delays when they enter school, the teacher first has to get the permission of the parents if testing outside the normal school testing is deemed necessary. The parents should be fully informed as to the reasons the teacher thinks this testing is necessary and be allowed to have input into the process. Once the tests results are final, there should be a meeting with the parents, teachers, school principal and the person who did the testing. The tester should be the person to deliver the report to the parents because of the detailed explanations of the results. Some parents may be upset when they find out that their child has a delay and the teacher has to be prepared to deal with this. However, it is important that the school support the parents in every way possible so that the child gets the needed help at an early age.

Skill 12.3 Strategies for supporting families in making decisions related to child development and parenting

Teachers have a responsibility to educate the children that come through the doors of their classrooms, but they also have a responsibility to help the parents/caregivers. Some parents may be expecting too much from their children at an early age, while others may not be providing them with the care they need. Teachers can help parents in this regard by helping them understand what children should be able to do at this age and to make sure that parents know how to access all avenues of service available to them.

When teachers notice that a child in the classroom does not have the normal development expected by school age, the teacher should contact the parents to set up a meeting. Through the discussion, the teacher can inform the parent of ways to help the child at home. In the case of children who are more advanced than their peers, teachers can help set up more challenging activities that the parents can continue with at home.

Some children come to school without breakfast or the proper clothing that will protect them from the weather. For parents who do not have the financial resources to provide for their children, the teacher can work with them to be able to access community resources that will help them. There are also courses available to help parents learn more about proper parenting.

Children who need special services can get them through the school and community. First the teacher has to arrange for the required testing and overcome objections from parents who may be fearful that the child will be negatively perceived based on the test results. The teacher has to convince the parents that such testing is in the best interest of the child and communicate that the testing is a required step before accessing community resources.

When meeting with parents, teachers should:

- Arrange the meetings at a time convenient for the parents and in a setting in which they will be comfortable
- Take the parents' comfort level into consideration when determining the number of school staff that will be present at this meeting
- Provide the parents with the topic of the meeting a few days in advance so that they will be prepared
- Encourage parents to bring a list of questions they would like to have answered at the meeting
- Discuss the bright side of some learning disabilities, such as ADHD
- Provide concrete examples of the child's behavior noticed through careful observation
- Don't pass judgment on either the child or the parents

Teachers need to communicate with parents on a regular basis to ensure that any strategies discussed are being worked on. Above all, communicate respect to the parents and ask for their advice about strategies they have used at home.

Skill 12.4 Ways of encouraging family involvement in the early childhood program

Research proves that the more families are involved in a child's educational experience, the more that child will succeed academically. Often teachers assume that involvement in education simply means that the parents show up to help at school events or participate in parental activities on campus. With this belief, many teachers devise clever strategies to increase parental involvement at school. However, just because a parent shows up to school and assists with an activity does not mean that the child will learn more. Many parents work all day long and cannot assist in the school. Teachers, therefore, have to think of different ways to encourage parental and family involvement in the educational process.

Quite often, teachers have great success within involving families by just informing families of what is going on in the classroom. Newsletters are particularly effective at this. Parents love to know what is going on in the classroom, and this way, they'll feel included. In newsletters, for example, teachers can provide suggestions on how parents can help with the educational goals of the school. For example, teachers can recommend that parents read with their children for twenty minutes per day. To add effectiveness to that, teachers can also provide suggestions on what to do when their children come across difficult words or when they ask a question about comprehension. This gives parents practical strategies.

Parents often equate phone calls from teachers with news about misbehaviors of their children. Teachers can change that tone by calling parents with good news. Or they can send positive notes home with students. By doing this, when negative phone calls need to be made, teachers will have greater success.

Teachers can also provide very specific suggestions to individual parents. For example, if a student needs additional assistance in a particular subject, th teacher can provide tips to parents to encourage and increase deeper understandings in the subject outside of class.

COMPETENCY 13.0 UNDERSTAND VARIATIONS IN FAMILY STRUCTURE AND SOCIAL AND CULTURAL BACKGROUNDS

Skill 13.1 The varying contexts and configurations of family

Family Configurations

At one time when one spoke of family, the typical setting was a mother, father and children. In the past it was common to see large families. Today's families are much different and come in all shapes and sizes, though for the most part families consist of only one or two children. Both parents are in the work force, which means that children are in the care of babysitters or attend daycare. Although the traditional family does exist, there are also many other configurations:

- Single parent families with either the mother or father raising the children
- Divorced parents where both parents have shared custody
- Children living with grandparents
- Children who are part of the Social Services system and are living in foster care
- Children living with a different family or with a relative
- Families where the parents have been married and divorced and bring two sets of children to a new relationship
- Families where the parents are living together without being married, with only one of the adults being the child's biological parent
- Children who are adopted
- Families where the parents are homosexual and raising children

Teachers today will deal with an increasingly diverse group of cultures in their classrooms. While this is an exciting prospect for most teachers, it creates new challenges in dealing with a variety of family expectations for school and teachers.

First, teachers must show respect to all parents and families. They need to set the tone that suggests that their mission is to develop students into the best people they can be. And then they need to realize that various cultures have different views of how children should be educated.

Second, teachers will have better success when they talk personally about the children. Even though teachers may have many students, when they share personal things about each child, parents will feel more confident that their child is "in the right hands."

Third, it is very important that teachers act like they are partners in the children's education and development. Parents know their children best, and it is important to get feedback, information, and advice from them.

Finally, teachers will need to be patient with difficult families, realizing that certain methods of criticism (including verbal attacks, etc.) are unacceptable. Such circumstances would require the teacher to get assistance from an administrator. This situation, however, is very unusual, and most teachers will find that when they really attempt to be friendly and personal with parents, the parents will reciprocate and assist in the educational program.

Skill 13.2   Strategies for creating a climate of respect and appreciation for both the diversity and the uniqueness of individuals, families, and community

SEE Skills 3.1, 12.1 and 13.1

COMPETENCY 14.0 UNDERSTAND HOW THE DYNAMICS, ROLES, AND RELATIONSHIPS WITHIN FAMILIES AND COMMUNITIES AFFECT CHILDREN

Skill 14.1 Ways in which physical and environmental factors (e.g., nutrition, health, economic issues, family issues) may affect children's success as learners

The student's capacity and potential for academic success within the overall educational experience are products of her or his total environment: classroom and school system; home and family; neighborhood and community in general. All of these segments are interrelated and can be supportive, one of the other, or divisive, one against the other.

As a matter of course, the teacher will become familiar with all aspects of the system, the school and the classroom pertinent to the students' educational experience. This would include not only process and protocols but also the availability of resources provided to meet the academic, health and welfare needs of students. But the teacher must also look beyond the boundaries of the school system to identify additional resources as well as issues and situations which will effect (directly or indirectly) a student's ability to succeed in the classroom.

Examples of Resources

- Libraries, museums, zoos, planetariums, etc.
- Clubs, societies and civic organizations, community outreach programs of private businesses and corporations and of government agencies
  These can provide a variety of materials and media as well as possible speakers and presenters
1) Departments of social services operating within the local community
   These can provide background and program information relevant to social issues which may be impacting individual students. And this can be a resource for classroom instruction regarding life skills, at-risk behaviors, etc.

Initial contacts for resources outside of the school system will usually come from within the system itself: from administration; teacher organizations; department heads; and other colleagues.

Examples of Issues/Situations

- <u>Students from multicultural backgrounds</u>:

  Curriculum objectives and instructional strategies may be inappropriate and unsuccessful when presented in a single format which relies on the student's understanding and acceptance of the values and common attributes of a specific culture which is not his or her own.

  - <u>Parental/family influences</u>: Attitude, resources and encouragement available in the home environment may be attributes for success or failure.

Families with higher incomes are able to provide increased opportunities for students. Students from lower income families will need to depend on the resources available from the school system and the community. This should be orchestrated by the classroom teacher in cooperation with school administrators and educational advocates in the community.

Family members with higher levels of education often serve as models for students, and have high expectations for academic success. And families with specific aspirations for children (often, regardless of their own educational background) encourage students to achieve academic success, and are most often active participants in the process.

A family in crisis (caused by economic difficulties, divorce, substance abuse, physical abuse, etc.) creates a negative environment which may profoundly impact all aspects of a student's life, and particularly his or her ability to function academically. The situation may require professional intervention. It is often the classroom teacher who will recognize a family in crisis situation and instigate an intervention by reporting this to school or civil authorities.

Regardless of the positive or negative impacts on the students' education from outside sources, it is the teacher's responsibility to ensure that all students in the classroom have an equal opportunity for academic success. This begins with the teacher's statement of high expectations for every student, and develops through planning, delivery and evaluation of instruction which provides for inclusion and ensures that all students have equal access to the resources necessary for successful acquisition of the academic skills being taught and measured in the classroom.

SEE also Skill 2.1

Skill 14.2 Strategies that build on positive factors and minimize the effects of environmental factors that may have a negative impact on children

Longitudinal studies have consistently documented that between half and two-thirds of children growing up in families with mentally ill, alcoholic, abusive, or criminally involved parents or in poverty-stricken or war-torn communities do overcome the odds and turn a life trajectory of risk into one that manifests "resilience," the term used to describe a set of qualities that foster a process of successful adaptation and transformation despite risk and adversity. We are all born with an innate capacity for resilience, by which we are able to develop social competence, problem-solving skills, a critical consciousness, autonomy, and a sense of purpose. Schools can become an environment that may alter or even reverse expected negative outcomes and enable individuals to overcome life stressors and manifest resilience despite risk. These "protective factors" or "protective processes" can be grouped into three major categories: caring and supportive relationships, positive and high expectations, and opportunities for meaningful participation.

Caring Relationships

The presence of at least one caring person--someone who conveys an attitude of compassion, who understands that no matter how awful a child's behavior, the child is doing the best he or she can given his or her experience--provides support for healthy development and learning. Werner and Smith's (1989) study, covering more than 40 years, found that, among the most frequently encountered positive role models in the lives of resilient children, outside of the family circle, was a favorite teacher who was not just an instructor for academic skills for the youngsters but also a confidant and positive model for personal identification.

High Expectations

Research has indicated that schools that establish high expectations for all children--and give them the support necessary to achieve them--have high rates of academic success. The conveying of positive and high expectations in a classroom and school occurs at several levels. The most obvious and powerful is at the relationship level in which the teacher and other school staff communicate the message that the student has everything he or she needs to be successful. As Tracy Kidder (1990) writes, "For children who are used to thinking of themselves as stupid or not worth talking to...a good teacher can provide an astonishing revelation. A good teacher can give a child at least a chance to feel, She thinks I'm worth something; maybe I am." Through relationships that convey high expectations, students learn to believe in themselves and in their futures, developing the critical resilience traits of self-esteem, self-efficacy, autonomy, and optimism.

Opportunities for Participation

Providing youth with opportunities for meaningful involvement and responsibility within the school is a natural outcome in schools that have high expectations. Participation, like caring and respect, is a fundamental human need. To foster the traits of resilience, school can that encourage critical thinking and dialogue (especially around current social issues), make learning more hands-on, involve students in curriculum planning, use participatory evaluation strategies, let students create the governing rules of the classroom, and use cooperative approaches (such as cooperative learning, peer helping, and cross-age mentoring.)

Research on resilience gives educators a blueprint for creating schools where all students can thrive socially and academically. To read more about children and resilience, see http://resilnet.uiuc.edu/library/benard95.html, and http://ohioline.osu.edu/b875/b875_1.html.

Other Environmental Factors

Abuse is not the only environmental factor that can have an impact of a child's development. Poor air quality can cause many health problems, such as asthma. Poor nutrition also causes problems, such as obesity, which can hamper a child's ability to learn and develop normally. The presence of mold can also cause health problems in children. School officials should make every effort to provide a classroom environment that is safe for children, and free of toxins.

TEACHER CERTIFICATION STUDY GUIDE

COMPETENCY 15.0 UNDERSTAND THE IMPORTANCE OF COORDINATION, COOPERATION, AND PROGRAM SUPPORT TO MEET CHILDREN'S NEEDS AND TO ENSURE LEARNING

Skill 15.1 The identification of institutions, agencies, programs, and organizations that advocate for and serve children and families (e.g., Head Start, social services, teacher associations)

One of the first things that a teacher learns is how to obtain resources and help for his/her students. When teachers notice social or academic problems with a student, they are obligated to refer the student for additional education services. The teacher will take this information to the appropriate committee for discussion and consideration. The committee will recommend the next step to be taken. Often subsequent steps include a complete psychological evaluation along with certain physical examinations such as vision and hearing screening and a complete medical examination by a doctor.

The referral of students for this process is usually relatively simple for the classroom teacher and requires little more than some initial paper work and discussion. The services and resources the student receives as a result of the process typically prove to be invaluable to the student with behavioral disorders.

Social Services
At times, the teacher must go beyond the school system to meet the needs of some students. An awareness of special services and resources and how to obtain them is essential to all teachers and their students. When the school system is unable to address the needs of a student, the teacher often must take the initiative and contact agencies within the community. Frequently there is no special policy for finding resources. It is simply up to the individual teacher to be creative and resourceful and to find whatever help the student needs. Meeting the needs of all students is certainly a team effort that is most often spearheaded by the classroom teacher.

Many families do not know that there are resources available in the community to help them with child rearing, health and nutrition. Teachers observe the children in the classroom and can discuss their needs with the parents. They can get the information for the parents as to what resources and skilled professionals are available for them and even set up meetings between the parents and these professionals.

National, State and Local Standards
Adherence to national, state and local standards for early childhood programs are of utmost importance. These standards set out the curriculum by detailing what the children should be able to know at do at specific stages of development.

Adherence to these standards can also give the teacher information about where some children may be lacking and need extra instruction or even testing by an outside agency. The standards set down for early childhood education programs prepare the children for Kindergarten and for the rest of their schooling.

Head Start
In 1965, the federal government provided unprecedented funds for the education of children from disadvantaged homes, especially preschool-age children. The Head Start program meant that large groups of preschool age children became readily available for research purposes concerning the effectiveness and improvement of programming for children of this age. The Head Start program also made educational programs available to **all** children, even children from poverty, for the first time.

The Head Start Program is a federally funded program, which monitors the health of children from low-income families. Children in this program engage in educational and play activities in a safe environment. They are provided with nutritional meals and their health is monitored. The curriculum and assessment techniques are carefully monitored to ensure that they are appropriate for the developmental age of each child.

At the same time, families receive the education they need to care for the child. There are classes for parents and caregivers to enable them to receive a High School Graduation certificate and training is also offered in child rearing, job skills, and health and nutrition.

Skilled professionals work with the families to ensure that children with special needs receive the help and support they need. The program also ensures that all the children receive their immunizations, have their hearing tested and receive dental care.

The health of young children has been identified as an area of special concern due to the research from Project Head Start that says a "child who is in poor health will function at a leave considerably lower than that of a well child." Effective early childhood programs will have policies that address the following areas:

1) Identifying health defects based on knowledge of developmental milestones for children at each stage of development
2) Providing or referring parents to preventive services (such as immunizations, dental checkups) to ensure a child's future health
3) Education for parents and children to improve the health of all members of the child's family

Teacher Associations

Parent-teacher associations, especially school councils, advocate for children in the school. These associations are cognizant of the demands being placed on teachers, but at the same time are always on the lookout for new sources of funding and resources that can help both the teachers and the students. Through these associations, teachers and parents can make their concerns known and get the help they need for lobbying government or for canvassing businesses in the community for the help they need.

Teacher associations can sponsor events in the school, which will bring the parents into the school, such as "Meet the Teacher Night". These associations have documents that are available to parents for further reading on a variety of topics to help them with parenting and in helping their children at home.

SEE also the website for Michigan Department of Education, Office of Special Education and Early Intervention Services (OSE-EIS) at http://www.michigan.gov/mde/0,1607,7-140-6530_6598-113565--,00.html.

Skill 15.2 Practices that ensure a smooth transition for both children and families to public schools

Most schools hold an Open House before children enter school. This is an opportunity for both the parents and the children to see the classroom, meet the teachers and administrators they will be dealing with and to receive a tour of the school. At this time, they will fill out an application form and receive literature related to entering the school as well as information about the program the child will be following.

Some schools also offer a pre-school program in which the children learn the routines of the school. During such programs, both the parents and the children come to school on selected days. This lets the parents know how the teacher conducts the classroom and lets them participate in the learning experiences. Just before school closes for the year, the students can come to school on their own for a day.

During the first days of school some parents like to come to school with the children just to make sure they are settled in. For the teacher, this may be a stressful time trying to get many of the children to feel comfortable away from the parents. However, it is important for the teacher to allow the parents this time and to gently ease them out of the classroom after the first week.

Teachers should establish regular communication with the students and their families even before school starts. By sending home a welcome letter a few weeks before the start of the school year, the children will be very excited about coming to school. This communication can also be a way in which the teacher introduces the parents to books they can buy and read to the students as well as giving them a list of school supplies that the child needs to have.

A child's ability to succeed in school takes a partnership—one that begins at home and continues in school. To increase learning and stop the summer learning decline, the Michigan Department of Education has developed summer literacy activities for preschool, prekindergarten, and early elementary students to practice at home. These activities can be found at the Family FUNdamentals website: http://www.michigan.gov/mde/0,1607,7-140-28753-69358--,00.html

Skill 15.3   The role of positive public relations

Establishing and maintaining positive public relations is extremely important for schools and teachers. The public image that the school has in the community will determine how much community and parental support the school receives for its activities and projects.

Positive relationships with the parents and the community at large will open up more opportunities for funding when the school needs to raise money for needed items. It will also bring more volunteers into the school to help out with activities and in the classrooms. When the school is viewed in a good light where parents are welcome, it will also be viewed as a great learning environment for the students. This will lead to parents praising the school to other parents and result in more students wanting to enroll in the classes.

Skill 15.4   Sources of funding

Since early childhood education is so important to a child's overall learning and future education, the federal government has established many different sources of funding that teachers and caregivers can access. In addition, there are many community groups and businesses that support local schools and their early education programs.

Some of the federal sources of funding include:

Head Start

This program is designed to help children from needy families and provides them with reading readiness skills as well as medical, dental and nutritional services. The programs include part time and full day accommodations for 8 – 9 months of the year.

Special Education Preschool Grants

Schools receive a base grant and then a portion of the remaining funds. For more information refer to the website at: http://www.ed.gov/programs/oseppsg/index.html

Early Reading First

This is a program that provides monies to schools and programs such as Head First in the form of grants for model programs. It also provides funds for teachers to get the training they need for teaching young children to read.

Even Start

This program provides monies for needy families with children who have disabilities. The program is designed to help these children obtain the skills necessary for them to enroll in school and experience success. The goal is to provide a type of intervention between pre-school and elementary school.

The Early Childhood Educator Professional Development Program

Teachers and other support personnel who work with needy families in areas of high poverty can access these grants to help them enroll in further professional development to enhance their skills. The focus of the professional development is on literacy to help get the children ready for Kindergarten.

There are also grants for early childhood education which are specific to Michigan, such as:

Early On

There is a formula employed to help distribute monies under this funding source to intermediate schools of a base grants of $50,00 to each school, $100 for each child in the target area and the rest of the money is distributed on the average number of children in the program.

TEACHER CERTIFICATION STUDY GUIDE

Even Start

This is a family literacy program with a base grant of $250,000 per year. The programs must include early childhood education, adult education parenting and interactive parent and child literacy experiences.

Michigan School Readiness Program

Four years olds at risk of failure qualify for funding under this program, which funds $3300 per child to districts that provide a half-day preschool program

Great Starts Collaboratives

This program is funded by the ECIC – Early Childhood Investment Corporation. It focuses on developing a comprehensive plan for children up to age 5.

Skill 15.5 Goals and benefits of collaborating with community Institutions and businesses

The community is a vital link to increasing learning experiences for students. Community resources can supplement the minimized and marginal educational resources of schools. With state and federal educational funding becoming increasingly subject to legislative budget cuts, schools welcome the financial support that community resources can provide in terms of discounted prices on high end supplies (e.g. computers, printers, and technology supplies), along with providing free notebooks, backpacks and student supplies for low income students who may have difficulty obtaining the basic supplies for school.

Community stores can provide cash rebates and teacher discounts for educators in struggling school districts and compromised school communities. Both professionally and personally, communities can enrich the student learning experiences by including the following support strategies:

- Provide programs that support student learning outcomes and future educational goals
- Create mentoring opportunities that provide adult role models in various industries to students interested in studying in that industry
- Provide financial support for school communities to help low-income or homeless students begin the school year with the basic supplies
- Offer parents without computer or Internet connection, stipends to purchase technology to create equitable opportunities for students to do research and complete word.doc paper requirements.
- Stop in classrooms and ask teachers and students what's needed to promote academic progress and growth.

Providing students with adult role models to reinforce the learning has become a crucial instructional strategy for teachers seeking to maximize student learning beyond the classroom. Mentoring has become an instrumental tool in addressing student achievement and access to learning. Adult mentors work individually with identified students on specific subject areas to reinforce the learning through tutorial instruction and application of knowledge.

Community resources are vital in providing that additional support to students, school communities and families struggling to remain engaged in declining educational institutions competing for federal funding and limited District funding. The commitment that a community shows to its educational communities is a valuable investment in the future. Community resources that are able to provide additional funding for tutors in marginalized classrooms or help schools reduce classrooms of students needing additional remedial instruction directly impact educational equity and facilitation of teaching and learning for both teachers and students.

Skill 15.6 Functions of an interagency council

It takes more than the teachers and the administration of a school to educate a child. There are many types of councils that operate in a school setting, the most common of which is the Parent Council. A parent council consists of a combination of parents, teachers, and administrators and in some cases, representatives from the business community. The purposes of a parent council include:
- Improving communication between the home and the school
- Assisting in school sponsored activities
- Representing the parents and the students in all aspects of the school life
- Providing a means of informing parents about what is happening in the school
- Providing input into staffing and the budget of the school
- Assisting the school with fundraising measures

This council is elected annually and there are regularly scheduled monthly meetings. During times of crisis in the school, the council may have to meet more frequently.

Other types of interagency councils that might exist in a school depend on the students themselves. For example, children with learning disabilities or special needs may have their own councils acting on their behalf. In these cases, the council consists of the classroom teacher, administrator, parents, any staff members dealing with the child in the school and any professionals from the community that may be involved, such as speech pathologists, itinerant teachers or mental health personnel. In this type of council, the child has an established IEP or a 504 plan, which needs to be monitored on a regular basis. The purpose for such an agency is to ensure that the child's needs are being met and that the strategies and recommendations included in the plan are being followed.

The administrator of the school may also be part of another council in the community. The purpose of this would be to bring attention to the needs of the school or to ensure that the community remains a safe place for the children.

DOMAIN IV. ASSESSMENT AND EVALUATION

COMPETENCY 16.0 UNDERSTAND INFORMAL ASSESSMENT STRATEGIES TO PLAN AND INDIVIDUALIZE CURRICULUM AND TEACHING PRACTICES

Skill 16.1 Ongoing observation, recording, and assessment of young children's development

There are many ways to evaluate a child's knowledge and assess his/her learning needs. In recent years, the emphasis has shifted from "mastery testing" of isolated skills to authentic assessments of what children know. Authentic assessments allow the teacher to know more precisely what each individual student knows, can do, and needs to do. Authentic assessments can work for both the student and the teacher in becoming more responsible for learning.

One of the simplest most efficient ways for the teacher to get to know his/her students is to conduct an entry survey. This is a record that provides useful background information about the students as they enter a class or school. Collecting information through an entry survey will give valuable insights into a student's background knowledge and experience. Teachers can customize entry surveys according to the type of information considered valuable. Some of the information that may be incorporated include student's name and age, family members, health factors, special interests, strengths, needs, fears, etc., parent expectations, languages spoken in the home, what the child likes about school, etc.

At the beginning of each school term the teacher will likely feel compelled to conduct some informal evaluations in order to obtain a general awareness of his/her students. These informal evaluations should be the result of a learning activity rather than a "test" and may include classroom observations, collections of reading and writing samples, and notations about the students' cognitive abilities as demonstrated by classroom discussions and participation including the students' command of language. The value of these informal evaluations cannot be underestimated. These evaluations, if utilized effectively, will drive instruction and facilitate learning.

After initial informal evaluations have been conducted and appropriate instruction follows, teachers will need to fine tune individual evaluations in order to provide optimum learning experiences. Some of the same types of evaluations can be used on an ongoing basis to determine individual learning needs as were used to determine initial general learning needs. It is somewhat more difficult to choose an appropriate evaluation instrument for elementary-aged students than for older students. Therefore, teachers must be mindful of developmentally appropriate instruments. At the same time, teachers must be cognizant of the information that they wish to attain from a specific evaluation instrument. Ultimately, these two factors—students' developmental stage and the information to be derived—will determine which type of evaluation will be most appropriate and valuable. There are few commercially designed assessment tools that will prove to be as effective as the tool that is constructed by the teacher.

A simple-to-administer, information-rich evaluation of a child's reading strengths and weaknesses is the running reading record. "This technique for recording reading behavior is the most insightful, informative, and instructionally useful assessment procedure you can use for monitoring a child's progress in learning to read." (Traill, 1993) The teacher uses a simple coding system to record what a child does while reading text out loud. At a later time the teacher can go back to the record and assess what the child knows about reading and what the teacher needs to address in an effort to help the student become a better reader.

If the teacher is evaluating a child's writing, it is a good idea to discourage the child from erasing his/her errors and to train the child to cross out errors with a single line so that the teacher can actually see the process that the student went through to complete a writing assignment. This writing becomes an important means of getting to know the students' writing and is an effective, valuable writing evaluation.

Mathematics skills can be evaluated informally by observing students as they work at their seats or perform at the board. Teachers can see if the students know basic computation skills, if they understand place value, or if they transpose numbers simply by watching them as they solve computation problems. Some teachers may prefer to administer some basic computation "tests" to determine a student's mathematics strengths and weaknesses. Although these "tests" are not as effective or thorough in assessing students, they are quick and easy to administer.

One of the most valuable and effective assessment tools available to any teacher is the classroom observation. As instructional decision makers, teachers must base their instructional strategies upon students' needs. An astute observer of student behaviors and performance is most capable of choosing instructional strategies that will best meet the needs of the learners. Classroom observations take place within the context of the learning environment thus allowing the observer the opportunity to notice natural behaviors and performances.

Classroom observations should be sensitive and systematic in order to permit a constant awareness of student progress. One of the shortcomings of classroom observations is that they are often performed randomly and frequently are focused on those students whose behaviors are less than desirable. If the teacher establishes a focused observation process then observations become more valuable. It has been suggested that a teacher focus his/her observations on five or six students at a time for a period of one to two weeks.

In order for observations to truly be useful, teachers must record the information obtained from observations. When doing a formal behavioral observation, the teacher will write what the child is doing for a designated time period. At times the teacher will tally the occurrences of specific behaviors within a designated time period. When making focused observations that are ongoing, the teacher may simply use a blank piece of paper with only the student's name and date written on it and space for the teacher to write anecdotal notes. Other teachers might write on post-it notes and put the information in a student's file. If it is not possible to record the information as it occurs and is observed, it is critical that it be recorded as soon as possible in order to maintain accuracy.

Sometimes it is helpful to do an observation simply to watch for frequency of a specific behavior. An observation can answer questions such as: Is the student on-task during independent work time? Is the student interacting appropriately with peers? Is the student using materials appropriately? These behaviors can be tallied on a piece of paper with the student's name and date of observation.

Classroom observations can provide the teacher with one of the most comprehensive means of knowing their students. Teachers can observe students to see how they interact with their peers, to see which activities they choose, what they like to read, and how frequently they choose to work alone. "Everything you hear a child say and see a child do is a glimpse into a mind and a source of information to 'know' from." (Traill, 1993)

Skill 16.2 The development and use of authentic, performance-based assessments

The teaching, learning, and assessing process is as follows:
1. Teachers know what is in the standards.
2. Teachers develop a plan for the school year to ensure that all the standards are covered.
3. Teachers develop objectives for specific lessons within the school year.
4. Teachers provide various assessments throughout the year to ensure that students are progressing adequately.
5. Teachers use the data from those assessments to make modifications to instruction (or to repeat certain topics).

Notice that all elements funnel back to instruction. All assessments, in fact, are designed in part to give teachers information about how they need to enhance or modify their instruction.

Each year teachers can use assessment data how well their students have done. But many people make the analogy that analyzing year-end test data provides as much information as the score of a basketball or baseball game gives people about the specific things that were done well and poorly throughout the game. When we just focus on the data from year-end tests, we see what areas students mastered and what areas they did not master. However, to really see how instruction can be modified, teachers need to focus on providing multiple opportunities for assessment throughout the year to get as much information within the year on what could be improved. A simple and short assessment at the end of a lesson tells a teacher, for example, if students mastered the material from the lesson. Or, a reading inventory kept throughout the year tells how much a student has progressed in reading skill, rather than just giving us a "score" at the end of the year, which will not show the ups and downs throughout the year.

When we say that common statistical methods should be used to identify students' strengths and weaknesses, we mean that different statistical methods should not be used to compare outcomes. Here's a good example: A teacher gives a student a 10 question quiz. A student gets 8 questions correct, and the teacher identifies performance as 80% correct. Yet, when the test scores from the state come back, and the teacher sees that the student is in the 60th %ile ("percentile"). This means that 60% of students taking the test scored LOWER than the student, not that the student only answered 60% correct. The teacher must understand what the scores mean and not compare one type of score to another type, as the numbers will not relate.

SEE also Skill 17.1

Skill 16.3   Ways to engage children in self-assessment

Engaging children in self-assessment of their work is a way of helping them to become more responsible and take an active part in their own learning. First of all, the teacher should make it known to the children what the objectives of the lesson/unit are so that they are clear about what they have to know at the end of the lesson/unit. By using exemplars, teachers can show the students the kind of work they need to produce to prove that they have achieved the objective. This is possible, even in early childhood grades, by rewriting the objectives into "I can" statements and posting them in the classroom. As the teacher discusses each of these statements with the students, there should be exemplars of work to show them what good work looks like and work that does not meet the standards, At an early age, children can see the difference between the two and are able to offer reasons why one piece of work is better than the other.

Students need to have models and guidelines for self-assessment so that they can develop their skills for this skill. Learning increases significantly when students are engaged in the assessment process.

For children in the early grades, a simple checklist of three to four items is sufficient for self-assessment. When students are finished writing a story, for example, the checklist could contain such items as:
- I did my best work
- I asked my friend to check my work
- Something I found hard to do was _____
- Next time I will try to _____

Students can also use happy and sad faces to tell whether they found something hard or easy to do. When children are working together in groups, teachers can use a self-assessment form that asks them how they thought they worked together and what they need to work on in the future.

Engaging the children in self-assessment also means that the teacher needs to conference with them after the assessment to discuss the work. Through the discussion, the students will be able to put some of their thoughts about their work into words and in so doing give the teacher more insight into where they may need a little extra help. Allowing the students to redo some parts of their work after the teacher has done an assessment will also help them in the self-assessment process as they see some of the mistakes they made or places where they can improve for the next time.

During the lesson, teachers can use a Pause and Think strategy with the students. In this strategy, students can:
- Turn to a partner and describe what they have learned
- Comment on a sample of their work that they think needs some improvement
- Explain how they think a sample of work meets the criteria set down by the teacher
- Use a rubric to help them determine whether or not their work meets the grade

Like all other aspects of their education, students need instruction in self-assessment and time to practice. Students need to know that making mistakes is a normal part of learning and the key is helping them to identify and correct the mistakes.

For more information on creating and using rubrics, go to http://rubistar.4teachers.org/index.php. This website provides a free tool to help teachers create quality rubrics.

Skill 16.4 The importance of matching assessments to the diverse needs of children

There is no such thing as one assessment for any objective that will meet the needs of all the children in the classroom. Children have different learning styles and thus different ways of demonstrating that they have achieved the objective of the lesson. When designing assessments, teachers need to carefully consider all the students in the class.

Some students may need more time than others to complete the work, depending on physical or other disabilities. For children with learning disabilities, the assessment may have to be tailored to their needs, such as having them give shorter answers, allowing for them to draw or use a computer to produce the work to show they have achieved the objective. There are also students in every class who find the work easy and therefore need challenging questions to make them think about what they have learned.

SEE also Skill 16.1 and Skill 16.5

Skill 16.5 The selection of appropriate assessments for a given purpose

Assessment should suit the objective being tested as well as the subject area and curriculum standard. This ensures that the assessment is relevant to the instruction and activities the children engage in during the lessons. There is a wide range of assessments teachers can use rather than depending on the traditional test to determine whether or not a child has achieved the objective.

Assessing how well a child performs on a given task can include such things as:

- Group activities, such as role-playing, dramatization
- Speaking activities, such as presentations to the class or participation in class discussions
- Artwork
- Writing stories and paragraphs

At the beginning of the lesson, the teacher should establish clear criteria for the assessment. The activities chosen for assessment should be age and grade appropriate and the students should know why and how they will be assessed. When assessment is designed with a purpose in mind, children know exactly what it is they have to do. Beginning with the end in mind is the basis of Understanding by Design. Understanding by Design (UbD) is a framework for designing curriculum units, performance assessments, and instruction that lead your students to deep understanding of the content you teach.

The purpose of assessment is to determine what the students know and where the teacher needs to go next with the instruction. For some children, it may mean that some of the content has to be retaught and for others it may mean they are ready to move on to a new concept.

SEE also Skill 16.1

For more information on Understanding by Design, refer to the website
http://www.grantwiggins.org/ubd.html

Skill 16.6   The use of informal assessments for the purpose of planning appropriate programs, environments, and interactions and adapting for individual differences

Informal assessments go a long way towards helping teachers know the needs of the students in the classroom. Some children have anxiety when it comes to tests. Therefore by using informal assessments, the children don't even realize they are being assessed.

At the beginning of the year, informal inventories and conversations with the students will guide the teacher in knowing where the interests of the students lie. This will help in planning the activities to meet the curriculum standards for the year. Watching and observing the students as they interact with one another helps the teacher know which students get along with one another and may be good working partners. In some cases, they may be too good together and this will not work well in a classroom setting because they may spend their time talking and not working.

Through informal assessments, teachers can also get a very good idea of which students will need extra help and which students will be able to work independently. Play time is an excellent opportunity to observe children and to get to know their interests and how well they can use their imagination. It will also give the teacher information for planning classroom activities.

Informal assessment also refers to the work the students doing during class time. The teacher is not giving a test on everything they do, but by working with students, the teacher can see which students need more instruction on a concept or skill than others. Anecdotal notes are an excellent way of recording this information so that the teacher has the information at hand when planning future lessons.

By observing the children in the classroom, the teacher can also make note of any problems with the seating arrangement or the placement of shelves or tables that may interfere with how children can get around the classroom environment. This is especially important for children with physical disabilities.

Questioning to elicit answers in the classroom, homework assignments, conversations with the students, learning logs and journals are other examples of informal ways to assess student learning.

SEE also Skills 16.1 and 16.2

TEACHER CERTIFICATION STUDY GUIDE

COMPETENCY 17.0   UNDERSTAND FORMAL ASSESSMENT STRATEGIES TO PLAN AND INDIVIDUALIZE CURRICULUM AND TEACHING PRACTICES

Skill 17.1   The selection, evaluation, and interpretation of formal, standardized assessment instruments and information used in the assessment of children

State and federal law requires that public schools administer various assessments. Furthermore, most districts have additional assessments. While all assessments can provide information for teachers so that they can modify and improve instruction, all required assessments also provide the district, the state, and the federal government with information regarding the academic growth of students. Therefore, policies and procedures for administering tests must be followed carefully and thoroughly. Whenever procedures are not followed carefully, the validity of the test scores is put into jeopardy. It is crucial that all teachers follow the same procedures so that all students get the same experiences. By doing so, there is much less chance that differences in test scores occur because of conditions outside of what students know. While schools will provide clear and specific information on test procedures, it is always worth asking for assistance when a procedure does not make sense.

Formal assessment is a structured infrequent measure of learner achievement. It involves the use of test sand exams. Exams are used to measure the learner's progress.

The purpose of informal assessment is to help our learners learn better. This form of assessment helps the teacher to how well the learners are learning and progressing. Informal assessment can be applied to home work assignments, field journals, daily class work, which are good indicators of student progress and comprehension.

Formal assessment on the other hand is highly structured keeping the learner in mind. It must be done at regular intervals and if the progress is not satisfactory, parent involvement is absolutely essential. A test or exam is a good example of formal assessment. A science project is also a formal assessment.

Assessments

The process of collecting, quantifying and qualifying student performance data using multiple assessment information on student learning is called assessment. A comprehensive assessment system must include a diversity of assessment tools such as norm-referenced, criterion-referenced, performance-based, or any student generated alternative assessments that can measure learning outcomes and goals for student achievement and success in school communities.

Norm-referenced Assessments

Norm-referenced tests (NRT) are used to classify students for homogenous groupings based on ability levels or basic skills into a ranking category. In many school communities, NRTs are used to classify students into AP (Advanced Placement), honors, regular or remedial classes that can significantly impact student future educational opportunities or success. NRTs are also used by national testing companies such as Iowa Test of Basic Skills (Riverside), Florida Achievement Test (McGraw-Hill) and other major test publishers to test a national sample of students to norm against standard test-takers. Stiggins (1994) states "Norm-referenced tests (NRT) are designed to highlight achievement differences between and among students to produce a dependable rank order of students across a continuum of achievement from high achievers to low achievers."

Educators may select NRTs to focus on students with lower basic skills which could limit the development of curriculum content that needs to provide students with academic learning's that accelerate student skills from basic to higher skill application to address the state assessments and core subject expectations.

NRT ranking ranges from 1-99 with 25% of students scoring in the lower ranking of 1-25 and 25% of students scoring in the higher ranking of 76-99.

Criterion-referenced Assessments

Criterion-referenced assessments look at specific student learning goals and performance compared to a norm group of student learners. According to Bond (1996) "Educators or policy makers may choose to use a Criterion-referenced test (CRT) when they wish to see how well students have learned the knowledge and skills which they are expected to have mastered." Many school districts and state legislation use CRTs to ascertain whether schools are meeting national and state learning standards. The latest national educational mandate of "No Child Left Behind" (NCLB) and Adequate Yearly Progress (AYP) use CRTs to measure student learning, school performance, and school improvement goals as structured accountability expectations in school communities. CRTs are generally used in learning environments to reflect the effectiveness of curriculum implementation and learning outcomes.

The Michigan Educational Assessment Program (MEAP) is criterion-referenced. The MEAP tests were developed to measure what Michigan educators believe all students should know and be able to achieve in five content areas: mathematics, reading, science, social studies, and writing. The test results paint a picture of how well Michigan students and Michigan schools are doing when compared standards established by the State Board of education. The MEAP test is the only common measure given statewide to all students. It serves as a measure of accountability for Michigan schools.

Performance-based Assessments

In today's classrooms, performance-based assessments in core subject areas must have established and specific performance criteria that start with pre-testing in a subject area and maintain daily or weekly testing to gauge student learning goals and objectives. To understand a student's learning is to understand how a student processes information. Effective performance assessments will show the gaps or holes in student learning which allows for an intense concentration on providing fillers to bridge non-sequential learning gaps. Typical performance assessments include oral and written student work in the form of research papers, oral presentations, class projects, journals, student portfolio collections of work, and community service projects.

Summary

With today's emphasis on student learning accountability, the public and legislature demands for school community accountability for effective teaching and assessment of student learning outcomes will remain a constant mandate of educational accountability. Before a state, district, or school community can determine which type of testing is the most effective, there must be a determination of testing outcome expectation; content learning outcome; and deciding effectiveness of the assessments in meeting the learning goals and objectives of the students

Skill 17.2 The integration of authentic classroom assessment data with formal assessment information

An authentic assessment usually includes a task for students to perform and a rubric by which their performance on the task will be evaluated. Formal assessment usually involves forced-choice measures of multiple-choice tests, fill-in-the-blanks, true-false, matching and the like that have been and remain so common in education. Students typically select an answer or recall information to complete the assessment. These tests may be standardized or teacher-created. They may be administered locally or statewide, or internationally.

Essentially, formal assessment is grounded in educational philosophy that adopts the following reasoning and practice:

1. A school's mission is to develop productive citizens.
2. To be a productive citizen an individual must possess a certain body of knowledge and skills.
3. Therefore, schools must teach this body of knowledge and skills.
4. To determine if it is successful, the school must then test students to see if they acquired the knowledge and skills.

In this model, the curriculum drives assessment. "The" body of knowledge is determined first. That knowledge becomes the curriculum that is delivered. Subsequently, the assessments are developed and administered to determine if acquisition of the curriculum occurred.

In contrast, authentic assessment springs from the following reasoning and practice:

1. A school's mission is to develop productive citizens.
2. To be a productive citizen, an individual must be capable of performing meaningful tasks in the real world.
3. Therefore, schools must help students become proficient at performing the tasks they will encounter when they graduate.
4. To determine if it is successful, the school must then ask students to perform meaningful tasks that replicate real world challenges to see if students are capable of doing so.

Thus, with authentic assessment, assessment drives the curriculum. That is, teachers first determine the tasks that students will perform to demonstrate their mastery, and then a curriculum is developed that will enable students to perform those tasks well, which would include the acquisition of essential knowledge and skills. This has been referred to as *planning backwards*.

If students were learning tennis they would be taught the skills required to perform well, but would not be assessed by a multiple choice test. To assess tennis skills the students would be placed on a tennis court and asked to perform. Although this is obvious with athletic skills, it is also true for academic subjects. We can teach students how to *do* math, *do* history and *do* science, not just *know* them. Then, to assess what our students learned, we can ask students to perform tasks that "replicate the challenges" faced by those using mathematics, doing history or conducting scientific investigation.

A teacher does not have to choose between authentic assessment and formal assessment. It is likely that some mix of the two will best meet your needs. If you had to choose an airplane pilot from between someone who passed the *flying* portion of the test but failed the *written* portion or someone who failed the flying portion and passed the written portion, you would probably choose the pilot who most directly demonstrated the ability to fly an airplane, that is, the one who passed the flying portion of the test. However, the best choice would the driver who passed both portions. The strongest students will have a good knowledge base about the subject area (which might best be assessed in a formal test) and will be able to apply that knowledge in a real context (which could be demonstrated through an authentic assessment).

Attributes of Traditional and Authentic Assessment

Another way that authentic assessment is commonly distinguished from formal assessment is in terms of its defining attributes. Typically, along the continuums of attributes listed below, formal assessment falls more towards the left end of each continuum and authentic assessment falls more towards the right end.

Formal -- Authentic

Selecting a Response ------------------------------------ Performing a Task

Contrived -- Real-life

Recall/Recognition -------------------------------- Construction/Application

Teacher-structured -- Student-structured

Indirect Evidence -- Direct Evidence

Skill 17.3 The use of formal assessments for the purpose of planning appropriate programs, environments, and interactions and adapting for individual differences

Formal assessment is essential for determining whether or not a student has met the objectives for a course of study. These include the quizzes, tests, writing assignments and projects that teachers assign in the classroom. The results of these assessments give teacher immediate feedback as to which students have met the objectives for the particular skill or concept that was taught in the class. However, teachers need to view these assessments as an integral part of the teaching and learning process and not just as something that needs to be done.

For one thing the material on the assessment has to be the same as what the student encountered in the class. Students shouldn't be surprised at what they find on the test because they have encountered it every day in class. The concepts, skills and content of the assessment should align perfectly with state curriculum standards and the outcomes teachers communicate to the students. When this takes place in a classroom, students understand that formal tests are an important measure of the learning goals.

Teachers should use the results of the formal assessment for more than assigning student grades. The grades should be analyzed along with the student answers to determine where the students are having problems or if they need to be challenged in the subsequent instruction and assessment. Individual differences in students also come into play with formal assessments. Some students do not react well to testing situations and even young children can have test anxiety as a result of high expectations from themselves and their parents. There may be times when children need some extra time to complete the assessment. For example, if a child completes half of a test and has everything correct, the teacher needs to investigate further to find out why the child did not complete the full test. It could be that the time was up, or that the students in the class who were finished were making noise which distracted the child, or some other reason.

Formal assessment will let teachers know what they did well in their teaching and areas that they need to work on with the students. Gathering information from the assessment, such as making a tally of how many children answered each question correctly or how many children missed a specific question provides valuable information for further instruction. The teacher can look at the question itself and if there is no problem, the answer may lie in using different teaching strategies in the classroom.

The same skill or concept may need to be taught in different ways for different students. Students may not have the prerequisite background knowledge for the instruction and therefore are at a disadvantage right from the beginning of the instruction.

Students who have difficulty with reading may need to have the questions read to them or may need a scribe to help them write their answers. This kind of information can be gained from analyzing the results of formal assessments.

TEACHER CERTIFICATION STUDY GUIDE

COMPETENCY 18.0   UNDERSTAND THE USE OF FORMATIVE AND SUMMATIVE PROGRAM EVALUATION TO ENSURE COMPREHENSIVE QUALITY OF THE TOTAL ENVIRONMENT, REFLECTING THE DIVERSITY OF CHILDREN, FAMILIES, AND COMMUNITY

Skill 18.1   The role of ongoing evaluations in program accountability and in making adjustments to the early childhood education program (e.g., curriculum, staffing, environment

Ongoing evaluation of early childhood classrooms is an effective for administrators making decisions about staffing and the environment of the classrooms. Teachers who engage in ongoing assessment can be mentors for other staff members. As the administrator observes what is taking place in the classroom, decisions can be made about retaining teachers or meeting with them to help them improve their teaching.

Ongoing assessment can also provide a framework to improve an academic program. In order for schools to be successful in achieving academic goals, it is essential for stakeholders in the school to assess the instructional programs they are teaching. Administrators, teachers, paraprofessionals – in short, all individuals who are responsible for devising, administering or overseeing the instructional program in the school must take a serious look at the way the school is approaching their role of guaranteeing that students are learning and making academic progress. Only through this careful analysis can schools hope to attain their AYP (Adequate Yearly Progress) addressed in the ***No Child Left Behind*** legislation.

So how does a school go about assessing its instructional program?   It is not the role of a single individual but is a collective responsibility. Working in collaborative groups, all individuals with a vested interest in student achievement must examine the current educational practices within the school and ask some key questions:

- Based on achievement data, is the current instructional program working?
- Are all students learning? If not, which students are not successful?
- Do our programs meet the needs of all students within our school, including but not limited to, regular and special education students, English speakers of other languages (ESOL students), advanced learners, and underachieving students?
- Are we working together as a school to address our achievement issues or are we working in isolation to try and resolve problems within our school?
- Do teachers know what steps to take in order to address the achievement deficiencies of students who are not successful?

- Are teachers teaching the right curriculum? Has there been a conscious effort to align the curriculum with the standards that must be taught and the standards on which students are tested?
- Are assessments clearly linked to the learning goals in every class in the school?
- Is there a continuous effort to add to the repertoire of strategies from which teachers can choose in order to meet the needs of students?
- Are teachers changing their approaches to addressing student learning needs or are they doing things "the same way they have for years?"

Some practitioners have reduced the assessment of school programs to an analysis of the results of tests that students take at the end of the school year. This approach is short sighted. Why would we wait until the year is over (and when most students are gone) to determine if we have met their learning needs? Program evaluation should be the on-going analysis of our instructional delivery throughout the school year. Teachers should be analyzing data on a routine basis? The constant and consistent questions teachers should ask themselves every day should be:

- Are these just **good** lessons or are they the **right** lessons to meet the needs of all my students?
- Do I regularly pre-assess the skills and knowledge of my students in order to plan appropriate units?
- Am I reteaching and reassessing students when they have shown that they have not learned curriculum content?
- Am I using students data (both the analysis of assessment results as well as the learning activities I provide for students) in order to determine what is working and what is not working.
- Am I collaborating with my colleagues as fellow professionals to elicit new ideas if I am frustrated and I feel that I need fresh ideas?
- Am I differentiating my approach to teaching by allowing my students to reach learning outcomes by following different pathways?

These essential questions may be just the beginning of the professional dialogues that must take place in a successful school. Good instruction and improved student learning can only come about when we assess the programs we are teaching, ask the tough questions, and make the appropriate adjustments.

Skill 18.2 The awareness of local, state, and national standards for various program models

The entire state system of education works to support each school, each classroom, and each teacher. The general structure, including the federal, U. S. Department of Education system, is explained below.

At the top is the U. S. Department of Education. The Secretary of this department is appointed by the President of the United States. While significant amounts of money do get distributed from this department for various projects and needs, its primary role, at least in this day and age, is to enforce the No Child Left Behind law.

Under the U. S. Department of Education are various research and "service" centers. Scattered around the country, these centers conduct research in education and distribute it to school systems around the country. Often, the research is posted online. See http://ies.ed.gov/ncee/edlabs/ for more information.

The next level is the state level. The state is the primary controller for public education. Each state has a set of laws and requirements for public education. All public schools in the state must follow these laws. In addition, the state sets standards for student learning and mandates and oversees achievement testing. These standards are the curriculum for each grade level. It doesn't matter what texts or resources the teacher uses – the instruction delivered in the classroom has to be closely correlated to these standards.

Under the state are local service centers. Usually, these are operated by counties. These service centers provide professional development to teachers and administrators, provide additional student services, and set instructional tones for all districts within the region.

Under these centers are the school districts themselves. Districts are set up to run the day-to-day operations of schools. They deal with the hiring of teachers, the management of bus and food services, the facilities of schools, and many more things. Under the districts are the schools. So while a teacher may work at a particular school, the teacher is really an employee of the district.

In the President's State of the Union Address in 1997, he listed seven priorities. One of the seven was that "All states and schools will have challenging and clear standards of achievement and accountability for all children, and effective strategies for reaching those standards."

In response to this charge, during the past decade there has been a movement to develop local, state and national education standards for every major school subject. You may find more information about this at http://www.education-world.com/standards/ and at http://eduscapes.com/tap/topic28.htm

TEACHER CERTIFICATION STUDY GUIDE

COMPETENCY 19.0 UNDERSTAND THE COMMUNICATION OF ASSESSMENT INFORMATION

Skill 19.1 Ways to communicate (e.g., checklists, portfolios, anecdotal records, progress reports, surveys) and their strengths and weaknesses

It is useful to consider the types of assessment procedures that are available to the classroom teacher. The types of assessment discussed below represent many of the more common types, but the list is not comprehensive.

Anecdotal records

These are notes recorded by the teacher concerning an area of interest or concern with a particular student. These records should focus on observable behaviors and should be descriptive in nature. They should not include assumptions or speculations regarding effective areas such as motivation or interest. These records are usually compiled over a period of several days to several weeks.

SEE also Skill 12.2

Rating scales & checklists

These assessments are generally self-appraisal instruments completed by the students or observations-based instruments completed by the teacher. The focus of these is frequently on behavior or effective areas such as interest and motivation.

Portfolio assessment

The use of student portfolios for some aspect of assessment has become quite common. The purpose, nature, and policies of portfolio assessment vary greatly from one setting to another. In general, though, a student's portfolio contains samples of work collected over an extended period of time. The nature of the subject, age of the student, and scope of the portfolio, all contribute to the specific mechanics of analyzing, synthesizing, and otherwise evaluating the portfolio contents.

In most cases, the student and teacher make joint decisions as to which work samples go into the student's portfolios. A collection of work compiled over an extended time period allows teacher, student, and parents to view the student's progress from a unique perspective. Qualitative changes over time can be readily apparent from work samples. uch changes are difficult to establish with strictly quantitative records typical of the scores recorded in the teacher's grade book.

Questioning

One of the most frequently occurring forms of assessment in the classroom is oral questioning by the teacher. As the teacher questions the students, she collects a great deal of information about the degree of student learning and potential sources of confusing for the students. While questioning is often viewed as a component of instructional methodology, it is also a powerful assessment tool.

Progress Reports

Progress reports serve as routine communication to inform parents/caregivers as to the child's progress in class. Ideally, progress reports should be supplied in both positive and negative social and academic circumstances. In cases where a student's performance is declining, progress reports serve to notify a caregiver so that steps may be taken to rectify the situation prior to report cards.

Surveys

SEE Skill 16.1

Skill 19.2 An understanding of a family's role as an active participant in the development, implementation, and interpretation of assessments

SEE Skill 12.2

Skill 19.3 The communication of assessment information to children, families, and others

One good reference for information on reporting assessment results is *Pencils Down! A Guide for Using and Reporting Test Results*, by Gucwa and Mastie (1989). This publication from the Michigan Department of Education presents descriptions of different procedures for reporting assessment results and includes a sample press release. The entire document can be found at http://www.ncrel.org/sdrs/areas/issues/methods/assment/as6penc2.htm

The following four sections describe methods that can be used when reporting assessment results to students, parents, the school board, and the public.

Reporting Results to Students: A two-step process is recommended for reporting assessment results to students. The first step is a briefing provided to the entire group of students who received individual results. The second step is individual follow-up meetings with students. These meetings should focus on how the teacher(s) will be addressing the individual needs of students.

Reporting Results to Parents: Parents want to know how their children are performing in school, so assessment information collected by schools is of great interest to them. Parents also want to know how the entire student body is performing in comparison with other schools. Reporting results to parents can satisfy both of these needs. Keep in mind that parents want to know how the school scored overall, even if their own children were not assessed.

The building administrator and teachers should be involved in carrying out both types of reporting activities. This collaboration helps build active partnerships between teachers and parents focused on the learning of children.

Four strategies are suggested for reporting results to parents. They are: (1) individual parent/teacher conferences, (2) an individual written report sent home, (3) parent group meetings, and (4) parent newsletter articles.

Although in-person meetings are generally more personal and effective, they are not always possible. Written reports may provide a more accessible form of communication between teachers and parents. In all types of reports, the information should include how well an individual student did on the assessment and what steps the educator will take to make improvements in instruction so that the student will learn what is needed. Written reports also should include information concerning how parents can actively participate in a plan of action to address the instructional needs of their child.

Reporting Results to the School Board: The school board is the legal policymaking entity at the district level. As such, it deserves to receive reports on the results of assessment. A three-part reporting strategy is recommended for reporting to the school board.

The first report provides background information about the assessment effort itself. It explains what was assessed, what type of assessments were used, why they were used, and how the results will be applied and reported. This report might best be given when the assessment information is being collected, but before assessment results become available. Such timing encourages the school board members to focus on the message of the assessment rather than the numbers.

The second report contains the results of the assessment at the school and district levels. It should answer typical questions raised by policymakers.

The third report follows up on the status of efforts to improve instruction at the school and the effectiveness of these changes. This report, though optional, goes a long way in conveying to the school board that the real purpose of student assessment is to help improve teaching and learning, not to serve as a scorecard on the quality of the school.

Reporting Results to the Public: Many educators are frustrated that communities receive most reports of assessment results through the news media. The public seems to know little else about schools other than test results. As a consequence, school districts may be leery about reporting assessment results or being candid with the public regarding the level of student performance.

The effectiveness of the entire reporting process will be greatly hindered if the school or district makes no effective use of the assessment information. If teachers, administrators, and parents do not learn from and act upon the information provided by the assessments, the entire process will be of little or no benefit to the children. Remember, the ultimate goal of assessment is to better educate children.

SEE also Skills 12.2, 12.4, and 22.2

DOMAIN V.   PROFESSIONALISM AND PROGRAM LEADERSHIP

COMPETENCY 20.0   UNDERSTAND THE FRAMEWORK OF THE EARLY CHILDHOOD PROFESSION

Skill 20.1   The multiple historical, philosophical, and social foundations of the early childhood profession and how these foundations influence current thought and practice

Major Theories of Child Development

Early in the twentieth century the study of child development began to explode. In previous studies, children were merely described as tiny adults. It was the expectation that a child's success was the result of the parents who had passed on the genes. However, in the new century the focus of childhood development study was shifted toward the abnormal. Studies began to recognize the advances in cognitive abilities, language usage, and physical growth, in addition to atypical development.

The following are just a few of the many theories of child development that have been proposed by theorists and researchers. More recent theories outline the developmental stages of children and identify the typical ages at which these growth milestones occur.

Psychoanalytic Theories

Sigmund Freud
The theories that Freud presented stressed the importance of childhood events and experiences. These theories only focus on the mental disorder side of functions rather than that of the normal functioning of students. According to Freud, there is a series of "psychosexual stages" that he outlined in "Three Essays on Sexuality" (1915). He proposes that at each stage satisfaction of desire is necessary and later plays a role in adult personality.

Erik Erikson
Erikson's development theory included development throughout the entire human lifespan. Erikson believed that each stage of development is involved in conflict resolution. Impact of overall functioning throughout childhood into adulthood would determine either success or failure. Erikson's theory of psychosocial development is one of the best-known theories of personality in psychology. Similar to Freud, Erikson believed that personality develops in a series of stages. Unlike Freud's theory of psychosexual stages, Erikson's theory describes the impact of social experience across the whole lifespan.

One of the main elements of Erikson's psychosocial stage theory is the development of **ego identity**. Ego identity is the conscious sense of self that we develop through social interaction. According to Erikson, our ego identity is constantly changing due to new experiences and information we acquire in our daily interactions with others. In addition to ego identity, Erikson also believed a sense of competence also motivates behaviors and actions. Each stage in Erikson's theory is concerned with becoming competent in an area of life. If the stage is handled well, the person will feel a sense of mastery. If the stage is managed poorly, the person will emerge with a sense of inadequacy.

In each stage, Erikson believed people experience a **conflict** that serves as a turning point in development. In Erikson's view, these conflicts are centered on either developing a psychological quality or failing to develop that quality. During these times, the potential for personal growth is high, but so is the potential for failure.

Cognitive Theories

Jean Piaget, a European scientist who died in the late 20th Century, developed many theories about the way humans learn. Most famously, he developed a theory about the stages of the development of human minds. It's very simple. The first stage is the "sensory-motor" stage that lasts until a child is in the toddler years. In this stage, children begin to understand their senses.

The next stage, called the "pre-operational" stage, is where children begin to understand symbols. For example, as they learn language, they begin to realize that words are symbols of thoughts, actions, items, and other elements in the world. This stage lasts into early elementary school.

The third stage is referred to as the "concrete operations" stage. This lasts until late elementary school. In this stage, children go one step beyond learning what a symbol is. They learn how to manipulate symbols, objects, and other elements. A common example of this stage is the displacement of water. In this stage, they can reason that a wide and short cup of water poured into a tall and thin cup of water can actually have the same amount of water.

The next stage is called the "formal operations" stage. It usually starts in adolescence or early teen years and it continues on into adulthood. This stage is what allows critical thinking, hypothesis, systematic organization of knowledge, etc.

Generally, when we say that children move from a stage of concrete thinking to logical and abstract thinking, we mean that they are moving from the "pre-operational" and "concrete" stage **TO** the "formal operations" stage. But as anyone who spends time with children knows, there are many bumps in the way to a person's ability to be a strong critical thinker. And remember, just because a child has moved into a particular stage does not mean that they will be able to completely function at the specified level. For example, adolescents may be able to think critically, but they need plenty of instruction and assistance to do so at an adequate level. This does not necessarily mean that critical thinking skills should be taught out of context; rather, through all lessons, teachers should work to instill components that help develop the thinking of children.

Behavioral Theories

Theories based upon behavior and interaction with the environment are considered behavioral theories. Several theorists contributed to the ideas of behavioral learning. Noted theorists are Watson, Pavlov, and Skinner. These theories deal only with observable behaviors. Development is considered a reaction to rewards, punishments, stimuli, and reinforcement. These behavioral theories are known as operant conditioning and classical conditioning.

Social Development Theories

Social development theories are still growing in popularity today. There is a great deal of research being done regarding the theories of early development, specifically regarding relationships with caregivers and role models. The idea is that these relationships continue to grow and influence social relationships throughout life. John Bowbly proposed one of the earliest theories of social development. His theory was known as the attachment theory.

Theories in Practice in the Classroom

Teachers must be able to acknowledge the various stages of development and theories and implement various practices into teaching and classroom management. Teachers must understand that some techniques will only be effective at certain stages during childhood. For example, if a child develops into the stage in which s/he has learned to master conflict resolution (later adolescence), students at this stage should be provided opportunities to engage in a scientific debate regarding a scientific topic of question (human genome project or was landing on the moon fact or fiction?)

Skill 20.2 The profession's code of ethical conduct

The ultimate goal of teachers when they enter the profession of teaching is to provide a comprehensive education for all students by providing challenging curriculum and setting high expectations for learning. In an ideal classroom, the mechanisms for providing the perfect teaching climate and instruction are the norm and not the exception. Given the diversity of learners from a multitude of cultural, ethnic, intellectual, socioeconomic and grade level prepared backgrounds, the reality is that teachers are confronted with classrooms that are infused with classroom management issues and differentiated learning among learners who are either positively engaged in the learning process or negatively removed from all aspects of learning.

Researchers have shown that for new teachers entering the profession, the two greatest obstacles are dealing with increasing behavioral issues in the classroom and dealing with student minimally engaged in their own learning process. The goal of teachers is to maintain a toolkit of resources to deal with an ever-changing landscape of learners and classroom environments.

> (1) The educator's primary professional concern will always be for the student and for the development of the student's potential. The educator will therefore strive for professional growth and will seek to exercise the best professional judgment and integrity.

In a student-centered learning environment, the goal is to provide the best education and opportunity for academic success for all students. Integrating the developmental patterns of physical, social and academic norms for students will provide individual learners with student learning plans that are individualized and specific to their skill levels and needs. Teachers who effectively develop and maximize a student's potential will use pre- and post-assessments to gain comprehensive data on the existing skill level of the student in order to plan and adapt curriculum to address and grow student skills. Maintaining communication with the student and parents will provide a community approach to learning where all stakeholders are included to maximize student-learning growth.

> (2) Aware of the importance of maintaining the respect and confidence of one's colleagues, of students, of parents, and of other members of the community, the educator strives to achieve and sustain the highest degree of ethical conduct.

The ethical conduct of an educator has undergone extensive scrutiny in today's classrooms. Teachers are under intense rules and regulations to maintain the highest degree of conduct and professionalism in the classroom. It is imperative that teachers educating today's young people have the highest regard for professionalism and be proper role models for students in and out of the classrooms.

The Michigan Professional Educator's Code of Ethics, adopted in December 2003, may be found at
http://www.michigan.gov/documents/Code_of_Ethics_Layout_128009_7.pdf

This Code of Ethics:
1. Highlights for all adults involved in PreK-16 educational arenas an agreed upon set of ethical principles to guide decisions;
2. Provides a consistent framework for thinking about the societal benefits of quality teachers;
3. Raises professional educators' awareness of the responsibility they carry when accepting a teaching certificate and/or position which involves touching the lives of students in Michigan's educational systems;
4. Makes a professional educator's ethical commitment transparent to the general public; and
5. Facilitates awareness and discussion for both pre-service and in-service educators on ethical standards.

Michigan Professional Educator's Code of Ethics

Preamble: Society has charged public education with trust and responsibility that requires of professional educators the highest ideals and quality service. The Michigan State Board of Education adopts this Code of Ethics to articulate the ethical standards to which professional educators are expected to adhere in their job performance.

Ethical Standards: The following ethical standards address the professional educator's commitment to the student and the profession.

1. *Service toward common good*
   Ethical Principle: The professional educator's primary goal is to support the growth and development of all learners for the purpose of creating and sustaining an informed citizenry in a democratic society.
2. *Mutual respect*
   Ethical principle: Professional educators respect the inherent dignity and worth of each individual.
3. *Equity*
   Ethical principle: Professional educators advocate the practice of equity. The professional educator advocates for equal access to educational opportunities for each individual.

4. *Diversity*
Ethical principle: Professional educators promote cross-cultural awareness by honoring and valuing individual differences and supporting the strengths of all individuals to ensure that instruction reflects the realities and diversity of the world.

5. *Truth and honesty*
Ethical principle: Professional educators uphold personal and professional integrity and behave in a trustworthy manner. They adhere to acceptable social practices, current state law, state and national student assessment guidelines, and exercise sound professional judgment.

Skill 20.3 Current research, trends, and issues in early childhood

There are many current issues, trends, educational innovations, and legislation that impact elementary school communities. National assessments and local evaluations of student academic performance in the areas of reading, writing and math have shown that there are gaps in learning from one cultural group to another in classrooms. The issue of student learning and performance has become a national debate on whether providing additional educational funding will alleviate or create academic access for students identified as at risk in schools.

Creating programs for literacy development and mathematical acquisition have become both the issues and the trends in the construct of new educational innovations. Differentiating instruction for learners who come to school in Pre-kindergarten has become a focus for educators seeking to increase the literacy and mathematical skills of its youngest learners. The development of effective programs and subsequent funding continue to be the goals of a legislative process dedicated to promoting educational equity for students.

Legislation issues of educational funding for teachers and program developments continue to impact existing educational implementations for students. With thousands of school communities failing to meet NCLB (No Child Left Behind) and AYP (Adequate Yearly Progress) standards, the cost of overhaul and providing additional financial support for effective school communities with over-capacity issues, is a major reason given for the decreased funding providing for current educational communities. Students who have been continually promoted from pre-K to higher elementary grade levels who have failed to attain the basic skills of reading, writing and math are becoming increasingly frustrated by school systems designed to promote rather than hold accountability for student learning and evaluation.

The cost of teacher turnover in school communities has been estimated to be in the range of 5-7 billion dollars which further impacts the legislature's ability to provide enough funding for all educational communities. Professional development training and required certification classes for teachers in elementary education also contribute to the comprehensive cost of educating students.

Early violence in elementary school communities coupled with classroom management issues have contributed to a reduction in teaching and instructional time for young learners. Providing young learners with ethical and social strategies to improve cooperative learning and communication will go a long way in reducing the time spent on conflict and increase the time spent on learning acquisition.

Educational innovations in technology and educational reform must address the issues that are creating conflict impacting educational development and implementation of effective curriculum for young learners. Current educational reform must continue to focus on addressing educational issues that promote learning opportunities and professional development for both students and educators.

TEACHER CERTIFICATION STUDY GUIDE

COMPETENCY 21.0 UNDERSTAND THE DEVELOPMENT AND ROLE OF AN ARTICULATED PHILOSOPHY IN AN EARLY CHILDHOOD EDUCATION PROGRAM

Skill 21.1 Purposes for developing an articulated philosophy (e.g., shaping the early childhood curriculum, accountability)

The early childhood education program should have a highly developed articulated philosophy, which shapes the curriculum of the early childhood program. The sources that contributed to the development of the philosophy, such as the research, standard, state guidelines, and national goals, should be stated. The recognition of the diverse needs of young students and their families should be uniquely articulated within the philosophy.

Detailed applications of the early childhood philosophy should include such as a comprehensive course outline or syllabus, with meticulous research on suggested reading assignments, textbook recommendations, and all inclusive lesson plans.

The guiding principle of the early childhood education program is the matching of curriculum and instruction to the child's needs, interests and developmental abilities. Early Childhood programs should implement planned instruction and effective communication system with parents. The program must always identify children with special needs; and demonstrate accountability.

An early childhood education program is based on child-initiated learning activities. The teacher's role is to support and facilitate these activities.

Skill 21.2 Sources of input in creating the philosophy

SEE Skill 21.1

Skill 21.3 Factors that should be reflected in the philosophy (e.g., research; national, state, and local goals, standards, and guidelines

When articulating a philosophy of early childhood education it is important to consider several factors. The first is current research that has been conducted in this area. All of the research points to the fact that children need hands-on experiences and that pre-school programs are fundamental in preparing children for school.

> For a list of researchers and organization in early childhood education:
> http://ceep.crc.uiuc.edu/poptopics/research.html#have

Developing a philosophy of early childhood education has to be closely aligned to the national, state and local goals, standards and guidelines. This is because in order to educate the children so that they can meet these standards for graduation, one has to teach the mandated curriculum. Activities must be based on the content and skills children of the early childhood grades are expected to know at the end of each year. The curriculum builds each year so that the skills and content a child learns in one year is further developed and enhanced in each successive school year.

The standards set out for all areas of education specifically state what the children are expected to know and be able to do. The curriculum also offers suggestions for teaching and assessing children so any philosophy of early childhood education must embrace the current methodologies for helping children to learn and grow so that they will become functional members of society.

The philosophy should be based upon sound theoretical principles of how children develop and learn. It should also:
- Be designed to include short and long term goals for teaching and learning
- Be realistic, even though a philosophy is theoretical in nature
- Reflect a belief that children need to be actively engaged
- Show that the teacher supports individual, cultural and linguistic diversity in the classroom
- Show that the teacher is flexible and can adapt the philosophy to different situations

SEE also Skill 24.1

Skill 21.4 Recognition of the diverse needs of children and their families

Any philosophy of early childhood education should reflect the diverse needs of the children in these grades and their families. In order for schools to meet the needs of all children, teachers must embrace a philosophy that includes curriculum and methodologies that engage and educate each and every child in the class.

When children enter school, they feel a sense of loss at leaving the safety of the home. Parents, too, feel a sense of loss when children start school. These are needs that must be met within the classroom environment, at least for the first month of school. The start of every school year is traumatic for some children, especially those that have moved to the area and for whom this is a new experience.

Along with the regular students in the class, there are students with special needs – physical disabilities and learning disabilities – as well as students from various ethnic backgrounds and students for whom English is not the native language. This will mean differentiated learning, adaptations being made to lesson plans and extra one-on-one teaching. There may also need to be accommodations made to the physical set up of the classroom. Parents of these children have special concerns as they want to make sure that the school and the classroom will meet the needs of their children.

One's philosophy of early childhood education must include information about the practices the teacher plans to implement in the classroom. The activities must be developmentally age appropriate and guidelines can be found at the National Association for the Education of Young Children. Decisions about such practices should be based on three types of information: what is known about child development and learning; what is known about the strengths, needs and interests of each individual child in the classroom; and the social and cultural context in which the children live. Developmentally age appropriate practice is important in every class, but more so in the early childhood class because it encourages a greater cultural sensitivity and allows for early intervention should the teacher notice any problems or deterrents to the child's learning.

Since the needs of children are so diverse, the teacher should use multiple methods and strategies to help them learn the new concepts and skills. When parents question the techniques or want more information, the teacher should be able to guide them to the appropriate research. Some parents may need assistance in how to help their children at home and the teacher can be a great asset to them in this regard. Allowing parents to come into the classroom to observe or to act as volunteers will put many of their fears and questions to rest.

SEE also Skill 21.1

Skill 21.5 The dissemination and application of the philosophy

An individual teacher's philosophy of early childhood education should give an overview of what the teacher believes about how young children learn and how they should be taught. Therefore reading this philosophy should give an insight into how the teacher will plan and carry out activities in the classroom.

A teacher whose philosophy of early childhood education states that children learn best by play should look for opportunities to bring play into the learning environment whenever possible or look for opportunities to teach the children through play.

It is not enough to have a philosophy of education just for the express purpose of being hired for a teaching position. Administrators should scrutinize each teacher's philosophy and set aside meeting time to discuss the philosophy at the beginning of each school year. The philosophy should also play a part in teacher evaluations as the administrator keeps it in mind when observing how the teacher conducts the lessons and interacts with the students. It is here that the application of the philosophy comes through – Are the teacher's words and actions in alignment with the philosophy?

TEACHER CERTIFICATION STUDY GUIDE

COMPETENCY 22.0   UNDERSTAND THE ASPECTS OF EFFECTIVE ADVOCACY TO IMPROVE THE QUALITY OF SERVICES FOR YOUNG CHILDREN AND THEIR FAMILIES

Skill 22.1   The conditions of children, families, and professionals

As an individual who spends a great deal of time with his or her students, the teacher is one who truly understands what students and schools need. It is important for teachers to vocalize concerns, issue and/or problems regarding their students, class, school and district.

To speak coherently and intellectually regarding any of these educational domains, teachers must maintain the highest professional standards for themselves. To do so, teachers must utilize their state's educational resources, including professional development, collaboration with peers, continuing higher education, professional organizations, community resources and other resources to stay current in the profession of teaching.

Skill 22.2   Legal issues

Student Records

The student permanent record is a file of the student's cumulative educational history. It contains a profile of the student's academic background as well as the student's behavioral and medical background. Other pertinent individual information contained in the permanent record includes the student's attendance, grade averages, and schools attended. Personal information such as parents' names and addresses, immunization records, child's height and weight, and narrative information about the child's progress and physical and mental well being is an important aspect of the permanent record. All information contained within the permanent record is strictly confidential and is only to be discussed with the student's parents or other involved school personnel.

The most essential fact to remember in regard to students' records is that the information within is confidential. Although specific policies may vary from one school or district to another, confidentiality remains constant and universal. Teachers never discuss any student or his/her progress with anyone other than the student's parents or essential school personnel. Confidentiality applies to all student information whether it is a student's spelling test, portfolio, standardized test information, report card, or the contents of the permanent record file.

The significance of the student's records is not to be taken lightly. In many instances, teachers have access to a student's records before she actually meets the student. It is important for the teacher to have helpful information about the student without developing any preconceived biases about the student. Careful regard must be given to all information that is added to a student's file without diluting the potential effectiveness of that information.

It is also important to be cognizant of the fact that the primary function of student records is that they are intended to be used as a means of developing a better understanding of the students' needs and to generate a more effective plan for meeting these needs.

Abuse Issues

SEE Skills 2.1, 14.2 and 24.5

Students' Rights

One of the first things that a teacher learns is how to obtain resources and help for his/her students. All schools have guidelines for receiving this assistance especially since the implementation of the Americans with Disabilities Act. The first step in securing help is for the teacher to approach the school's administration or exceptional education department for direction in attaining special services or resources for qualifying students. Many schools have a committee designated for addressing these needs such as a Child Study Team or Core Team. These teams are made up of both regular and exceptional education teachers, school psychologists, guidance counselors, and administrators. The particular student's classroom teacher usually has to complete some initial paper work and will need to do some behavioral observations.

The teacher will take this information to the appropriate committee for discussion and consideration. The committee will recommend the next step to be taken. Often subsequent steps include a complete psychological evaluation along with certain physical examinations such as vision and hearing screening and a complete medical examination by a doctor.

The referral of students for this process is usually relatively simple for the classroom teacher and requires little more than some initial paper work and discussion. The services and resources the student receives as a result of the process typically prove to be invaluable to the student with behavioral disorders.

At times, the teacher must go beyond the school system to meet the needs of some students. An awareness of special services and resources and how to obtain them is essential to all teachers and their students. When the school system is unable to address the needs of a student, the teacher often must take the initiative and contact agencies within the community. Frequently there is no special policy for finding resources. It is simply up to the individual teacher to be creative and resourceful and to find whatever help the student needs. Meeting the needs of all students is certainly a team effort that is most often spearheaded by the classroom teacher.

Parent's Rights

When children enter school parents do not automatically lose their rights for the time students are within the school environment. Parents who do not agree with what is happening in the classroom have several avenues open to them. The first step a parent should take is to contact the child's teacher and discuss the problem. In most cases, this resolves the problem and nothing further needs to be done.

If however, a meeting with the teacher is not effective, the parent should then contact the school principal. Often the principal will talk to the teacher and go further to set up a meeting between the parents and the teacher, which the principal will attend. Parents can also contact the school district if they still have problems remaining unresolved at the school level.

The school council is also an avenue for parents in the school on issues that do not involve curriculum. The school council meets on a regular basis and parents can attend these meetings and request items to be placed on the agenda, but this has to be done in advance by contacting the chairperson of the council.

Parents have the right to be treated with respect in the school, but they do not have the right to disrupt the daily activity. They do not have the right to force their way into the school, use profane language or treat any staff member in a manner that could result in legal action.

Teacher's Rights

Teachers have rights that need to be respected in the classroom. They do have a professional code of conduct that they must follow, and issues arising from problems with employers and staff members can be addressed through their Teacher Union.

Within the school, teachers have the right to be respected by student, parents and colleagues. Teachers that have a problem with another staff member should first of all speak to that person. The principal is also a mediator in disputes and should be informed of any problems within the school staff.

Students do not have the right to be verbally or physically abusive to teachers and should be removed from the classroom if this situation arises. Students in the classroom with severe physical or learning disabilities need to have a teacher assistant with them so that the teacher has time to devote to all students in the class.

Teachers have the right to ask parents to leave the classroom if they are disrupting the lessons. Teachers also have the right to ask for the principal or another staff member to be present when meeting with parents.

Special Education

Under the IDEA, parent/guardian involvement in the development of the student's IEP is required and absolutely essential for the advocacy of the disabled student's educational needs. IEPs must be tailored to meet the student's needs, and no one knows those needs better than the parent/guardian and other significant family members. Optimal conditions for a disabled student's education exist when teachers, school administrators, special education professionals and parents/guardians work together to design and execute the IEP.

Due process
Under the IDEA, Congress provides safeguards for students against schools' actions, including the right to sue in court, and encourages states to develop hearing and mediation systems to resolve disputes. No student or their parents/guardians can be denied due process because of disability.

Inclusion, mainstreaming, and least restrictive environment
Inclusion, mainstreaming and least restrictive environment are interrelated policies under the IDEA, with varying degrees of statutory imperatives.
- Inclusion is the right of students with disabilities to be placed in the regular classroom.
- Lease restrictive environment is the mandate that children be educated to the maximum extent appropriate with their non-disabled peers.
- Mainstreaming is a policy where disabled students can be placed in the regular classroom, as long as such placement does not interfere with the student's educational plan.

SEE also Skill 2.2

Skill 22.3 Legislation and public policies affecting children, families, programs for young children, and the early childhood profession

Educators should recognize that fact that early childhood is the phase in a child's life that is a critical time in which the young child is developing their physical, emotional, social, and cognitive skills.

Current legislation supports the idea that all children must begin school with an equal chance at achievement in order that no child is left behind. The Bush Administration has proposed a new early childhood initiative *Good Start, Grow Smart* to help States and local communities strengthen early learning for young children. This program emphasizes the fact that young children should be equipped with the educational skills they will need to start school.

The Bush Administration's *Good Start, Grow Smart* initiative addresses several major areas:

- **Partnering with States to Improve Early Childhood Education:** The Bush administration proposes a stronger Federal-State partnership in the delivery of quality early childhood programs. This new approach will ask States to develop quality criteria for early childhood education, including voluntary guidelines on pre-reading and language skills activities that align with State K-12 standards.

- **Providing Information to Teachers, Caregivers and Parents:** In order to close the gap between the best research and current practices in early childhood education, the Department of Education will establish a range of partnerships as part of a broad public awareness campaign targeted toward parents, early childhood educators, child care providers, and other interested parties.

For more information on Good Start, Grow Smart go to the website:
http://www.acf.hhs.gov/programs/ccb/initiatives/gsgs/fedpubs/GSGSBooklet.pdf

---

The *No Child Left Behind Act* is important because it ensures that public schools are teaching students what they need to know to be successful in life. It also draws attention to the need to prepare children before they start school. What children learn before coming to school is vital to their success.

Programs administered through the Department of Education

Title I Preschool Programs
Many school districts support preschool programs with their Title I (Education for the Disadvantaged) funds. Title I pre-school programs help more than 300,000 children in high-poverty communities enter kindergarten with the skills they need to succeed in school.

Early Reading First
This program, established in the No Child Left Behind Act, provides competitive grants to school districts and pre-school programs, such as Head Start centers. The grants fund the development of model programs to support the school readiness of preschool-aged children, particularly those from low-income families. Program activities will prepare teachers to provide high-quality language, literacy, and pre-reading activities.

Even Start
This program improves the educational opportunities of children and their parents in low-income areas by integrating early childhood education, adult education, parenting education, and interactive literacy activities between parents and their children.

The Early Childhood Educator Professional Development Program
The professional development activities focuses on furthering children's language and literacy skills to help set them on the road to reading proficiency once they enter kindergarten.

Skill 22.4 Methods for improving the quality of programs and services for young children

Efforts to improve early childhood learning should involve each state and their school districts, which shoulder the primary responsibility for providing public education. Since every state and their corresponding school district are directly responsible for student learning and achievement in school, preparing children to learn before they start school is in their best interest. This is particularly true now that the *No Child Left Behind* law requires standards and accountability for every school in America.

The Bush administration's plan requires all states to implement methods that help prepare children before they enter school. States should coordinate childhood programs with the public schools that serve the children they later educate.

This can be accomplished in part by making available to early childhood programs information on what will be expected of children once they reach school and what skills children will need to learn before school in order to meet State standards in school.

Methods for improving the quality of programs would include:

- **Early Learning Guidelines**. State guidelines implemented for literacy, language, and pre-reading skills activities for children ages 3 to 5 that align with State K-12 standards.
- **Professional development**. A plan for offering education and training activities to child care and pre-school teachers and administrators.
- **Program Coordination**. A program for coordinating childhood programs, which may include Head Start, and other programs in the public schools,

Training could also be provided on the scientifically-based research on cognitive development and highlight practical ideas to pre-k teachers and child care providers.

Skill 22.5 Ways of enhancing professional status and improving working conditions for early childhood educators

Experts agree that early childhood care and education will improve only if states build the infrastructure to support high-quality programs. That means careful standards and regulations for early-childhood providers; a sufficient system for training; a system of teacher credentialing; and higher salaries for early-childhood teachers.

Training should be provided in a variety of ongoing professional development activities which include:
- in-service training,
- professional workshops,
- courses at institutions of higher learning
- coaching

An effective early childhood program would provide specific requirements for maintaining and continuing teacher certification. Early childhood professionals would participate each year in developmental activities such as; college courses, in-service activities, workshops, seminars, or training programs.

Early childhood educators should be aware that teaching young children is often difficult and uniquely challenging. Often, teaching in early education programs that target children who live below the poverty line can be even more challenging, especially if the class includes youngsters who may require extra support. Teachers in these programs may require even more assistance than is generally assumed.

Training in child development which emphasizes knowledge in working with underprivileged young children; and also support systems which focus on their instructional behaviors and classroom management are extremely vital. Knowledge of child development and application of that knowledge in preschool settings are emphasized as much in two-year training programs as in four-year programs, if not more.

Additionally, a strong and knowledgeable administrative leadership is a key component to an effective early childhood program.

COMPETENCY 23.0 UNDERSTAND HOW TO WORK WITH AND SUPERVISE COLLEAGUES AND OTHERS IN AN EARLY CHILDHOOD PROGRAM

Skill 23.1 Strategies for coordinating activities with members of the classroom team, families, and the community (e.g., social services departments, administrators, other school personnel)

The bridge to effective learning for students begins with a collaborative approach by all stakeholders that support the educational needs of students. Underestimating the power and integral role of the community institutions in impacting the current and future goals of students can carry high stakes for students beyond the high school years who are competing for college access, student internships, and entry level jobs in the community. Researchers have shown that school involvement and connections with community institutions have greater retention rates of students graduating and seeking higher education experiences. The current disconnect and autonomy that has become commonplace in today's society must be reevaluated in terms of promoting tomorrow's citizens.

When community institutions provide students and teachers with meaningful connections and input, the commitment is apparent in terms of volunteering, loyalty and professional promotion. Providing students with placements in leadership positions such as the ASB (Associated Student Body); the PTSA (Parent Teacher Student Association); School Boards; neighborhood sub-committees addressing political or social issues; or government boards that impact and influence school communities creates an avenue for students to explore ethical, participatory, collaborative, transformational leadership that can be applied to all areas of a student's educational and personal life.

Community liaisons provide students with opportunities to experience accountability and responsibility so that students learn about life and how organizations work with effective communication and teams working together to accomplish goals and objectives. Teaching students skills of inclusion, social and environmental responsibility and creating public forums that represent student voice and vote foster student interest and access to developing and reflecting on individual opinions and understanding the dynamics of the world around them.

In communications with other teachers, administration, and parents, respectful, reciprocal communication solves many problems. This is especially true if the teacher truly respects the opinions and ideas of others involved in the life of the students. The teacher may be the classroom expert, but parents may be the experts in what is going on with their child. Bringing them into the decision-making process in dealing with their child may lead to solutions and success beyond what the teacher could envision. A sense of partnership between parents and teacher is vital and useful.

Part of being an effective teacher is to not only get the students to grow educationally, but to allow oneself to also continue to grow. Working with other members of the school community—peers, supervisors, and other staff—will provide the grounding needed to increase skills and knowledge sets. Identifying possible mentors, teachers you respect and whom you would like to emulate, is one step. Search out other teachers who have had an amount of success in the area you wish to learn more about. Ask them questions and ask for advice on improving your lesson plans. Talk to your supervisor or the principal when you are having difficulties, or when you want to learn more. They may know of development training seminars, books, journals, or other resources that might help you. Teachers should remember that they are part of a team of professionals, and that their personal success is part of a greater success that everyone hopes to achieve.

Social services departments are available to help the school and the teachers. Social workers will come to the school at the request of the teacher when a problem is suspected. They will also be part of a team dealing with the student and the family and often become the bridge between the home and the school.

SEE also Skill 15.1 and Skill 23.2

Skill 23.2 Appropriate roles and responsibilities of various personnel (e.g., paraprofessionals, associate teachers, volunteers)

Depending on the educational situation, team-teaching or the use of aides or assistants in the classroom, often serves to modify the behavior of students positively. It is not just the presence of more authority figures, but a more diverse environment, more opportunity for individual attention and a perceived sense of increased security, which engenders a positive attitude among the students.

People skills and management skills are necessary for the teacher to work effectively with assistants in the classroom. These are not unlike the skills necessary to manage a classroom, but the individuals involved will quite likely consider themselves as peers to the teacher. Perceived attitudes and actual interactions will be on a different level than between teacher and student; but there is ultimately one authority in the classroom, and that must be the teacher.

A paraprofessional is often brought into a classroom for the benefit of the special needs student. The role of the paraprofessional or any teaching assistant or aide in the classroom must be clearly defined to promote the learning experience for all children and avoid an unnecessary hindrance (or worse, conflict of wills) in the classroom. It is the responsibility of the teacher, often in concert with a team consisting of special education personnel and parents, to clearly define this role.

The primary objective is to determine and define what activities the individual should undertake to support the teacher's mission to provide the highest standards of education for each student and the class as a whole.

By appropriate planning and continual monitoring, the teacher can avoid the following situations which have been experienced by other teachers:
- Teacher neglect (or "surrender" of responsibility) for a student under the direct care of a paraprofessional
- Allowing an assistant to separate students with disabilities from classmates during a classroom activity although the students' needs and abilities were compatible with classmates regarding the activity
- Allowing an assistant to distract students through activities or discussions which are not related to the current lesson activity
- Allowing an assistant to provide a barrier (intentional or not) between students under the assistant's care and interaction with other classmates
- Allowing an assistant to question or comment upon the teacher's lesson plan, presentation, evaluation methods, etc., in front of the students
- Allowing an assistant to intervene in a matter of classroom disciplined
- Allowing an assistant to initiate and conduct conversations with parents without authority or prior approval

Skill 23.3   Types and sources of professional development activities and organizations that help maintain and improve the effectiveness of the early childhood education program

The level of knowledge available to teachers to improve practice is unprecedented. New knowledge is widely available in instructional methods, content, and child development. Teachers could continue to learn more and more and still be far behind the most current understandings of educational practice. To make the most of all this new knowledge, particularly as teachers have limited time, teachers should be strategic about how they pursue new knowledge and support.

Many schools now have instructional coaches. Instructional coaches are available to observe lessons, provide feedback, and model lessons. Instructional coaches have been shown to dramatically influence the instructional practice of teachers as they are able to provide personalized suggestions. While it may seem scary to have someone in the classroom watching what you are doing, coaches can be very helpful, encouraging, and assistive.

In addition to coaches, mentors can be assigned to teachers to provide suggestions and feedback outside of the classroom. While the mentor may not be in the actual classroom, he or she can still review lesson strategies, provide new techniques, and be a critical listener.

Outside of the school, service centers provide professional development opportunities. Often, teachers can get this information through principals and other school administrators. Usually, these service centers will provide workshops on specific instructional topics. While teachers may need to get permission to attend, these types of workshops can be very effective at giving teachers good strategies to use in their classrooms.

State initiatives often provide unique ways of approaching common educational problems. For example, many schools get extra funding for reading programs, community service learning programs, and math programs. These programs typically involve intensive teacher learning.

Finally, universities often are looking for schools and classrooms to experiment in. When teachers get opportunities to participate, they will definitely be amazed at what can happen. Usually, universities are hoping to test new strategies and activities with students. While teachers learn new techniques, the universities get terrific data.

Professional organizations and associations for educators can provide current research on best practices, information about new legislation, and training opportunities.

> For a list of Professional Education Associations & Educational Journals resources, go online to:
> http://www.highered.nysed.gov/org_jnl.htm#Associations
>
> For more information about the Michigan Education Association go online to:
> http://www.mea.org/members/index.html

In general, teachers really need to consider themselves as life-long learners. As a teacher, there is no end to learning!

TEACHER CERTIFICATION STUDY GUIDE

COMPETENCY 24.0 **UNDERSTAND THE BASIC PRINCIPLES OF ADMINISTRATION, ORGANIZATION, AND OPERATION OF EARLY CHILDHOOD PROGRAMS**

Skill 24.1 Local, state, and national standards, rules, and regulations regarding early childhood programs and work environments (e.g., licensing, accreditation, health and safety requirements)

A young child's mental, physical health, nutrition, and safety are essential to their overall development and learning. Intellectual development can only occur when children's basic health needs are met. The early childhood classroom should provide settings which supports their emotional well-being. A quality early childhood education program should address these needs, in cooperation with state and local regulations.

Accreditation is a description of quality awarded to child care programs that meet national standards set by accrediting organizations such as the National Association for the Education of Young Children (NAEYC). The National Association for the Education of Young Children evaluates these areas:

- Curriculum
- Professional qualifications and development of staff
- Physical environment
- Teacher/child interactions
- Teacher/family relationships
- Health & safety
- Nutrition
- Administration

The early childhood program should promote the nutrition and health of children and also protect children and staff from illness and injury. The program should also employ and support teaching staff that has the educational qualifications, knowledge, and the professional commitment necessary to promote children's learning and development and to support families' diverse needs and interests.

The effective program provides a curriculum that is consistent with its goals for children and promotes learning and development in each of the following areas: social, emotional, physical, language and cognitive skills.

Early childhood programs should implement a safe and healthful environment that provides appropriate and well-maintained indoor and outdoor physical environments. The environment includes facilities, equipment, and materials to facilitate child learning and development.

Skill 24.2 Communication skills and techniques

The best early childhood teachers know child development and develop children's interests. Educators interact with young children in order to promote developmental change, which may involve structured lessons. Effective early childhood teachers of young children must competently connect instructional activities to activities that allow children choices to explore and play.

Strategies of effective communication skills and techniques that early childhood teachers may implement include:

- Explicit instruction in key skills
- Sensitive and emotionally warm interactions
- Immediate and responsive feedback
- Verbal engagement with the young child
- Classroom environment that is not overly structured

An effective early childhood classroom should provide exposure to literacy-related activities, including narrative storytelling, practice with letters, rhyming games, and listening activities. Productive instructional activities with caring and responsive adults who consistently provide feedback, challenges to think, and offer social support enable young children to become ready for regular school.

Skill 24.3 Funding streams and funded programs such as Head Start

See Skill 15.1 and 15.4

Skill 24.4 The enrollment, qualification, and recruitment of children

The policies and practices of an early childhood program should support the enrollment and participation of all children, including those with disabilities. This program should also promote an environment of acceptance that supports and respects gender, culture, language, ethnicity, individual abilities, and family structures.

An effective early childhood program should:
- Practice nondiscriminatory enrollment and personnel policies.
- Encourage staff to demonstrate a genuine respect for each child's family, culture, and life-style.
- Provide a learning environment that reflects the cultures of all children in the program in an integrated and positive manner.
- Foster children's first language, while encouraging the development of the English language.

TEACHER CERTIFICATION STUDY GUIDE

Skill 24.5 **The responsibility and procedures for recognizing, reporting, and making referrals of children and families to other resources (e.g., other early childhood programs, child abuse prevention and treatment agencies)**

Child abuse is a significant social problem with far-reaching and serious consequences for children and society. School professionals and educators are in a unique position to protect children from this dangerous condition, through awareness of the possible indicators of child maltreatment. Early childhood educators should possess requirements of the legal/ethical obligation in order to promptly report suspected abuse.

Mandatory reporting statutes in 49 states and the District of Columbia require the reporter to act on reasonable "suspicion of abuse" In most states, therefore, failure to report suspected child abuse carries both criminal and civil sanctions and could elicit charges that jeopardize professional licensure/certification

Responsibility of care givers to look for these signs:

Some signs of physical abuse are more obvious than others: bruise marks, scratches, welts, marks from belts, and the young child's verbal disclosure of abuse. Other more subtle indicators are extreme physical aggression to others, emotional distress, and externalizing improper behavior.

There are also more reserved signs of physical abuse that should be noted which may include: a sudden onset of academic or social problems at school, extreme submission or aggression when reprimanded, acute suspicion of perceived threatening situations, and extreme fear of adults should also be noted.

Skill 24.6 **Principles of management**

Early childhood education can be an extremely rewarding and satisfying career. But given the sensitive nature of the field, combined with the unique mindsets of young students, professionals in this field should be prepared for a wide variety of challenges. In addition to the usual frustrations that accompany teaching, early childhood educators must be prepared to stand, walk, stoop, and lift throughout the course of a typical workday. You should possess an inherent love for children in addition to patience, a creative mind, and the ability to nurture and teach. You must also have organizational, administrative, and leadership qualities. Training programs should emphasize designing appropriate learning environments, developing individual and adaptive curricula, and delivering instructional strategies and techniques to maximize learning outcomes.

Managers for early childhood programs must also have knowledge of the principles of sound financial management and the ability to apply those principles to the financial planning and management of early childhood programs. Gaining a better understanding of the critical relationship between financial management and program quality for children, parents, families and staff is a critical skill.

Today's early childhood educators face management and strategic challenges in an increasingly turbulent environment; rapid growth demands increased managerial proficiency. In order to meet these critical challenges, agency leaders must develop entrepreneurial competencies and a firm understanding of core management theories and principles. At times, even the most successful organizations need to redefine business goals and create innovative strategies to excel at a new level.

Pre Test

Subarea I. Child Development and Learning

1. According to Piaget's theory of human development, at which stage would a child understand abstract terms such as honesty and justice? (Rigorous)

    A. Concrete operations

    B. Pre-operational

    C. Formal operations

    D. Sensory-motor

2. Which of the following is NOT one of Gardner's Multiple Intelligences? (Average rigor)

    A. Intrapersonal

    B. Musical

    C. Technological

    D. Logical/mathematical

3. Which of the following is a true statement? (Average rigor)

    A. Physical development does not influence social development.

    B. Social development does not influence physical development.

    C. Cognitive development does not influence social development.

    D. All domains of development are integrated and influence other domains.

4. What is the most significant development emerging in children at age two? (Rigorous)

    A. Immune system development

    B. Language development

    C. Socialization development

    D. Perception development

5. **What developmental patterns should a professional teacher assess to meet the needs of each student? (Average rigor)**

    A. Academic, regional, and family background

    B. Social, physical, and academic

    C. Academic, physical, and family background

    D. Physical, family, and ethnic background

6. **Which of the following best describes how different areas of development impact each other? (Average rigor)**

    A. Development in other areas cannot occur until cognitive development is complete.

    B. Areas of development are inter-related and impact each other.

    C. Development in each area is independent of development in other areas.

    D. Development in one area leads to a decline in other areas.

7. **Which of the following is a TRUE statement? (Rigorous)**

    A. Younger children tend to process information at a slower rate than older children (age eight and older).

    B. Older children tend to process information at a slower rate than younger children (younger than age 8).

    C. Children process information at the same rate as adults.

    D. All children process information at the exact same rate.

8. **Which of the following best explains why emotional upsets can reduce a child's classroom performance? (Rigorous)**

    A. They reduce the energy that students put towards schoolwork.

    B. They lead to a reduction in cognitive ability.

    C. They contribute to learning disorders such as dyslexia.

    D. They result in the development of behavioral problems.

9. What is a student who has extreme trouble spelling most likely to be identified as? (Average rigor)

   A. Dyslexic

   B. Gifted

   C. Autistic

   D. Hyperactive

10. In successful inclusion of students with disabilities: (Average rigor)

    A. A variety of instructional arrangements is available.

    B. School personnel shift the responsibility for learning outcomes to the student.

    C. The physical facilities are used as they are.

    D. Regular classroom teachers have sole responsibility for evaluating student progress.

11. A teacher can help instill confidence in the parents of diverse children by talking about the child: (Rigorous)

    A. Unemotionally

    B. Indirectly

    C. Personally

    D. Logically

12. Research into students who are learning English as a second language has found that they have difficulty manipulating the sound system of English. This difficulty is in which area of reading development? (Rigorous)

    A. Comprehension

    B. Fluency

    C. Phonics

    D. Phonemic Awareness

13. When developing lessons, it is important that teachers provide equity in pedagogy so that: (Rigorous)

    A. Unfair labeling of students will not occur

    B. Student experiences will be positive

    C. Students will achieve academic success

    D. All of the above

14. **Mrs. Peck wants to justify the use of personalized learning communities to her principal. Which of the following reasons should she use? (Rigorous)**

    A. They are likely to engage students and maintain their interest.

    B. They provide a supportive environment to address academic and emotional needs.

    C. They encourage students to work independently.

    D. They are proactive in their nature.

15. **Children from age 2 through 5 develop patterns of language from the words and sentences: (Rigorous)**

    A. They hear on a daily basis.

    B. They encounter in learning situations.

    C. They read in grade-level books.

    D. They learn from other students.

16. **Why is repetition an important part of child's play? (Easy)**

    A. It allows the child to master the skill and then move into creativity.

    B. It prevents caregivers from becoming bored with activities.

    C. It allows all children to learn at the same rate.

    D. It decreases the amount of planning required for lessons.

17. **What is one of the main advantages of portfolio assessment for students? (Average rigor)**

    A. It promotes creativity.

    B. It generates opportunities to use diverse skills.

    C. It encourages students to reflect on their own work.

    D. It develops communication skills.

18. When is utilization of instructional materials most effective? (Average rigor)

    A. When the activities are sequenced

    B. When the materials are prepared ahead of time

    C. When the students choose the pages to work on

    D. When the students create the instructional materials

19. Ms. Beckham is teaching students how to revise their work. She does this by using a draft of her own writing and revising it, while telling students what she is doing at each step. What teaching strategy is Ms. Beckham using? (Average rigor)

    A. Inquiry

    B. Modeling

    C. Cooperative learning

    D. Hands-on learning

Subarea II. Curriculum Development and Implementation

20. What is the main benefit of teaching science in a context where it is relevant to the lives of students? (Average rigor)

    A. It reduces costs for the school.

    B. It allows science to be integrated with other subjects.

    C. It increases student motivation.

    D. It promotes independence.

21. Mrs. Gomez has a fully integrated early childhood curriculum. This is beneficial to students because it: (Rigorous)

    A. Is easier to plan for and maintain

    B. Allows students to apply their unique skills

    C. Helps the students see the relationships between subjects and concepts

    D. Provides opportunities for social interaction

22. **Which of the following would be most useful for an ESOL student? (Average rigor)**

    A. Placing the student in a mixed learning group

    B. Making content two grades below the student's level

    C. Encouraging the student to use complex language

    D. Having the student complete activities independently

23. **The three areas of differentiated instruction are content, process, and: (Easy)**

    A. Application

    B. Product

    C. Assessment

    D. Structure

24. **Which of the following is an example of content which has been differentiated to meet the needs of individual learners? (Rigorous)**

    A. Flexible group activities on various levels

    B. Accepting different final projects from various students

    C. Research projects based on student's interests

    D. Individual tutoring by the teacher to address student weaknesses

25. **A learning activity for students below age eight should focus on: (Rigorous)**

    A. Complex activities

    B. Applying the information

    C. Short time frames

    D. Challenging students

26. Playing team sports at young ages should be done for the following purpose: (Rigorous)

   A. To develop the child's motor skills

   B. To prepare children for competition in high school

   C. To develop the child's interests

   D. Both A and C

27. Students who are learning English as a second language often require which of the following to process new information? (Average rigor)

   A. Translators

   B. Reading tutors

   C. Instruction in their native language

   D. Additional time and repetitions

28. Mr. Gorman has taught a concept to his class. All of the students have grasped the concept except for Sam. Mr. Gorman should: (Rigorous)

   A. Reteach the concept to the whole class in exactly the same way

   B. Reteach the concept to Sam in exactly the same way

   C. Reteach the concept to Sam in a different way

   D. Reteach the concept to the whole class in a different way

29. Mrs. Smith writes an encouraging note to each student in her classroom every week. These notes encourage the students to improve upon their previous work and to strive to do even better in the future. Mrs. Smith is most likely trying to: (Rigorous)

   A. Maintain good discipline

   B. Hold the students to high standards

   C. Meet the needs of individual students

   D. Improve her test scores

30. **Which of the following has been shown to have the greatest impact on a student's academic performance? (Easy)**

    A. The teacher's expectations

    B. Strict discipline

    C. The student's social skills

    D. Measurable objectives

31. **What should a teacher do when students have not responded well to an instructional activity? (Average rigor)**

    A. Reevaluate learner needs

    B. Request administrative help

    C. Continue with the activity another day

    D. Assign homework on the concept

32. **Which of the following is an effective method for helping young children cope with stress? (Average rigor)**

    A. Reading them books

    B. Encouraging them to play sports

    C. Helping them make friends

    D. Persuading them not to focus on their feelings

33. **Michael keeps using phrases such as "she go to the store." Which of the following areas should Michael's teacher work on to improve Michael's skills? (Average rigor)**

    A. Morphology

    B. Syntax

    C. Phonics

    D. Semantics

34. Children who are having difficulty understanding non-literal expressions are having difficulties with which of the following areas? (Rigorous)

    A. Syntax

    B. Morphology

    C. Semantics

    D. Phonics

35. Which of the following types of children's literature would you be unlikely to utilize in a kindergarten classroom? (Easy)

    A. Fable

    B. Science fiction

    C. Epic

    D. Fairy tale

36. Mr. Stine put puppet making materials in his art center after he read the children a story. He asked the students who had chosen to make puppets to use them to retell the story he read in front of the class. Mr. Stine was helping the children: (Rigorous)

    A. Improve their art skills

    B. Respond to literature

    C. Improve their oral presentation skills

    D. Increase their listening skills

37. Which of the following is NOT a good example of fine motor practice for young students? (Easy)

    A. Throwing a ball

    B. Manipulating clay

    C. Cutting

    D. Tearing

38. What is the most important factor in improving the developmental and educational gains for students with language delays? (Average rigor)

    A. Varied teaching procedures

    B. The social environment

    C. Early intervention

    D. Encouraging independence

39. Which of the following is an important criterion for evaluating children's literature? (Easy)

    A. Character development

    B. Appropriate reading level

    C. Cultural diversity

    D. All of the above

40. Which of the following approaches to student writing assignments is most likely to lead to students becoming disinterested? (Average rigor)

    A. Designing assignments where students write for a variety of audiences.

    B. Designing assignments where the teacher is always the audience.

    C. Designing assignments where students write to friends and family.

    D. Designing assignments where students write to real people such as mayors, the principle, or companies.

41. To build efficacy, the instructor must not only raise the student's belief in his/her capabilities, but also: (Rigorous)

    A. Create classroom activities that require higher levels of thinking

    B. Structure situations that breed success and limit repeated failure.

    C. Group students by ability

    D. Use a grading scale with tougher standards

42. The principal walks into your classroom during math class. He sees your students making cake mixtures. Later, the principal questions your lesson. What would be the best explanation for your lesson? (Rigorous)

    A. The students earned a reward time and it was free choice.

    B. You were teaching the students how math is used in real-life situations.

    C. You had paperwork to complete and needed the time to complete it.

    D. It kept the students interested in math and prevented boredom.

43. A teacher plans an activity that involves students calculating how many chair legs are in the classroom, given that there are 30 chairs and each chair has 4 legs. This activity is introducing the ideas of: (Average rigor)

    A. Probability

    B. Statistics

    C. Geometry

    D. Algebra

44. Students are working with a set of rulers and various small objects from the classroom. Which concept are these students exploring? (Average rigor)

    A. Volume

    B. Weight

    C. Length

    D. Temperature

45. Kindergarten students are participating in a calendar time activity. One student adds a straw to the "ones can" to represent that day of school. What math principle is being reinforced? (Rigorous)

    A. Properties of a base ten number system

    B. Sorting

    C. Counting by twos

    D. Even and odd numbers

46. When you find it necessary to communicate with a parent regarding a concern about a student, it is important that you: (Easy)

    A. Allow yourself a "cooling off" period

    B. Raise your voice to let them know you are serious

    C. Remain professional and objective

    D. Both A and C

47. Which of the following is a social skill gained from participation in physical activities? (Easy)

    A. Problem-solving skills

    B. Communication skills

    C. Judgment skills

    D. All of the above

48. Which of the following benefits can physical education provide? (Easy)

    A. A sense of belonging

    B. Increased self-esteem

    C. Appreciation of beauty

    D. All of the above

49. A student who is observed to often collide with other people while taking part in physical education probably has poor awareness of: (Rigorous)

    A. Balance

    B. Space

    C. Speed

    D. Force

50. Which activity would be most suitable for beginning students of visual arts? (Rigorous)

    A. Analyzing famous works of arts

    B. Reflecting on the possible meanings of art work

    C. Observing the shapes and forms of common objects

    D. Using blocks to construct three dimensional shapes

51. What should the arts curriculum for early childhood avoid? (Average rigor)

    A. Judgment

    B. Open expression

    C. Experimentation

    D. Discovery

52. What would the viewing of a dance company performance be most likely to promote? (Average rigor)

   A. Critical-thinking skills

   B. Appreciation of the arts

   C. Improvisation skills

   D. Music vocabulary

Subarea III. Family and Community Relationships

53. Which of the following should NOT be a purpose of a parent teacher conference? (Average rigor)

   A. To involve the parent in their child's education

   B. To establish a friendship with the child's parents

   C. To resolve a concern about the child's performance

   D. To inform parents of positive behaviors by the child

54. In regards to dealing with parents, which term best describes the role that teachers should play in the education of children? (Average rigor)

   A. Friends

   B. Leaders

   C. Partners

   D. Managers

55. Which of the following is a right of parents? (Easy)

   A. To be informed of the teacher's concerns about their child

   B. To require the teacher to use the teaching method that works for the child

   C. To administer discipline to their child in the classroom

   D. To attend all classes to support their child

56. **What is the purpose of a parent-teacher conference? (Average rigor)**

   A. Sharing information with the parents

   B. Obtaining information from the parents

   C. Requesting parent support

   D. Any or all of the above

57. **How should a teacher respond to criticism about her teaching strategies from a parent? (Rigorous)**

   A. Explain to the parent that negative feedback is hurtful and mean-spirited

   B. Dismiss the criticism as an attempt to undermine her performance

   C. Think about the criticism objectively and consider that it might be true

   D. Change her teaching strategies to eliminate the aspect being criticized

58. **When is it appropriate for a teacher to talk to parents about another student's performance? (Rigorous)**

   A. When the parents of the student have been invited to participate

   B. When the student is having a negative impact on other students

   C. When the student is performing well and only positive information will be communicated

   D. When permission to discuss the student has been given by the principal

59. **You receive a phone call from a parent who is angry about the grade their child receives on the report card. As the conversation continues, the parent becomes verbally abusive and uses curse words. What should you do? (Rigorous)**

   A. Raise your voice to establish your authority

   B. Hang up and get assistance from your administrator

   C. Blame the parent for the poor grade

   D. Apologize over and over and hope that the parent will calm down and stop cursing

60. There has been a lot of research on how birth order in a family affects the development of young children. Researchers have identified typical characteristics that can apply to the eldest child in the family. Which of the following are characteristics of an oldest child? (Rigorous)

   A. Expects to have things done for him/her

   B. May feel left out

   C. Tries to control other children

   D. Adapts easily to situations

61. A teacher has a class with several students from low income families in it. What would it be most important for a teacher to consider when planning homework assignments to ensure that all students have equal opportunity for academic success? (Rigorous)

   A. Access to technology

   B. Ethnicity

   C. Language difficulties

   D. Gender

62. Which of the following is NOT an economic factor that may influence the health of a child? (Easy)

   A. Pollution

   B. Malnutrition

   C. Neglect

   D. Poor medical care

63. Which of the following problems are likely to be faced by migrant, homeless, and abandoned children? (Easy)

   A. Poor attendance

   B. Language barriers

   C. Social isolation

   D. All of the above

64. Head Start programs were created in what decade? (Easy)

   A. 2000's

   B. 1990's

   C. 1980's

   D. 1960's

65. IDEA is a federal law passed in 1990 that has a direct impact on classrooms. The acronym IDEA stands for: (Average rigor)

   A. Individuals with Disabilities Education Act

   B. Individualized Differentiation for Education Always

   C. Idealistic Dedicated Educational Access

   D. Instructional Differentiation Education Act

66. Local businesses are an important resource for schools because they are a source of: (Easy)

   A. Students

   B. Employment

   C. Teachers

   D. Funding

67. In terms of positive public relations, it is most important for teachers to remember that they are: (Rigorous)

   A. Solely responsible for educating students

   B. Representatives of their school

   C. Only viewed by the public when at school

   D. Positive role models for all students

68. Researchers have shown that school involvement and connections with community institutions yield greater retention rates of students graduating and seeking higher education experiences. What is a current barrier to community involvement? (Rigorous)

   A. The current disconnect and autonomy that has become common in today's society.

   B. The amount of gang activity in many communities.

   C. The tough economic times we are facing.

   D. The introduction of standardized testing.

Subarea IV. Assessment and Evaluation

69. Which type of assessment has the main purpose of helping learners learn better? (Average rigor)

    A. Formal assessment

    B. Observation

    C. Informal assessment

    D. Exam

70. Which of the following is an effective method of evaluating a child's writing skills? (Average rigor)

    A. Have the child erase his/her writing errors

    B. Have the child start writing assignments over again

    C. Have the child cross out errors with a single line

    D. Have the child complete writing assignments at home

71. Proponents of formal assessment believe that to determine if a school is successful: (Average rigor)

    A. Assessments will drive the curriculum.

    B. Students must be able to perform meaningful tasks that replicate real world challenges.

    C. Students must be tested to see if they learned the required knowledge and skills.

    D. None of the above.

72. Which of the following is a common self-appraisal instrument? (Average rigor)

    A. Rating scales

    B. Questioning

    C. Portfolio assessment

    D. Anecdotal records

73. A teacher wishes to identify the sources of confusion that are resulting in students performing poorly on standardized tests. What would be the best method to use for this purpose? (Rigorous)

    A. Rating scales

    B. Questioning

    C. Portfolio assessment

    D. Anecdotal records

74. Which strategy for adapting the curriculum would be most useful for the purpose of reducing the effect of a student's learning disability on completing an assessment task? (Rigorous)

    A. Differentiated instruction

    B. Alternative assessments

    C. Testing modifications

    D. Total Physical Response

75. Which type of social skill assessment involves students ranking their classmates on set criteria? (Average rigor)

    A. Direct observation

    B. Paired-comparison

    C. Peer nomination

    D. Peer rating

76. Which factor is it most important to consider when choosing structured assessment methods? (Rigorous)

    A. The authenticity of the methods

    B. The results of informal evaluations

    C. The formal assessments required

    D. The developmental stage of students

77. Which type of assessment is the least structured? (Easy)

    A. Observation

    B. Informal continuous assessment

    C. Formal assessment

    D. Standardized testing

78. Which of the following is the best method for a teacher to use to get to know the students initially? (Average rigor)

   A. Running reading record

   B. Entry survey

   C. Norm-referenced test

   D. Oral presentations

79. Which type of assessment would be used to place students into honors, regular, and remedial classes? (Rigorous)

   A. Norm-referenced assessments

   B. Criterion-referenced assessments

   C. Performance-based assessments

   D. Observation-based assessments

80. Which type of assessment is most likely to be used to assess student interest and motivation? (Average rigor)

   A. Rating scales

   B. Questioning

   C. Portfolio assessment

   D. Anecdotal records

81. Which of these actions taken by a teacher would improve planning for instruction? (Average rigor)

   A. Describe the role of the teacher and student

   B. Evaluate the outcomes of instruction

   C. Rearrange the order of activities

   D. Give outside assignments

82. Which of the following types of assessment is most likely to be required to be administered in a specific format by state and federal laws? (Rigorous)

   A. Informal evaluations

   B. Classroom observation

   C. Peer ratings

   D. Standardized tests

83. Which of the following statements would not be appropriate in an anecdotal record about a student? (Rigorous)

    A. Jasmine completed only half of the homework assigned.

    B. Jasmine contributed only slightly to class discussions.

    C. Jasmine was not interested in learning the material.

    D. Jasmine did not volunteer to answer any questions.

84. Teachers should regard a student's test results as: (Average rigor)

    A. Exact indications of the student's ability

    B. Ballpark figures indicating the student's ability

    C. Possible indicators of a student's ability

    D. Unlikely to be a true indication of a student's ability

85. What is it most important for a teacher to consider when reading another teacher's observations of a student? (Average rigor)

    A. Mood

    B. Discrimination

    C. Dishonesty

    D. Bias

Subarea V. Professional and Program Leadership

86. Which of the following is a widely known curriculum model for early childhood programs? (Easy)

    A. Creative Curriculum

    B. DISTAR method

    C. Success for All

    D. Voyager

87. Which of the following is considered a current trend in education? (Easy)

    A. Differentiated instruction so that no child is left behind

    B. Innovations in technology

    C. Instruction in the 3 Rs

    D. A and B

88. What criteria are used to assess whether a child qualifies for services under IDEA? (Rigorous)

    A. Having a disability only

    B. Having a disability and demonstrating educational need only

    C. Demonstrating educational need only

    D. Having a disability, demonstrating educational need, and having financial support

89. A student who is deaf has an Individual Family Service Plan (IFSP) in place. This legal document is a way of providing: (Average rigor)

    A. Early intervention

    B. Help for the family and the child

    C. Services to deal with the child's disability

    D. All of the above

90. Which federal law has directed states to construct curriculum models specific to the development of early childhood and elementary programs for academic enhancement? (Rigorous)

    A. IDEA

    B. Head Start

    C. FERPA

    D. NCLB

91. To determine if a child has a disability that may qualify the child for services under IDEA, which of the following pieces of information should the school collect? (Average rigor)

    A. The present levels of academic achievement

    B. Vision and hearing screening information

    C. A complete psychological evaluation

    D. All of the above

92. **What would be put into place to assist students with special needs who are in a regular education classroom? (Rigorous)**

    A. 504 plan

    B. IEP

    C. IFSP

    D. All of the above

93. **Failure to make a report when abuse or neglect is suspected is punishable by which of the following? (Average rigor)**

    A. Revocation of certification and license

    B. A monetary fine

    C. Criminal charges

    D. All of the above

94. **When should a teacher report child abuse? (Average rigor)**

    A. Only when the teacher has sufficient evidence

    B. Once the child confirms the abuse

    C. Any time that it is suspected

    D. After the student's parents have been contacted

95. **Which of the following is NOT a sign of child abuse? (Easy)**

    A. Awkward social behavior around other children

    B. Participation in class discussions

    C. Awkward social behavior around adults

    D. Bruises

96. **A teacher notices that a student is quiet, and has several bruises on his head, arms, and legs. When asked, the student tells the teacher that his dad hit him, but then begs her not to tell. The teacher should: (Rigorous)**

    A. Report suspected abuse to the school counselor

    B. Attempt to get more information from the student

    C. Respect the child's wishes and withhold the information

    D. Wait and see if other signs of abuse become evident

97. Who should you talk to if you suspect child abuse? (Easy)

    A. The child

    B. The child's parent

    C. Your supervisor

    D. Another teacher

98. Physical accommodations may need to be done in the school or the classroom to make it possible for children with disabilities to come to school. Which of the following is NOT a demonstration of accommodation? (Easy)

    A. Building wheelchair ramps

    B. Installing an elevator

    C. Repainting the classroom

    D. Enlarging the doorways

99. General classroom safety should include the following: (Average rigor)

    A. Adequate traffic flow

    B. Entry and exit accessibility

    C. Adequate ventilation and climate control

    D. All of the above

100. Which of the following is NOT a communication issue that the teacher in a diverse classroom should be aware of? (Rigorous)

    A. Body language that is intimidating or offensive to some cultures

    B. Emphasizing the importance of different viewpoints and opinions

    C. Planning and directing interactive "hands-on" learning experiences

    D. Knowing and using the current terms that ethnic and cultural groups use to identify themselves

TEACHER CERTIFICATION STUDY GUIDE

Pre Test Answer Key

1.	C	35.	C	69.	C
2.	C	36.	B	70.	C
3.	D	37.	A	71.	C
4.	B	38.	C	72.	A
5.	B	39.	D	73.	B
6.	B	40.	B	74.	C
7.	A	41.	B	75.	D
8.	A	42.	B	76.	D
9.	A	43.	D	77.	A
10.	A	44.	C	78.	B
11.	C	45.	A	79.	A
12.	D	46.	D	80.	A
13.	D	47.	D	81.	B
14.	B	48.	D	82.	D
15.	A	49.	B	83.	C
16.	A	50.	C	84.	B
17.	C	51.	A	85.	D
18.	A	52.	B	86.	A
19.	B	53.	B	87.	D
20.	C	54.	C	88.	B
21.	C	55.	A	89.	D
22.	A	56.	D	90.	D
23.	B	57.	C	91.	D
24.	C	58.	A	92.	A
25.	C	59.	B	93.	D
26.	D	60.	C	94.	C
27.	D	61.	A	95.	B
28.	C	62.	A	96.	A
29.	B	63.	D	97.	C
30.	A	64.	D	98.	C
31.	A	65.	A	99.	D
32.	A	66.	D	100.	C
33.	B	67.	B		
34.	C	68.	A		

TEACHER CERTIFICATION STUDY GUIDE

Pre Test Rigor Table

	Easy %20	Average rigor %40	Rigorous %40
Question #	16, 23, 30, 35, 37, 39, 46, 47, 48, 55, 62, 63, 64, 66, 77, 86, 87, 95, 97, 98	2, 3, 5, 6, 9, 10, 17, 18, 19, 20, 22, 27, 31, 32, 33, 38, 40, 43, 44, 51, 52, 53, 54, 56, 65, 69, 70, 71, 72, 75, 78, 80, 81, 84, 85, 89, 91, 93, 94, 99	1, 4, 7, 8, 11, 12, 13, 14, 15, 21, 24, 25, 26, 28, 29, 34, 36, 41, 42, 45, 49, 50, 57, 58, 59, 60, 61, 67, 68, 73, 74, 76, 79, 82, 83, 88, 90, 92, 96, 100

TEACHER CERTIFICATION STUDY GUIDE

Pre Test Rationales with Sample Questions

Subarea I. Child Development and Learning

1. According to Piaget's theory of human development, at which stage would a child understand abstract terms such as honesty and justice? (Rigorous)

    A. Concrete operations
    B. Pre-operational
    C. Formal operations
    D. Sensory-motor

Answer C: Formal operations

Jean Piaget's theory describes how human minds develop through four stages. The first stage is the sensory-motor stage. This occurs up to age 2 and involves understanding the world via the senses. The second stage is the pre-operational stage. It occurs from ages 2 to 7 and involves understanding symbols. The concrete operations stage occurs from ages 7 to 11 and is where children begin to develop reason. The final stage is the formal operations stage. It involves the development of logical and abstract thinking.

2. Which of the following is NOT one of Gardner's Multiple Intelligences? (Average rigor)

    A. Intrapersonal
    B. Musical
    C. Technological
    D. Logical/mathematical

Answer C: Technological

The Multiple Intelligence Theory, developed by Howard Gardner, suggests that students learn in (at least) seven different ways. These include visually/spatially, musically, verbally, logically/mathematically, interpersonally, intrapersonally, and bodily/kinesthetically.

TEACHER CERTIFICATION STUDY GUIDE

3. Which of the following is a true statement? (Average rigor)

    A. Physical development does not influence social development.
    B. Social development does not influence physical development.
    C. Cognitive development does not influence social development.
    D. All domains of development are integrated and influence other domains.

Answer D: All domains of development are integrated and influence other domains.

Child development does not occur in a vacuum. Each element of development impacts other elements of development. For example, as children develop physically, they develop the dexterity to demonstrate cognitive development, such as writing something on a piece of paper.

4. What is the most significant development emerging in children at age two? (Rigorous)

    A. Immune system development
    B. Language development
    C. Socialization development
    D. Perception development

Answer B: Language development

The most significant development emerging in children at age two is language development. General researchers have shown that children at 2 years old should have speech patterns that are about 70% intelligible.

5. What developmental patterns should a professional teacher assess to meet the needs of each student? (Average rigor)

    A. Academic, regional, and family background
    B. Social, physical, and academic
    C. Academic, physical, and family background
    D. Physical, family, and ethnic background

Answer B: Social, physical, and academic

The effective teacher applies knowledge of physical, social, and academic developmental patterns and of individual differences, to meet the instructional needs of all students in the classroom.

6. Which of the following best describes how different areas of development impact each other? (Average rigor)

   A. Development in other areas cannot occur until cognitive development is complete.
   B. Areas of development are inter-related and impact each other.
   C. Development in each area is independent of development in other areas.
   D. Development in one area leads to a decline in other areas.

Answer B: Areas of development are inter-related and impact each other.

Child development does not occur in a vacuum. Each element of development impacts other elements of development. For example, as cognitive development progresses, social development often follows. The reason for this is that all areas of development are fairly inter-related.

7. Which of the following is a TRUE statement? (Rigorous)

   A. Younger children tend to process information at a slower rate than older children (age eight and older).
   B. Older children tend to process information at a slower rate than younger children (younger than age 8).
   C. Children process information at the same rate as adults.
   D. All children process information at the exact same rate.

Answer A: Younger children tend to process information at a slower rate than older children (age eight and older).

Younger children tend to process information at a slower rate than older children (age eight and older). Because of this, the learning activities selected for younger students (below age eight) should focus on short time frames in highly simplified form. The nature of the activity and the content in which the activity is presented affects the approach that the students will take in processing the information.

8. Which of the following best explains why emotional upsets can reduce a child's classroom performance? (Rigorous)

    A. They reduce the energy that students put towards schoolwork.
    B. They lead to a reduction in cognitive ability.
    C. They contribute to learning disorders such as dyslexia.
    D. They result in the development of behavioral problems.

Answer A: They reduce the energy that students put towards schoolwork.

Although cognitive ability is not lost due to emotional upsets, the child will most likely not be able to provide as much intellectual energy as the child would if none of these things were present. This explains why classroom performance is often negatively impacted.

9. What is a student who has extreme trouble spelling most likely to be identified as? (Average rigor)

    A. Dyslexic
    B. Gifted
    C. Autistic
    D. Hyperactive

Answer A: Dyslexic

Dyslexia is a common learning disability that requires intervention strategies. Students with dyslexia often have difficulty reading and have extreme trouble spelling.

10. In successful inclusion of students with disabilities: (Average rigor)

    A. A variety of instructional arrangements is available
    B. School personnel shift the responsibility for learning outcomes to the student
    C. The physical facilities are used as they are
    D. Regular classroom teachers have sole responsibility for evaluating student progress

Answer A: A variety of instructional arrangements is available

All students have the right to an education, but there cannot be a singular path to that education. A teacher must acknowledge the variety of learning styles and abilities among students within a class apply multiple instructional and assessment processes to ensure that every child has appropriate opportunities to master the subject matter, demonstrate such mastery, and improve and enhance learning skills with each lesson.

TEACHER CERTIFICATION STUDY GUIDE

11. A teacher can help instill confidence in the parents of diverse children by talking about the child: (Rigorous)

    A. Unemotionally
    B. Indirectly
    C. Personally
    D. Logically

Answer C: Personally

When speaking to the parents of children, teachers often have greater success when they speak about the child personally, rather than talking about the group of students as a whole. Speaking about the child personally helps instill confidence in the parents and makes it more likely they will believe that the child is in good hands.

12. Research into students who are learning English as a second language has found that they have difficulty manipulating the sound system of English. This difficulty is in which area of reading development? (Rigorous)

    A. Comprehension
    B. Fluency
    C. Phonics
    D. Phonemic Awareness

Answer D: Phonemic Awareness

As is the case with many students who struggle with reading, it has also been found that students who are learning English as a second language often have difficulties with phonemic awareness skills.

13. When developing lessons, it is important that teachers provide equity in pedagogy so that: (Rigorous)

    A. Unfair labeling of students will not occur
    B. Student experiences will be positive
    C. Students will achieve academic success
    D. All of the above

Answer D: All of the above

When there is equity in pedagogy, teachers can use a variety of instructional styles to facilitate diversity in cooperative learning and individualized instruction that will provide more opportunities for positive student experiences and academic success. Empowering the school culture and climate by establishing an anti-bias learning environment and promoting multicultural learning inclusion will also discourage unfair labeling of certain students.

14. Mrs. Peck wants to justify the use of personalized learning communities to her principal. Which of the following reasons should she use? (Rigorous)

    A. They are likely to engage students and maintain their interest.
    B. They provide a supportive environment to address academic and emotional needs.
    C. They encourage students to work independently.
    D. They are proactive in their nature.

Answer B: They provide a supportive environment to address academic and emotional needs.

Personalized learning communities provide supportive learning environments that address the academic and emotional needs of students. In personalized learning communities, relationships and connections between students, staff, parents and community members promote lifelong learning for all students. School communities that promote an inclusion of diversity in the classroom, community, curriculum and connections enable students to maximize their academic capabilities and educational opportunities.

15. **Children from age 2 through 5 develop patterns of language from the words and sentences: (Rigorous)**

    A. They hear on a daily basis
    B. They encounter in learning situations
    C. They read in grade-level books
    D. They learn from other students

Answer A: They hear on a daily basis

Children develop patterns of language by learning from the vocal experiences of word and sentence usage that they hear on a daily basis. As children continue through the language development years, the words they hear on a daily basis continue to add to their understanding of language.

16. **Why is repetition an important part of child's play? (Easy)**

    A. It allows the child to master the skill and then move into creativity.
    B. It prevents caregivers from becoming bored with activities.
    C. It allows all children to learn at the same rate.
    D. It decreases the amount of planning required for lessons.

Answer A: It allows the child to master the skill and then move into creativity.

Repetition is an important aspect of children's play. Doing the same thing over and over may be boring to the adult caregiver, but the repetition allows the child to master the new skill and then move on to experimentation and creativity.

17. **What is one of the main advantages of portfolio assessment for students? (Average rigor)**

    A. It promotes creativity.
    B. It generates opportunities to use diverse skills.
    C. It encourages students to reflect on their own work.
    D. It develops communication skills.

Answer C: It encourages students to reflect on their own work.

One of the main advantages of portfolio assessment for students is that it provides them with the opportunity to assess and reflect on their own work. This also encourages self-directed learning.

TEACHER CERTIFICATION STUDY GUIDE

18. **When is utilization of instructional materials most effective? (Average rigor)**

    A. When the activities are sequenced
    B. When the materials are prepared ahead of time
    C. When the students choose the pages to work on
    D. When the students create the instructional materials

Answer A: When the activities are sequenced.

Most assignments will require more than one educational principle. It is helpful to explain to students the proper order in which these principles must be applied to complete the assignment successfully. Subsequently, students should also be informed of the nature of the assignment (i.e., cooperative learning, group project, individual assignment, etc). This is often done at the start of the assignment.

19. **Ms. Beckham is teaching students how to revise their work. She does this by using a draft of her own writing and revising it, while telling students what she is doing at each step. What teaching strategy is Ms. Beckham using? (Average rigor)**

    A. Inquiry
    B. Modeling
    C. Cooperative learning
    D. Hands-on learning

Answer B: Modeling

Teachers have a range of teaching strategies they can use to instruct students. Modeling is a strategy where teachers show students how to complete a process, usually while explaining what they are doing at each step of the process. By watching the teacher use the process, the students learn how to use it themselves.

TEACHER CERTIFICATION STUDY GUIDE

Subarea II. Curriculum Development and Implementation

20. **What is the main benefit of teaching science in a context where it is relevant to the lives of students? (Average rigor)**

    A. It reduces costs for the school.
    B. It allows science to be integrated with other subjects.
    C. It increases student motivation.
    D. It promotes independence.

Answer C: It increases student motivation.

If learning is connected to everyday life, students are motivated because they can easily see its relevance. If they are taught about something remote, they will not be able to relate, and the result is decreased interest, decreased motivation to study, and a general decrease in learning.

21. **Mrs. Gomez has a fully integrated early childhood curriculum. This is beneficial to students because it: (Rigorous)**

    A. Is easier to plan for and maintain
    B. Allows students to apply their unique skills
    C. Helps the students see the relationships between subjects and concepts
    D. Provides opportunities for social interaction

Answer C: Helps the students see the relationships between subjects and concepts

An integrated curriculum is a curriculum in which lessons are taught in several different subject areas according to the outcomes that deal with the same concepts. It may also be known as thematic teaching or interdisciplinary teaching.

TEACHER CERTIFICATION STUDY GUIDE

22. **Which of the following would be most useful for an ESOL student? (Average rigor)**

    A. Placing the student in a mixed learning group
    B. Making content two grades below the student's level
    C. Encouraging the student to use complex language
    D. Having the student complete activities independently

Answer A: Placing the student in a mixed learning group

ESOL approaches are often based on social learning methods. One common method is to place the student in a mixed learning group. This allows the student the chance to practice English in a non-threatening environment. Activities such as making the content lower than the grade, encouraging the student to use complex language, or having the student complete activities independently would be likely to isolate the student.

23. **The three areas of differentiated instruction are content, process, and: (Easy)**

    A. Application
    B. Product
    C. Assessment
    D. Structure

Answer B: Product

Differentiated instruction includes the areas of content, process, and product. Content focuses on what is going to be taught. Process focuses on how the content is going to be taught. Product focuses on the expectations and requirements placed on students, where the product refers to the product expected of students.

24. **Which of the following is an example of content which has been differentiated to meet the needs of individual learners? (Rigorous)**

    A. Flexible group activities on various levels
    B. Accepting different final projects from various students
    C. Research projects based on student's interests
    D. Individual tutoring by the teacher to address student weaknesses

Answer C: Research projects based on student's interests

Differentiated instruction encompasses several areas: content, process, and product. Differentiating content means that students will have access to content that piques their interest about a topic, with a complexity that provides an appropriate challenge to their intellectual development.

25. **A learning activity for students below age eight should focus on: (Rigorous)**

    A. Complex activities
    B. Applying the information
    C. Short time frames
    D. Challenging students

Answer C: Short time frames

Younger children tend to process information at a slower rate than older children (age eight and older). Learning activities selected for younger students (below age eight) should focus on short time frames in highly simplified form.

26. **Playing team sports at young ages should be done for the following purpose: (Rigorous)**

    A. To develop the child's motor skills
    B. To prepare children for competition in high school
    C. To develop the child's interests
    D. Both A and C

Answer D: Both A and C

Sports, for both boys and girls, can be very valuable. Parents and teachers, though, need to remember that sports at young ages should only be for the purpose of development of interests and motor skills—not competition. Many children will learn that they do not enjoy sports, and parents and teachers should be respectful of these decisions.

27. **Students who are learning English as a second language often require which of the following to process new information? (Average rigor)**

    A. Translators
    B. Reading tutors
    C. Instruction in their native language
    D. Additional time and repetitions

Answer D: Additional time and repetitions

While there are varying thoughts and theories into the most appropriate instruction for ESL students, much ground can be gained by simply providing additional repetitions and time for new concepts. It is also important to include visuals and the other senses into every aspect of this instruction.

28. **Mr. Gorman has taught a concept to his class. All of the students have grasped the concept except for Sam. Mr. Gorman should: (Rigorous)**

    A. Reteach the concept to the whole class in exactly the same way
    B. Reteach the concept to Sam in exactly the same way
    C. Reteach the concept to Sam in a different way
    D. Reteach the concept to the whole class in a different way

Answer C: Reteach the concept to Sam in a different way

There is always more than one way to approach a problem, an example, a process, fact or event, or any learning situation. Varying approaches for instruction helps to maintain the students' interest in the material and enables the teacher to address the diverse needs of individuals to comprehend the material.

29. Mrs. Smith writes an encouraging note to each student in her classroom every week. These notes encourage the students to improve upon their previous work and to strive to do even better in the future. Mrs. Smith is most likely trying to: (Rigorous)

   A. Maintain good discipline
   B. Hold the students to high standards
   C. Meet the needs of individual students
   D. Improve her test scores

Answer B: Hold the students to high standards

Time and again, a direct correlation has been demonstrated between the teacher's expectations for a particular student and that student's academic performance. A note encouraging the students to improve and do even better in the future is one way to hold students to high standards.

30. Which of the following has been shown to have the greatest impact on a student's academic performance? (Easy)

   A. The teacher's expectations
   B. Strict discipline
   C. The student's social skills
   D. Measurable objectives

Answer A: The teacher's expectations

Time and again, a direct correlation has been demonstrated between the teacher's expectations for a particular student and that student's academic performance. This may be unintended and subtle but the effects are manifest and measurable.

31. What should a teacher do when students have not responded well to an instructional activity? (Average rigor)

   A. Reevaluate learner needs
   B. Request administrative help
   C. Continue with the activity another day
   D. Assign homework on the concept

Answer A: Reevaluate learner needs

The value of teacher observations cannot be underestimated. Through the use of observations, the teacher is able to informally assess the needs of the students during instruction. These observations will drive the lesson and determine the direction that the lesson will take based on student behavior.

32. **Which of the following is an effective method for helping young children cope with stress? (Average rigor)**

    A. Reading them books
    B. Encouraging them to play sports
    C. Helping them make friends
    D. Persuading them not to focus on their feelings

Answer A: Reading them books

For younger children, reading books is an effective method for helping them deal with stress. By seeing how other characters deal with stress, students can learn how to cope with stress and understand that feeling stressed is normal.

33. **Michael keeps using phrases such as "she go to the store." Which of the following areas should Michael's teacher work on to improve Michael's skills? (Average rigor)**

    A. Morphology
    B. Syntax
    C. Phonics
    D. Semantics

Answer B: Syntax

Syntax is the understanding of the rules of the English language to put words together in a grammatically appropriate manner. Michael is having difficulty with this concept and could benefit from some more instruction in this area.

34. **Children who are having difficulty understanding non-literal expressions are having difficulties with which of the following areas? (Rigorous)**

    A. Syntax
    B. Morphology
    C. Semantics
    D. Phonics

Answer C: Semantics

Listening and understanding the intentions of speakers (teacher/peers) involves semantics. A student that is having difficulty understanding non-literal expressions is having difficulty with semantics.

35. Which of the following types of children's literature would you be unlikely to utilize in a kindergarten classroom? (Easy)

    A. Fable
    B. Science fiction
    C. Epic
    D. Fairy tale

Answer C: Epic

It would be unlikely that you would use a full epic in a kindergarten classroom. The complexity of a combination poem and story to the extent of an epic story would be difficult for this particular age range to understand.

36. Mr. Stine put puppet making materials in his art center after he read the children a story. He asked the students who had chosen to make puppets to use them to retell the story he read in front of the class. Mr. Stine was helping the children: (Rigorous)

    A. Improve their art skills
    B. Respond to literature
    C. Improve their oral presentation skills
    D. Increase their listening skills

Answer B: Respond to literature

The purpose of the activity was to allow students to respond to literature. There are numerous strategies which can be used to allow students the opportunity to interact with literature. Mr. Stine incorporated one that allows students an opportunity to utilize different areas of multiple intelligences as well.

37. Which of the following is NOT a good example of fine motor practice for young students? (Easy)

    A. Throwing a ball
    B. Manipulating clay
    C. Cutting
    D. Tearing

Answer A: Throwing a ball

Manipulating clay, cutting, and tearing are all good examples of fine motor practice for young students. Throwing a ball is an activity that develops gross motor skills.

TEACHER CERTIFICATION STUDY GUIDE

38. **What is the most important factor in improving the developmental and educational gains for students with language delays?** (Average rigor)

    A. Varied teaching procedures
    B. The social environment
    C. Early intervention
    D. Encouraging independence

Answer C: Early intervention

Teachers and parents who have concerns about a child's language development should be proactive in addressing language delays. Early intervention is the key to addressing children's language delays or differences.

39. **Which of the following is an important criterion for evaluating children's literature?** (Easy)

    A. Character development
    B. Appropriate reading level
    C. Cultural diversity
    D. All of the above

Answer D: All of the above

In selecting appropriate literature for children, teachers must consider several factors. Primary among these factors is the composition of the class (including diversity) and the preferences of the children. Children love to identify with the characters in books; therefore it is important to select books with characters that provide positive role models for children. Books should be chosen at an appropriate reading level and should be challenging enough to promote vocabulary growth.

40. **Which of the following approaches to student writing assignments is most likely to lead to students becoming disinterested?** (Average rigor)

 A. Designing assignments where students write for a variety of audiences.
 B. Designing assignments where the teacher is always the audience.
 C. Designing assignments where students write to friends and family.
 D. Designing assignments where students write to real people such as mayors, the principle, or companies.

Answer B: Designing assignments where the teacher is always the audience.

In the past, teachers have assigned reports, paragraphs and essays that focused on the teacher as the audience with the purpose of explaining information. However, for students to be meaningfully engaged in their writing, they must write for a variety of reasons. Writing for different audiences and aims allows students to be more involved in their writing. If they write for the same audience and purpose, they will continue to see writing as just another assignment

41. **To build efficacy, the instructor must not only raise the student's belief in his/her capabilities, but also:** (Rigorous)

 A. Create classroom activities that require higher levels of thinking
 B. Structure situations that breed success and limit repeated failure.
 C. Group students by ability
 D. Use a grading scale with tougher standards

Answer B: Structure situations that breed success and limit repeated failure.

Efficacy describes a person's belief about his/her capability to produce designated levels of performance that exercise influence over events that affect their lives. A strong sense of efficacy enhances human accomplishment and personal well-being in many ways. People with high assurance in their capabilities view difficult tasks as challenges rather than threats. A student with high self-efficacy will be highly motivated to participate in classroom activities. To build efficacy, the instructor must not only raise the student's belief in his/her capabilities, but also structure situations that breed success and limit repeated failure.

TEACHER CERTIFICATION STUDY GUIDE

42. The principal walks into your classroom during math class. He sees your students making cake mixtures. Later, the principal questions your lesson. What would be the best explanation for your lesson? (Rigorous)

    A. The students earned a reward time and it was free choice.
    B. You were teaching the students how math is used in real-life situations.
    C. You had paperwork to complete and needed the time to complete it.
    D. It kept the students interested in math and prevented boredom.

Answer B: You were teaching the students how math is used in real-life situations.

Providing the students with the opportunity to explore how math is around them and how it is utilized in everyday experiences is important. As students identify and realize the importance of the skills being learned to their lives at home, they will become more involved in the learning, as it has new and better value for them.

43. A teacher plans an activity that involves students calculating how many chair legs are in the classroom, given that there are 30 chairs and each chair has 4 legs. This activity is introducing the ideas of: (Average rigor)

    A. Probability
    B. Statistics
    C. Geometry
    D. Algebra

Answer D: Algebra

This activity involves recognizing patterns. It could also involve problem-solving by developing an expression that represents the problem. Activities such as this do not introduce the terms of algebra, but they introduce some of the ideas of algebra.

44. Students are working with a set of rulers and various small objects from the classroom. Which concept are these students exploring? (Average rigor)

    A. Volume
    B. Weight
    C. Length
    D. Temperature

Answer C: Length

The use of a ruler indicates that the activity is based on exploring length.

45. Kindergarten students are participating in a calendar time activity. One student adds a straw to the "ones can" to represent that day of school. What math principle is being reinforced? (Rigorous)

    A. Properties of a base ten number system
    B. Sorting
    C. Counting by twos
    D. Even and odd numbers

Answer A: Properties of a base ten number system

As the students group craft sticks into groups of tens to represent the days of school, they are learning the properties of our base ten number system.

46. When you find it necessary to communicate with a parent regarding a concern about a student, it is important that you: (Easy)

    A. Allow yourself a "cooling off" period
    B. Raise your voice to let them know you are serious
    C. Remain professional and objective
    D. Both A and C

Answer D: Both A and C

When you find it necessary to communicate (whether by phone, letter, or in person) with a parent regarding a concern about a student, allow yourself a "cooling off" period before making contact with the parent. It is important that you remain professional and objective.

TEACHER CERTIFICATION STUDY GUIDE

47. **Which of the following is a social skill gained from participation in physical activities? (Easy)**

    A. Problem-solving skills
    B. Communication skills
    C. Judgment skills
    D. All of the above

Answer D: All of the above

Participation in physical activities helps students develop a number of social skills. Problem-solving skills and judgment skills are developed in both individual and team sports. Communication skills are especially developed in team sports.

48. **Which of the following benefits can physical education provide? (Easy)**

    A. A sense of belonging
    B. Increased self-esteem
    C. Appreciation of beauty
    D. All of the above

Answer D: All of the above

Physical education provides a wide range of benefits, including physical, emotional, and social benefits. These include a sense of belonging, increased self-esteem, appreciation of beauty, good sportsmanship, increased humanism, valuable social experiences, and improved health.

49. **A student who is observed to often collide with other people while taking part in physical education probably has poor awareness of: (Rigorous)**

    A. Balance
    B. Space
    C. Speed
    D. Force

Answer B: Space

When performing physical activities, students incorporate space, direction, and speed concepts. Students who understand these concepts generally move with confidence and avoid collisions. The space concept is most beneficial in helping a student avoid collisions.

50. Which activity would be most suitable for beginning students of visual arts? (Rigorous)

    A. Analyzing famous works of arts
    B. Reflecting on the possible meanings of art work
    C. Observing the shapes and forms of common objects
    D. Using blocks to construct three dimensional shapes

Answer C: Observing the shapes and forms of common objects

Beginning students of visual arts should be learning to develop their observation skills, such as by observing objects or the environment and noting features such as shape, color, size, repeating patterns, or other aspects. Students can then progress to hands-on activities and later to analysis activities.

51. What should the arts curriculum for early childhood avoid? (Average rigor)

    A. Judgment
    B. Open expression
    C. Experimentation
    D. Discovery

Answer A: Judgment

The arts curriculum for early childhood should focus on the experimental and discovery aspects of the arts. The emphasis should be on creative processes with little judgment and minimal criticism.

52. What would the viewing of a dance company performance be most likely to promote? (Average rigor)

    A. Critical-thinking skills
    B. Appreciation of the arts
    C. Improvisation skills
    D. Music vocabulary

Answer B: Appreciation of the arts

Live performances are an important part of learning arts and help to develop aesthetic appreciation of the arts. A dance company performance is one example of a live performance that students could attend.

TEACHER CERTIFICATION STUDY GUIDE

Subarea III. Family and Community Relationships

53. **Which of the following should NOT be a purpose of a parent teacher conference? (Average rigor)**

    A. To involve the parent in their child's education
    B. To establish a friendship with the child's parents
    C. To resolve a concern about the child's performance
    D. To inform parents of positive behaviors by the child

Answer B: To establish a friendship with the child's parents.

The purpose of a parent teacher conference is to involve parents in their child's education, address concerns about the child's performance and share positive aspects of the student's learning with the parents. It would be unprofessional to allow the conference to degenerate into a social visit to establish friendships.

54. **In regards to dealing with parents, which term best describes the role that teachers should play in the education of children? (Average rigor)**

    A. Friends
    B. Leaders
    C. Partners
    D. Managers

Answer C: Partners

It is important for teachers to act as partners in the education of children. This means accepting that parents know their children best and utilizing the feedback, information, and advice received from parents.

TEACHER CERTIFICATION STUDY GUIDE

55. Which of the following is a right of parents? (Easy)

- A. To be informed of the teacher's concerns about their child
- B. To require the teacher to use the teaching method that works for the child
- C. To administer discipline to their child in the classroom
- D. To attend all classes to support their child

Answer A: To be informed of the teacher's concerns about their child.

It is a parent's right to be involved in their child's education and to be informed of the teacher's reports on his/her progress as well as the teacher's concerns about their child's learning or behavior. Since parents are entrusting the child to the teacher's professional care, they are entitled to know what concerns the teacher about their child during their absence.

56. What is the purpose of a parent-teacher conference? (Average rigor)

- A. Sharing information with the parents
- B. Obtaining information from the parents
- C. Requesting parent support
- D. Any or all of the above

Answer D: Any or all of the above

A parent-teacher conference can be held for a number of reasons. These include allowing the teacher to provide parents with information, allowing the teacher to obtain information from the parents, and asking the parents for involvement in the student's learning activities.

57. How should a teacher respond to criticism about her teaching strategies from a parent? (Rigorous)

- A. Explain to the parent that negative feedback is hurtful and mean-spirited
- B. Dismiss the criticism as an attempt to undermine her performance
- C. Think about the criticism objectively and consider that it might be true
- D. Change her teaching strategies to eliminate the aspect being criticized

Answer C: Think about the criticism objectively and consider that it might be true

Any time a teacher receives negative feedback her reaction should be to think about its validity. This approach would benefit the teacher's skills of self-assessment and awareness of her teaching, as well as being the appropriate professional response to negative feedback.

TEACHER CERTIFICATION STUDY GUIDE

58. **When is it appropriate for a teacher to talk to parents about another student's performance? (Rigorous)**

    A. When the parents of the student have been invited to participate
    B. When the student is having a negative impact on other students
    C. When the student is performing well and only positive information will be communicated
    D. When permission to discuss the student has been given by the principal

Answer A: When the parents of the student have been invited to participate

Information about a student's school performance is confidential and comes under the Privacy Act. Information can be given only to the student's parents or guardians. If another student must be spoken about, that student's parents or guardians must be invited to participate.

59. **You receive a phone call from a parent who is angry about the grade their child receives on the report card. As the conversation continues, the parent becomes verbally abusive and uses curse words. What should you do? (Rigorous)**

    A. Raise your voice to establish your authority
    B. Hang up and get assistance from your administrator
    C. Blame the parent for the poor grade
    D. Apologize over and over and hope that the parent will calm down and stop cursing

Answer B: Hang up and get assistance from your administrator

Teachers will need to be patient with difficult families, but should help them realize that certain methods of criticism are unacceptable. In the described circumstance, it would be appropriate for the teacher to hang up so they could get assistance from an administrator. This situation, however, is very unusual, and most teachers will find that when they really attempt to be friendly and personal with parents, the parents will reciprocate and assist in the educational program.

60. There has been a lot of research on how birth order in a family affects the development of young children. Researchers have identified typical characteristics that can apply to the eldest child in the family. Which of the following are characteristics of an oldest child? (Rigorous)

   A. Expects to have things done for him/her
   B. May feel left out
   C. Tries to control other children
   D. Adapts easily to situations

Answer C: Tries to control other children

The eldest child is the one most likely to succeed in school, while the middle children are those with the most negative self-concepts. The eldest child often tries to control other children. They often may feel unloved because of the birth of the second child. They tend to be very protective of younger children and strive to please their parents and teachers.

61. A teacher has a class with several students from low income families in it. What would it be most important for a teacher to consider when planning homework assignments to ensure that all students have equal opportunity for academic success? (Rigorous)

   A. Access to technology
   B. Ethnicity
   C. Language difficulties
   D. Gender

Answer A: Access to technology

Families with higher incomes are able to provide increased opportunities for students. Students from lower income families will need to depend on the resources available from the school system and the community. To ensure that all students have equal opportunity for academic success, teachers should plan assessments so that not having access to technology does not disadvantage students from low income families.

62. Which of the following is NOT an economic factor that may influence the health of a child? (Easy)

   A. Pollution
   B. Malnutrition
   C. Neglect
   D. Poor medical care

Answer A: Pollution

Malnutrition, neglect, and poor medical care are economic factors that may influence the health of a child. Pollution could influence the health of a child, but it is not an economic factor.

63. Which of the following problems are likely to be faced by migrant, homeless, and abandoned children? (Easy)

   A. Poor attendance
   B. Language barriers
   C. Social isolation
   D. All of the above

Answer D: All of the above

Migrant, homeless, and abandoned children face a number of educational problems. Common problems faced include poor attendance, language barriers, and social isolation. These can lead to poor school performance.

64. Head Start programs were created in what decade? (Easy)

   A. 2000's
   B. 1990's
   C. 1980's
   D. 1960's

Answer D: 1960's

Head Start Programs were created in the early 1960's to provide a comprehensive curriculum model for preparation of low-income students for success in school communities.

TEACHER CERTIFICATION STUDY GUIDE

65. IDEA is a federal law passed in 1990 that has a direct impact on classrooms. The acronym IDEA stands for: (Average rigor)

    A. Individuals with Disabilities Education Act
    B. Individualized Differentiation for Education Always
    C. Idealistic Dedicated Educational Access
    D. Instructional Differentiation Education Act

Answer A: Individuals with Disabilities Education Act

IDEA (Individuals with Disabilities Education Act) passed in 1990 has a direct impact on classrooms. This law ensures that all children with disabilities and their families receive the help and support they need. It governs how states and public agencies can provide intervention services and how schools can provide special education services for these children.

66. Local businesses are an important resource for schools because they are a source of: (Easy)

    A. Students
    B. Employment
    C. Teachers
    D. Funding

Answer D: Funding

The main importance of local businesses to schools is that they are a source of funding. Local businesses can often provide assistance to purchase school supplies. They can also support projects run by the school, sponsor academic and athletic teams, or provide assistance to students in need.

67. In terms of positive public relations, it is most important for teachers to remember that they are: (Rigorous)

    A. Solely responsible for educating students
    B. Representatives of their school
    C. Only viewed by the public when at school
    D. Positive role models for all students

Answer B: Representatives of their school

Teachers are the public face of their school. The impression that teachers make can make a significant difference to how the school is viewed by the community. This can influence enrolments, financial support, and the level of community support.

68. Researchers have shown that school involvement and connections with community institutions yield greater retention rates of students graduating and seeking higher education experiences. What is a current barrier to community involvement? (Rigorous)

    A. The current disconnect and autonomy that has become common in today's society.
    B. The amount of gang activity in many communities.
    C. The tough economic times we are facing.
    D. The introduction of standardized testing.

Answer A: The current disconnect and autonomy that has become common in today's society.

Daily life is more isolated than it used to be. With the ability to communicate easily and cheaply, families have scattered all over the globe, with few living in one community their whole life. Neighbors are isolated from neighbors, no longer sharing community activities. The general disconnectedness in our society is a barrier to school/community involvement.

Subarea IV. Assessment and Evaluation

69. Which type of assessment has the main purpose of helping learners learn better? (Average rigor)

    A. Formal assessment
    B. Observation
    C. Informal assessment
    D. Exam

Answer C: Informal assessment

The main purpose of informal assessment is to help learners learn better. It aims to help the teacher understand how the student is learning and progressing.

70. **Which of the following is an effective method of evaluating a child's writing skills?** (Average rigor)

    A. Have the child erase his/her writing errors
    B. Have the child start writing assignments over again
    C. Have the child cross out errors with a single line
    D. Have the child complete writing assignments at home

Answer C: Have the child cross out errors with a single line

If the teacher is evaluating a child's writing, it is a good idea to discourage the child from erasing his/her errors and to train the child to cross out errors with a single line so that the teacher can actually see the process that the student went through to complete a writing assignment. This is an effective means of getting to know the student's writing and is a valuable writing evaluation technique.

71. **Proponents of formal assessment believe that to determine if a school is successful**: (Average rigor)

    A. Assessments will drive the curriculum.
    B. Students must be able to perform meaningful tasks that replicate real world challenges.
    C. Students must be tested to see if they learned the required knowledge and skills.
    D. None of the above.

Answer C: Students must be tested to see if they learned the required knowledge and skills.

In formal assessment, the curriculum drives assessment. "The" body of knowledge is determined first. That knowledge becomes the curriculum that is delivered. Subsequently, the assessments are developed and administered to determine if acquisition of the curriculum occurred.

In contrast, proponents of authentic assessment believe that assessment drives the curriculum. Teachers first determine the tasks that students will perform to demonstrate their mastery, and then a curriculum is developed that will enable students to perform those tasks well, which would include the acquisition of essential knowledge and skills. This has been referred to as *planning backwards*.

72. **Which of the following is a common self-appraisal instrument? (Average rigor)**

    A. Rating scales
    B. Questioning
    C. Portfolio assessment
    D. Anecdotal records

Answer A: Rating scales

Rating scales and checklists can be self-appraisal instruments completed by the student. They can also be completed by the teacher.

73. **A teacher wishes to identify the sources of confusion that are resulting in students performing poorly on standardized tests. What would be the best method to use for this purpose? (Rigorous)**

    A. Rating scales
    B. Questioning
    C. Portfolio assessment
    D. Anecdotal records

Answer B: Questioning

Oral questioning is an assessment method often used by teachers. While asking questions, the teacher can identify the degree of student knowledge as well as the areas where students may by experiencing confusion or misunderstandings.

74. **Which strategy for adapting the curriculum would be most useful for the purpose of reducing the effect of a student's learning disability on completing an assessment task? (Rigorous)**

    A. Differentiated instruction
    B. Alternative assessments
    C. Testing modifications
    D. Total Physical Response

Answer C: Testing modifications

Testing modifications are changes made to assessments that allow students with disabilities equal opportunity to demonstrate their knowledge and ability on the task.

75. **Which type of social skill assessment involves students ranking their classmates on set criteria? (Average rigor)**

    A. Direct observation
    B. Paired-comparison
    C. Peer nomination
    D. Peer rating

Answer D: Peer rating

There are many ways to assess student's social skills. Peer rating is a method where students rate their peers on set criteria.

76. **Which factor is it most important to consider when choosing structured assessment methods? (Rigorous)**

    A. The authenticity of the methods
    B. The results of informal evaluations
    C. The formal assessments required
    D. The developmental stage of students

Answer D: The developmental stage of students

The structured assessment methods used in class take into account two major factors. The first is the developmental stage of students, where teachers must choose assessment methods that are appropriate for the developmental level of students. The second consideration is the purpose of the assessment.

77. **Which type of assessment is the least structured? (Easy)**

    A. Observation
    B. Informal continuous assessment
    C. Formal assessment
    D. Standardized testing

Answer A: Observation

Observation is an assessment activity that involves noticing someone and judging their action. It is the least structured type of assessment.

78. Which of the following is the best method for a teacher to use to get to know the students initially? (Average rigor)

   A. Running reading record
   B. Entry survey
   C. Norm-referenced test
   D. Oral presentations

Answer B: Entry survey

An entry survey is a survey a teacher takes to get to know the students straight away. It typically focuses on finding out the students' backgrounds and experiences. Questions asked on an entry survey might ask about the student's interests, fears, and language spoken at home.

79. Which type of assessment would be used to place students into honors, regular, and remedial classes? (Rigorous)

   A. Norm-referenced assessments
   B. Criterion-referenced assessments
   C. Performance-based assessments
   D. Observation-based assessments

Answer A: Norm-referenced assessments

Norm-references assessments are used to classify students into a ranking category. Norm-references assessments are used to place students into honors, remedial, and regular classes.

80. Which type of assessment is most likely to be used to assess student interest and motivation? (Average rigor)

   A. Rating scales
   B. Questioning
   C. Portfolio assessment
   D. Anecdotal records

Answer A: Rating scales

Rating scales are often used to assess behavior and effective areas. They can be used to assess interest and motivation, whereas most other assessment types are not appropriate for this purpose.

81. Which of these actions taken by a teacher would improve planning for instruction? (Average rigor)

    A. Describe the role of the teacher and student
    B. Evaluate the outcomes of instruction
    C. Rearrange the order of activities
    D. Give outside assignments

Answer B: Evaluate the outcomes of instruction

An important part of the planning process is for the teacher to constantly adapt all aspects of the curriculum to what is actually happening in the classroom. Planning frequently misses the mark or fails to allow for unexpected factors. Evaluating the outcomes of instruction regularly and making adjustments accordingly will have a positive impact on the overall success of a teaching methodology.

82. Which of the following types of assessment is most likely to be required to be administered in a specific format by state and federal laws? (Rigorous)

    A. Informal evaluations
    B. Classroom observation
    C. Peer ratings
    D. Standardized tests

Answer D: Standardized tests

State and federal law requires that public schools administer various standardized assessments. Policies and procedures for administering these tests must be followed carefully and thoroughly. Whenever procedures are not followed carefully, the validity of the test scores can be placed into jeopardy.

83. Which of the following statements would not be appropriate in an anecdotal record about a student? (Rigorous)

    A. Jasmine completed only half of the homework assigned.
    B. Jasmine contributed only slightly to class discussions.
    C. Jasmine was not interested in learning the material.
    D. Jasmine did not volunteer to answer any questions.

Answer C: Jasmine was not interested in learning the material.

Anecdotal records of a student should include observable behaviors. Anecdotal records should not include assumptions or speculations about the student's motivation or interest. "Jasmine was not interested in learning the material" is not appropriate to include because it is speculation.

84. Teachers should regard a student's test results as: (Average rigor)

    A. Exact indications of the student's ability
    B. Ballpark figures indicating the student's ability
    C. Possible indicators of a student's ability
    D. Unlikely to be a true indication of a student's ability

Answer B: Ballpark figures indicating the student's ability

The test results achieved by students should be regarded as indications of the student's ability, but ballpark figures rather than exact indications. This occurs because other factors can influence the test results, such as the student's mood on the day of the test or other factors.

85. What is it most important for a teacher to consider when reading another teacher's observations of a student? (Average rigor)

    A. Mood
    B. Discrimination
    C. Dishonesty
    D. Bias

Answer D: Bias

When reading another teacher's observations of a student, teachers must be aware that the teacher may be biased. This could result in either a more positive or a more negative assessment.

TEACHER CERTIFICATION STUDY GUIDE

Subarea V. Professional and Program Leadership

86. **Which of the following is a widely known curriculum model for early childhood programs? (Easy)**

    A. Creative Curriculum
    B. DISTAR method
    C. Success for All
    D. Voyager

Answer A: Creative Curriculum

Creative Curriculum is used by Head Start, child care, preschool, Pre-kindergarten and kindergarten programs. It focuses on ten interest areas or activities in the program environment: blocks, house corner, table toys, art, sand and water, library corner, music and movement, cooking, computers, and the outdoors.

87. **Which of the following is considered a current trend in education? (Easy)**

    A. Differentiated instruction so that no child is left behind
    B. Innovations in technology
    C. Instruction in the 3 Rs
    D. A and B

Answer D: A and B

Differentiated instruction so that no child is left behind is an important trend that will allow schools to address the needs of all learners as required by the NCLB law. In the global economy, skills in technology have become increasingly important and teachers must stay current in the use of technology for instruction.

88. What criteria are used to assess whether a child qualifies for services under IDEA? (Rigorous)

   A. Having a disability only
   B. Having a disability and demonstrating educational need only
   C. Demonstrating educational need only
   D. Having a disability, demonstrating educational need, and having financial support

Answer B: Having a disability and demonstrating educational need only

Based on IDEA, eligibility for special education services is based on a student having one of a listed set of disabilities (or a combination thereof) and demonstration of educational need through professional evaluation.

89. A student who is deaf has an Individual Family Service Plan (IFSP) in place. This legal document is a way of providing: (Average rigor)

   A. Early intervention
   B. Help for the family and the child
   C. Services to deal with the child's disability
   D. All of the above

Answer D: All of the above

An IFSP is an Individual Family Service Plan and is a legal document. This plan is put in place for young children who have disabilities, such as deafness or other special needs. The focus of the plan is to help the family and the child by providing services, such as family based programs and the services of professionals to deal with the child's disability. The IFSP is a way of providing early intervention under IDEA (Individuals with Disabilities Education Act). It is not only designed to enhance the child's education but it is also designed to help the family facilitate the child's development.

TEACHER CERTIFICATION STUDY GUIDE

90. **Which federal law has directed states to construct curriculum models specific to the development of early childhood and elementary programs for academic enhancement? (Rigorous)**

    A. IDEA
    B. Head Start
    C. FERPA
    D. NCLB

Answer D: NCLB

The NCLB (No Child Left Behind) Act has directed the growth of both federal and state mandates in constructing curriculum models specific to the development of early childhood and elementary programs for academic enhancement.

91. **To determine if a child has a disability that may qualify the child for services under IDEA, which of the following pieces of information should the school collect? (Average rigor)**

    A. The present levels of academic achievement
    B. Vision and hearing screening information
    C. A complete psychological evaluation
    D. All of the above

Answer D: All of the above

To begin the process of determining if a child has a disability, the teacher will take information about the child's present levels of academic achievement to the appropriate school committee for discussion and consideration. The committee will recommend the next step to be taken. Often subsequent steps may include a complete psychological evaluation along with certain physical examinations such as vision and hearing screening and a complete medical examination by a doctor.

TEACHER CERTIFICATION STUDY GUIDE

92. **What would be put into place to assist students with special needs who are in a regular education classroom? (Rigorous)**

    A. 504
    B. IEP
    C. IFSP
    D. All of the above

Answer A: 504

A 504 plan is a legal document falling under the provisions of the Rehabilitation Act of 1973. It is designed to plan a program of instructional services to assist students with special needs who are in a regular education setting. A 504 plan is not an Individualized Education Program (IEP) as is required for special education students.

93. **Failure to make a report when abuse or neglect is suspected is punishable by which of the following? (Average rigor)**

    A. Revocation of certification and license
    B. A monetary fine
    C. Criminal charges
    D. All of the above

Answer D: All of the above

Failure to make a report when abuse or neglect is suspected is punishable by revocation of certification and license, a fine, and criminal charges. It is the duty of any citizen who suspects abuse and neglect to make a report, and it is especially important and required for State licensed and certified persons (like teachers) to make a report. All reports can be kept confidential if required.

94. **When should a teacher report child abuse? (Average rigor)**

    A. Only when the teacher has sufficient evidence
    B. Once the child confirms the abuse
    C. Any time that it is suspected
    D. After the student's parents have been contacted

Answer C: Any time that it is suspected

It is important that teachers report child abuse any time that it is suspected. Failure or delay in reporting suspected abuse may be a cause for further abuse to the student. Teachers are not required to investigate abuse for themselves or verify their suspicions.

TEACHER CERTIFICATION STUDY GUIDE

95. Which of the following is NOT a sign of child abuse? (Easy)

    A. Awkward social behavior around other children
    B. Participation in class discussions
    C. Awkward social behavior around adults
    D. Bruises

Answer B: Participation in class discussions

While the symptoms of abuse are usually thought to be physical (and therefore visible, like bruises), mental and emotional abuse is also possible. The impact of abuse on a child's development in other domains is often extensive. Abused children can be socially withdrawn, and typically, as one might suspect, their minds will not always be on their schoolwork.

96. A teacher notices that a student is quiet, and has several bruises on his head, arms, and legs. When asked, the student tells the teacher that his dad hit him, but then begs her not to tell. The teacher should: (Rigorous)

    A. Report suspected abuse to the school counselor
    B. Attempt to get more information from the student
    C. Respect the child's wishes and withhold the information
    D. Wait and see if other signs of abuse become evident

Answer A: Report suspected abuse to the school counselor.

The most important concern is for the safety and well being of the student. Teachers should not promise students that they won't tell because they are required by law to err on the side of caution and report suspected abuse.

97. Who should you talk to if you suspect child abuse? (Easy)

    A. The child
    B. The child's parent
    C. Your supervisor
    D. Another teacher

Answer C: Your supervisor

The best action to take when children abuse is suspected is immediately contact a superior at the school, such as your supervisor. It is the duty of any citizen who suspects abuse and neglect to make a report, and it is especially important and required for State licensed and certified persons to make a report.

98. **Physical accommodations may need to be done in the school or the classroom to make it possible for children with disabilities to come to school. Which of the following is NOT a demonstration of accommodation? (Easy)**

    A. Building wheelchair ramps
    B. Installing an elevator
    C. Repainting the classroom
    D. Enlarging the doorways

Answer C: Repainting the classroom

Students with disabilities are now being accommodated in the regular classroom. Physical accommodations may need to be done in the school or the classroom to make it possible for children with disabilities to come to school. This includes such things as building wheelchair ramps or installing elevators, making the doors larger, or having special chairs for the children to use while in the classroom.

99. **General classroom safety should include the following: (Average rigor)**

    A. Adequate traffic flow
    B. Entry and exit accessibility
    C. Adequate ventilation and climate control
    D. All of the above

Answer D: All of the above

For safety reasons, rows of desks must have adequate space between them for students to move and for the teacher to circulate. Another consideration is adequate ventilation and climate control. Local fire and safety codes dictate entry and exit standards. In all cases, proper care must be taken to ensure student safety.

100. **Which of the following is NOT a communication issue that the teacher in a diverse classroom should be aware of? (Rigorous)**

    A. Body language that is intimidating or offensive to some cultures
    B. Emphasizing the importance of different viewpoints and opinions
    C. Planning and directing interactive "hands-on" learning experiences
    D. Knowing and using the current terms that ethnic and cultural groups use to identify themselves

Answer C: Planning and directing interactive "hands-on" learning experiences

Communication issues that the teacher in a diverse classroom should be aware of include knowing and using the current terms that ethnic and cultural groups use to identify themselves (e.g., "Latinos" (favored) vs. "Hispanics"). Teachers should be aware of body language that is intimidating or offensive to some cultures, such as direct eye contact, and adjust their teaching style accordingly. Teachers should emphasize the importance of discussing and considering different viewpoints and opinions. They should also demonstrate and express value for all opinions and comments and encourage their students to do the same.

Post Test

Subarea I. Child Development and Learning

1. **At what age would a child be expected to have developed speech patterns with 100% intelligibility? (Average rigor)**

    A. Age 2

    B. Age 3

    C. Age 4

    D. Age 5

2. **The stages of play development from infancy stages to early childhood includes a move from: (Rigorous)**

    A. Cooperative to solitary

    B. Solitary to cooperative

    C. Competitive to collaborative

    D. Collaborative to competitive

3. **According to Piaget, during what stage do children learn to manipulate symbols and objects? (Average rigor)**

    A. Concrete operations

    B. Pre-operational

    C. Formal operations

    D. Conservative operational

4. **What does the Multiple Intelligence Theory developed by Howard Gardner explain? (Easy)**

    A. How the intelligence of students depends on the environment

    B. How the intelligence of students constantly change

    C. How students have different levels of overall intelligence

    D. How students learn in at least seven different ways

5. Above what age does learning a language become increasingly difficult? (Average rigor)

   A. Age 3

   B. Age 5

   C. Age 7

   D. Age 10

6. The various domains of development are best described as: (Average rigor)

   A. Integrated

   B. Independent

   C. Simultaneous

   D. Parallel

7. A student has developed and improved their vocabulary. However, the student is not confident enough to use their improved vocabulary, and the teacher is not aware of the improvement. What is this an example of? (Rigorous)

   A. Latent development

   B. Dormant development

   C. Random development

   D. Delayed development

8. A child exhibits the following symptoms: inability to appreciate humor, indifference to physical contact, abnormal social play, and abnormal speech. What is the likely diagnosis for this child? (Rigorous)

   A. Separation anxiety

   B. Mental retardation

   C. Autism

   D. Hypochondria

9. The complex linguistic deficiency marked by the inability to remember and recognize words by sounds and the inability to break words down into component units describes: (Average rigor)

   A. Oral processing disorder

   B. Attention deficit disorder

   C. Dyslexia

   D. Autism

10. **What is a good strategy for teaching ethnically diverse students? (Rigorous)**

    A. Don't focus on the students' culture

    B. Expect them to assimilate easily into your classroom

    C. Imitate their speech patterns

    D. Use instructional strategies of various formats

11. **When teaching in a diverse classroom, teachers should: (Rigorous)**

    A. Plan, devise, and present material in a multicultural manner

    B. Research all possible cultures and expose the children to those

    C. Focus on the curriculum and whatever multicultural opportunities are built into it already

    D. Utilize single format instruction to present material in a multicultural manner

12. **Because teachers today will deal with an increasingly diverse group of cultures in their classrooms, they must: (Average rigor)**

    A. Ignore the cultures represented

    B. Show respect to all parents and families

    C. Provide a celebration for each culture represented

    D. Focus on teaching the majority

13. **What is an effective way to help a non-English speaking student succeed in class? (Rigorous)**

    A. Refer the child to a specialist

    B. Maintain an encouraging, success-oriented atmosphere

    C. Help them assimilate by making them use English exclusively

    D. Help them cope with the content materials you presently use

14. Jose moved to the United States last month. He speaks little to no English at this time. His teacher is teaching the class about habitats in science and has chosen to read a story about various habitats to the class. The vocabulary is difficult. What should Jose's teacher do with Jose? (Rigorous)

    A. Provide Jose with additional opportunities to learn about habitats

    B. Read the story to Jose multiple times

    C. Show Jose pictures of habitats from his native country

    D. Excuse Jose from the assignment

15. IDEA sets policies that provide for inclusion of students with disabilities. What does inclusion mean? (Rigorous)

    A. Inclusion is the name of the curriculum that must be followed in special education classes.

    B. Inclusion is the right of students with disabilities to be placed in the regular classroom.

    C. Inclusion refers to the quality of instruction that is important for student's academic success.

    D. Inclusion means that students with disabilities should always be placed in special classes.

16. What is one component of the instructional planning model that must be given careful evaluation? (Average rigor)

    A. Students' prior knowledge and skills

    B. The script the teacher will use in instruction

    C. Future lesson plans

    D. Parent participation

17. Which of the following is a true statement? (Rigorous)

    A. Recess is not important to a child's development.

    B. Playtime is only provided in schools to help children release energy.

    C. Play has an important and positive role in child development.

    D. Solitary play is always an indication that a child has development issues.

18. Which type of learning involves the formulation of questions that convert new information into an active application of knowledge? (Rigorous)

    A. Hands-on learning

    B. Guided reading

    C. Inquiry-based learning

    D. Teacher directed model

19. Which of the following is portfolio assessment most likely to encourage? (Rigorous)

    A. Self-esteem

    B. Self-directed learning

    C. Conflict management skills

    D. Time management skills

Subarea II. Curriculum Development and Implementation

20. Which of the following is the most important reason for integrating the curriculum? (Average rigor)

    A. It increases ease of lesson planning.

    B. It meets the needs of diverse students.

    C. It breaks down barriers between subjects.

    D. It narrows the focus of study.

21. Mrs. Potts is conducting a language development task with her students. She forms students into small mixed-ability groups. She then gives each group a discussion question. Each group is asked to discuss the question, while ensuring that each person has a chance to give their opinion. What approach to language development is this activity based on? (Rigorous)

    A. Linguistic approach

    B. Cognitive approach

    C. Socio-cognitive approach

    D. Learning approach

22. **A teacher attempting to create a differentiated classroom should focus on incorporating activities that: (Rigorous)**

    A. Favor academically advanced students

    B. Challenge special education students to achieve more

    C. Are suitable for whichever group of students is the majority

    D. Meet the needs of all the students in the class

23. **Why is it most important for teachers to ensure that students from different economic backgrounds have access to the resources they need to acquire the academic skills being taught? (Rigorous)**

    A. All students must work together on set tasks.

    B. All students must achieve the same results in performance tasks.

    C. All students must have equal opportunity for academic success.

    D. All students must be fully included in classroom activities.

24. **A teacher is planning to get all of her students involved in sports for the purpose of helping develop hand-eye coordination and teamwork skills. What would be the most appropriate approach when planning the sports activities? (Rigorous)**

    A. Encourage competition among students so they become used to the pressure of competing.

    B. Ensure that students who dislike sports continue until they enjoy sports.

    C. Choose activities that are beyond the student's current abilities so students are prompted to improve.

    D. Maintain a relaxed atmosphere and remind students that the sport is designed to be fun.

25. **Which is the best approach to the holistic teaching of a concept? (Rigorous)**

    A. Start with the whole concept and then move on to the parts.

    B. Teach only the parts and avoid focusing on the whole.

    C. Focus only on the whole to avoid students becoming confused by the parts.

    D. Begin with parts until students have developed their own understanding of the whole.

26. **Young children do not concentrate for long periods of time. Generally, young children should be changing academic activities every: (Rigorous)**

    A. 5-10 minutes

    B. 15-20 minutes

    C. 20-45 minutes

    D. 45 minutes-1 hour

27. **Providing instruction from various points of view, not only helps students academically, but it also allows them to: (Rigorous)**

    A. Work cooperatively and contribute to a team

    B. Develop the personal skill of being able to view situations from multiple viewpoints

    C. Become problem solvers with the ability to apply creative thinking to common problems

    D. Develop tolerance and patience

28. **What area of differentiated instruction is a teacher focusing on when planning what material to teach? (Easy)**

    A. Process

    B. Content

    C. Product

    D. Assessment

29. Which of the following best describes how different areas of development impact each other? (Average rigor)

    A. Development in other areas cannot occur until cognitive development is complete.

    B. Areas of development are inter-related and impact each other.

    C. Development in each area is independent of development in other areas.

    D. Development in one area leads to a decline in other areas.

30. Teachers must create personalized learning communities where every student is a valued member and contributor of the classroom experiences. Which of the following are effects of a personalized learning environment? (Rigorous)

    A. Decreased drop-out rates among marginalized students

    B. Increased learning affect for students

    C. Decreased unproductive student behavior

    D. All of the above

31. What is a conflict resolution principle? (Average rigor)

    A. Attack the person

    B. React immediately

    C. Find common ground

    D. Focus on the past

32. What should a teacher do first when they notice a student appears stressed? (Average rigor)

    A. Praise the student

    B. Hold a class discussion

    C. Inform the parents

    D. Ask the student what the problem is

33. Johnny loves to listen to stories and points to signs all around the room that have letters on them. This suggests that Johnny: (Average rigor)

    A. Will be a good reader

    B. Has good emergent literacy skills

    C. Has good phonemic awareness skills

    D. Understands grammar

34. Children having difficulties with spelling, reading accuracy, and reading comprehension skills are also likely to have difficulties with: (Rigorous)

   A. Cognitive skills

   B. Development factors

   C. Math skills

   D. Speech and language skills

35. Children typically develop oral language by listening to: (Easy)

   A. Teachers

   B. Parents

   C. Peers

   D. All of the above

36. Mr. Phillips has called a parent meeting with Maria's parents. Maria is struggling to acquire the necessary comprehension skills to maintain grade level standards. Maria's parents speak Spanish in the home and are eager and willing to do anything to help Maria succeed in school. Which of the following strategies will help Maria, while maintaining and fostering the importance of her native language? (Rigorous)

   A. Encouraging Maria's parents to enroll in an English language course

   B. Making sure Maria speaks only English during classroom activities

   C. Encouraging Maria's parents to read and discuss books written in Spanish

   D. Ensuring that Maria's parents only speak English in the home

37. In her kindergarten classroom, Mrs. Thomas has been watching the students in the drama center. She has watched the children pretend to complete a variety of magic tricks. Mrs. Thomas decides to use stories about magic to share with her class. Her decision to incorporate their interests into the reading shows that Mrs. Thomas understands that: (Rigorous)

   A. Including student interests is important at all times

   B. Teaching by themes is crucial for young children

   C. Young children respond to literature that reflects their lives

   D. Science fiction and fantasy are the most popular genres

38. Young children learning to write commonly grip the pencil: (Average rigor)

   A. Too far from the point

   B. With the wrong hand

   C. With too many fingers

   D. Too tightly

39. Mr. Adams uses a short story about early train travel as part of a history lesson. This shows that literature: (Average rigor)

   A. Can be used to expand students' vocabulary

   B. Can be used to build students' communication skills

   C. Can be used to help students empathize

   D. Can be used to enhance other areas of the curriculum

40. A classroom activity involves students writing letters to a mayor to ask for more bike paths to be built. What type of discourse are the students engaged in? (Easy)

   A. Exposition

   B. Persuasion

   C. Narration

   D. Description

41. Ms. Smith considers the use of quality children's literature to be one of the most important qualities of an early childhood teacher. She is asked to justify her reasons behind this consideration to her principal. Which of the following is an appropriate justification? (Rigorous)

   A. There are many different types of children's literature, so there will be something to which every child can relate.

   B. Children's literature in early childhood classrooms provides the students with the opportunity to learn to read and process language.

   C. Children are like adults in many ways and need to be exposed to a variety of types of literature.

   D. Children's literature helps children improve their mental, social, and psychological skills and aids in the development in all of these areas.

42. When teaching science, which of the following is a method of focusing on students' intrinsic motivation? (Average rigor)

   A. Adapting the lessons to students' interests

   B. Providing regular feedback

   C. Supplying rewards for the highest achievers

   D. Having regular science tests

43. What math principle is reinforced by matching numerals with number words? (Rigorous)

   A. Sequencing

   B. Greater than and less than

   C. Number representations

   D. Rote counting

44. Recognizing if the word *fill* belongs in the word family of *bill, hill,* and *mill* or the word family of *king, sing,* and *wing* is an example of using what math principle? (Rigorous)

    A. Pattern recognition

    B. Letter counting

    C. Counting by threes

    D. Identity property

45. Students using a measuring cylinder are exploring what concept? (Average rigor)

    A. Volume

    B. Weight

    C. Length

    D. Temperature

46. Science and technology are best described as: (Average rigor)

    A. Different names for the same thing

    B. Competing against each other

    C. Closely related and intertwined

    D. Independent of each other

47. Which type of physical education activity is most likely to encourage appreciation of diversity? (Average rigor)

    A. Solitary activities

    B. Teamwork activities

    C. Competitive activities

    D. Creative activities

48. Maintaining body weight is best accomplished by: (Average rigor)

    A. Dieting

    B. Aerobic exercise

    C. Lifting weights

    D. Equalizing caloric intake relative to output

49. Which of the following is the main source of energy in the diet? (Easy)

    A. Vitamins

    B. Minerals

    C. Water

    D. Carbohydrates

50. According to Charles Fowler, why is it important for arts to be incorporated into the teaching of other subject areas? (Rigorous)

   A. It reduces loss of interest in the subject.

   B. It enhances the likelihood that students will retain the information.

   C. It provides a three dimensional view of the subject.

   D. It encourages the development of personal connections with the subject.

51. What should the arts curriculum for early childhood students focus on? (Average rigor)

   A. Judgment

   B. Criticism

   C. Interpretation

   D. Experimentation

52. What venues offer suitable opportunities for allowing students to view live performances? (Easy)

   A. Symphonies

   B. Dance companies

   C. Art museums

   D. All of the above

Subarea III. Family and Community Relationships

53. Teachers and parents should be: (Easy)

   A. Enemies

   B. Friends

   C. Partners

   D. Strangers

54. Which of the following is NOT a right of parents? (Average rigor)

   A. To be informed of the teacher's concerns about their child

   B. To require the teacher to use the teaching method that works for the child

   C. To administer discipline to their child in the classroom

   D. Both B and C

55. When addressing issues of concern in a parent-teacher conference, what is it best to focus on? (Easy)

    A. Likely explanations

    B. Personal opinions

    C. Statements from other students

    D. Observable behaviors

56. What should a teacher begin a parent-teacher conference with? (Average rigor)

    A. Student weaknesses

    B. Positive comments

    C. Entertaining anecdotes

    D. Issues of concern

57. When dealing with a difficult family, what is most important for a teacher to display? (Average rigor)

    A. Strength

    B. Excitement

    C. Authority

    D. Patience

58. When considering a student's family, teachers should be aware that families: (Easy)

    A. Can be in a range of forms

    B. Are commonly nuclear families

    C. Always have at least one parent

    D. Are always a positive influence on students

59. When communicating with parents for whom English is not the primary language you should: (Average rigor)

    A. Provide materials whenever possible in their native language

    B. Use an interpreter

    C. Provide the same communication as you would to native English speaking parents

    D. All of the above

TEACHER CERTIFICATION STUDY GUIDE

60. Tommy is a student in your class. His parents are deaf. Tommy is struggling with math and you want to contact the parents to discuss the issues. How should you proceed? (Rigorous)

    A. Limit contact due to the parents' inability to hear

    B. Use a TTY phone to communicate with the parents

    C. Talk to your administrator to find an appropriate interpreter to help you communicate with the parents personally

    D. Both B and C

61. Which of the following is a sign of emotional neglect? (Average rigor)

    A. Jealousy of other children

    B. Aggression

    C. Lack of attention to schoolwork

    D. All of the above

62. Which of the following is the most likely cause of a child becoming easily agitated in class? (Average rigor)

    A. Lack of sleep

    B. Lack of training in manners

    C. Being raised in a single parent home

    D. Watching too much television

63. What type of problems are children who have been abandoned or neglected most likely to have? (Rigorous)

    A. Behavioral problems

    B. Medical problems

    C. Social problems

    D. Physical problems

64. **Assigning an adult mentor to a student is an effective tool for addressing student achievement because: (Average rigor)**

   A. The mentor can reinforce learning through tutorial instruction

   B. It provides the student with an appropriate adult role model

   C. The mentor can help the student with the practical application of the lesson

   D. All of the above

65. **The NCLB Act requires schools to establish AYP. What does the acronym AYP stand for? (Easy)**

   A. Advocates for Youth Programs

   B. Adequate Yearly Progress

   C. All Young People

   D. Adequate Yearly Preparation

66. **Head Start programs were created in the early 1960's to provide for the needs of: (Average rigor)**

   A. Non-English speaking students

   B. Students with disabilities

   C. Low-income students

   D. Gifted students

67. **Businesses are most likely to play an important role in supporting education in the community by: (Rigorous)**

   A. Providing work training as an alternative to school

   B. Encouraging students to increase their education

   C. Providing additional financial assistance to schools

   D. Allowing workers time off to attend school functions

68. The commitment that a community shows to its educational communities is: (Average rigor)

   A. Judged by how much money is contributed

   B. Something that doesn't matter much to the school

   C. A valuable investment in the future

   D. Something that will cause immediate gains

Subarea IV. Assessment and Evaluation

69. Which of the following are included in a student's permanent record? (Easy)

   A. Student's attendance

   B. Grade averages

   C. Immunization records

   D. All of the above

70. What are entry surveys, collections of reading and writing samples, and classroom observations examples of? (Average rigor)

   A. Informal assessments

   B. Structured assessments

   C. Formal assessments

   D. Criterion-referenced assessments

71. Traditional assessment methods include the following: (Easy)

   A. Multiple choice questions

   B. Questions that require self-reflection

   C. True/false questions

   D. Both A and C

72. What does a student's portfolio typically contain? (Easy)

   A. Results of standardized tests

   B. Competed self-appraisal checklists

   C. Samples of work

   D. Results of all assessment activities completed to date

73. Flexible scheduling and use of mechanical aids are examples of: (Easy)

   A. Alternative assessments

   B. Testing modifications

   C. Differentiated instruction

   D. Classroom observations

74. **Portfolio assessment provides what kind of opportunities for monitoring student progress? (Rigorous)**

    A. Formative

    B. Summative

    C. Both formative and summative

    D. Neither formative nor summative

75. **The financial support that can be made available by community resources is best described as: (Rigorous)**

    A. The only financial support available

    B. Only available to students performing well

    C. A valuable additional source of funding

    D. Limited and rarely worth considering

76. **Portfolio assessment is especially useful for identifying: (Easy)**

    A. Quantitative changes

    B. Qualitative changes

    C. Behavioral changes

    D. Attitude changes

77. **Which type of social skills assessment involves the teacher observing students in structured scenarios? (Average rigor)**

    A. Role play

    B. Teacher ratings

    C. Peer nomination

    D. Peer rating

78. **What are tests, exams, and a science project all examples of? (Easy)**

    A. Observation

    B. Informal assessment

    C. Formal assessment

    D. Norm-referenced assessment

79. **What type of assessment is a running reading record? (Average rigor)**

   A. Observation

   B. Structured assessment

   C. Informal assessment

   D. Formal assessment

80. **Which type of assessment would be used to determine if students are meeting national and state learning standards? (Average rigor)**

   A. Norm-referenced assessments

   B. Criterion-referenced assessments

   C. Performance-based assessments

   D. Observation-based assessments

81. **Why are student records often a good indicator of student progress? (Easy)**

   A. They contain information from several people.

   B. They show changes over time.

   C. They contain information gathered over a period of time.

   D. All of the above

82. **When should a classroom management plan be implemented? (Easy)**

   A. When a parent requests one

   B. When behavioral issues are impacting students

   C. At the start of the school year

   D. On the first instance that undesired behaviors are observed

83. **Which of the following should teachers remember when reading observations recorded by other teachers? (Average rigor)**

   A. Teachers may be manipulative.

   B. Teachers may be biased.

   C. Teachers may be dishonest.

   D. Teachers may be indifferent.

84. What should a teacher record in anecdotal records of a student? (Rigorous)

   A. Assumptions about the student's interest

   B. Theories explaining the student's attitude

   C. Speculations about the student's motivation

   D. Observed behaviors of the student

85. Which factor is it most important to consider when choosing structured assessment methods? (Rigorous)

   A. The ease of administering the assessment

   B. The benefits of observing students

   C. The opinions of parents on testing methods

   D. The purpose of the assessment

Subarea V. Professional and Program Leadership

86. Which of the following is a widely known curriculum model for early childhood programs? (Easy)

   A. Montessori method

   B. DISTAR method

   C. Success for All

   D. Voyager

87. Under the IDEA, Congress provides safeguards for students against schools' actions, including the right to sue in court, and encourages states to develop hearing and mediation systems to resolve disputes. This is known as: (Rigorous)

   A. Due process

   B. Mediation

   C. Safe Schools Initiative

   D. Parent involvement

88. **As teachers select instructional materials, it is important that teachers remember that:** (Average rigor)

   A. It is unlawful for students to study from textbooks or materials that are brought from home.

   B. It is unlawful for students to study from textbooks or materials that are more than 10 years old.

   C. It is unlawful to require students to study from textbooks or materials other than those approved by the state Department of Education.

   D. None of the above

89. **What is the most important factor in raising academic outcomes for all students as required in the NCLB law?** (Rigorous)

   A. The curriculum model used

   B. The quality of instruction in the classroom

   C. The location of the school

   D. The number of years of experience the teacher has

90. **Which factor would it be most important to consider when developing an early childhood program?** (Rigorous)

   A. The state standards and guidelines

   B. The interests of students

   C. The background of teachers

   D. The resources of the school

91. **According to IDEA, who must be involved in developing a child's IEP?** (Average rigor)

   A. A medical doctor

   B. The school psychologist

   C. The parents or guardians

   D. The principal

92. Why should teachers view the websites of professional organizations like the IRA? (Rigorous)

    A. To find new video games for teaching children

    B. To chat with other early childhood educators

    C. To find strategies to improve early childhood education for students

    D. To post student's work for viewing by parents

93. A teacher notices that a student is sullen, and has several bruises on his head, arms, and legs. When asked, the student responds that he hit his arm getting out of bed that morning. The teacher should: (Average rigor)

    A. Attempt to get more information from the student

    B. Report the suspected abuse

    C. Inform the parents

    D. Wait and see if other signs of abuse become evident

94. If child abuse is suspected, what action should a teacher take? (Average rigor)

    A. Wait to see if the child talks about it again

    B. Talk to your supervisor about your concerns

    C. Call the child's parent

    D. Take no action unless there is proof

95. When considering whether child abuse could be occurring, what types of abuse should teachers be aware of? (Rigorous)

    A. Physical abuse

    B. Mental abuse

    C. Emotional abuse

    D. All of the above

96. Which skill would be most important for a senior teacher working with associate teachers and paraprofessionals? (Rigorous)

    A. Delegation skills

    B. Problem-solving skills

    C. Conflict management skills

    D. Decision-making skills

97. **Which of the following is a sign of child abuse? (Average rigor)**

    A. Awkward social behavior around other children

    B. Bruises

    C. Withdrawn

    D. All of the above

98. **Students with disabilities may demonstrate difficulty in academic skills requiring a specialized education program. Which of the following is a program of special education intervention? (Rigorous)**

    A. NTA

    B. IEP

    C. NCLB

    D. CIA

99. **It is important to make a report when abuse or neglect is suspected because: (Average rigor)**

    A. Failure to do so could result in revocation of certification and license

    B. Failure to do so could result in a monetary fine

    C. Both A and B

    D. None of the above

100. **A positive classroom environment is a critical factor in creating an effective learning environment. Which of the following are factors in creating an effective learning environment for students? (Easy)**

    A. Classroom rules prominently displayed

    B. Praise delivered by the teacher

    C. Teacher is in control of the behavior of all students

    D. All of the above

Post Test Answer Key

1.	D	35.	D	69.	D
2.	B	36.	C	70.	A
3.	A	37.	C	71.	D
4.	D	38.	D	72.	C
5.	C	39.	D	73.	B
6.	A	40.	B	74.	C
7.	A	41.	D	75.	C
8.	C	42.	A	76.	B
9.	C	43.	C	77.	A
10.	D	44.	A	78.	C
11.	A	45.	A	79.	B
12.	B	46.	C	80.	B
13.	B	47.	B	81.	D
14.	A	48.	D	82.	C
15.	B	49.	D	83.	B
16.	A	50.	C	84.	D
17.	C	51.	D	85.	D
18.	C	52.	D	86.	A
19.	B	53.	C	87.	A
20.	C	54.	D	88.	C
21.	C	55.	D	89.	B
22.	D	56.	B	90.	A
23.	C	57.	D	91.	C
24.	D	58.	A	92.	C
25.	A	59.	D	93.	B
26.	B	60.	D	94.	B
27.	B	61.	D	95.	D
28.	B	62.	A	96.	A
29.	B	63.	B	97.	D
30.	D	64.	D	98.	B
31.	C	65.	B	99.	C
32.	D	66.	C	100.	D
33.	B	67.	C		
34.	D	68.	C		

Post Test Rigor Table

	Easy %20	Average rigor %40	Rigorous %40
Question #	4, 28, 35, 40, 49, 52, 53, 55, 58, 65, 69, 71, 72, 73, 76, 78, 81, 82, 86, 100	1, 3, 5, 6, 9, 12, 16, 20, 29, 31, 32, 33, 38, 39, 42, 45, 46, 47, 48, 51, 54, 56, 57, 59, 61, 62, 64, 66, 68, 70, 77, 79, 80, 83, 88, 91, 93, 94, 97, 99	2, 7, 8, 10, 11, 13, 14, 15, 17, 18, 19, 21, 22, 23, 24, 25, 26, 27, 30, 34, 36, 37, 41, 43, 44, 50, 60, 63, 67, 74, 75, 84, 85, 87, 89, 90, 92, 95, 96, 98

TEACHER CERTIFICATION STUDY GUIDE

Post Test Rationales with Sample Questions

Subarea I. Child Development and Learning

1. At what age would a child be expected to have developed speech patterns with 100% intelligibility? (Average rigor)

    A. Age 2
    B. Age 3
    C. Age 4
    D. Age 5

Answer D: Age 5

Speech intelligibility guidelines provide a tracking of a child's oral speech development. Children at 2 years old should have speech patterns that are about 70% intelligible. Children at 3 years old should have an increased 10% speech pattern that is about 80% intelligible. Children at 4 years old should have a 20% speech pattern that is about 90% intelligible. Children at 5 years old should have a speech pattern that is 100% intelligible.

2. The stages of play development from infancy stages to early childhood includes a move from: (Rigorous)

    A. Cooperative to solitary
    B. Solitary to cooperative
    C. Competitive to collaborative
    D. Collaborative to competitive

Answer B: Solitary to cooperative

The stages of play development move from mainly solitary in the infancy stages to cooperative in early childhood. However, even in early childhood, children should be able to play on their own and entertain themselves from time to time.

TEACHER CERTIFICATION STUDY GUIDE

3. According to Piaget, during what stage do children learn to manipulate symbols and objects? (Average rigor)

    A. Concrete operations
    B. Pre-operational
    C. Formal operations
    D. Conservative operational

Answer A: Concrete operations

In the pre-operational stage, children begin to understand symbols. In the concrete operations stage, children go one step beyond this and begin to learn to manipulate symbols, objects and other elements.

4. What does the Multiple Intelligence Theory developed by Howard Gardner explain? (Easy)

    A. How the intelligence of students depends on the environment
    B. How the intelligence of students constantly change
    C. How students have different levels of overall intelligence
    D. How students learn in at least seven different ways

Answer D: How students learn in at least seven different ways

Gardner's Multiple Intelligence Theory suggests that students learn in (at least) seven different ways. These include visually/spatially, musically, verbally, logically/mathematically, interpersonally, intrapersonally, and bodily/kinesthetically.

5. Above what age does learning a language become increasingly difficult? (Average rigor)

    A. Age 3
    B. Age 5
    C. Age 7
    D. Age 10

Answer C: Age 7

The most important concept to remember regarding the difference between learning a first language and a second one is that if the learner is approximately age seven or older, learning a second language will occur very differently in the learner's brain than it will had the learner been younger. The reason for this is that there is a language-learning function that exists in young children that appears to go away as they mature. Learning a language prior to age seven is almost guaranteed, with relatively little effort.

6. The various domains of development are best described as: (Average rigor)

    A. Integrated
    B. Independent
    C. Simultaneous
    D. Parallel

Answer A: Integrated

The most important premise of child development is that all domains of development (physical, social, and academic) are integrated.

7. A student has developed and improved their vocabulary. However, the student is not confident enough to use their improved vocabulary, and the teacher is not aware of the improvement. What is this an example of? (Rigorous)

    A. Latent development
    B. Dormant development
    C. Random development
    D. Delayed development

Answer A: Latent development

Latent development refers to the way that development in students may not always be observable. A student that has developed and improved their vocabulary, but lacks the confidence to use the vocabulary would not show any outward signs of the development, and so the change may remain hidden. Teachers should be aware of this in order to identify a child's future or near-future capabilities.

8. **A child exhibits the following symptoms: inability to appreciate humor, indifference to physical contact, abnormal social play, and abnormal speech. What is the likely diagnosis for this child? (Rigorous)**

   A. Separation anxiety
   B. Mental retardation
   C. Autism
   D. Hypochondria

Answer C: Autism

According to many psychologists who have been involved with treating autistic children, it seems that these children have built a wall between themselves and everyone else, including their families and even their parents. They are often indifferent to physical contact, engage in abnormal social play, display abnormal speech, are unable to appreciate humor, and cannot empathize with others.

9. **The complex linguistic deficiency marked by the inability to remember and recognize words by sounds and the inability to break words down into component units describes: (Average rigor)**

   A. Oral processing disorder
   B. Attention deficit disorder
   C. Dyslexia
   D. Autism

Answer C: Dyslexia

Dyslexia is a very common reading disorder. It is a complex linguistic deficiency that typically causes problems recalling or recognizing words, as well as the inability to decode words. Oral processing disorder refers to a student's ability to listen and process audible information; attention deficit disorder labels a student's ability to focus and maintain attention; and autism is a disorder that influences social interaction.

10. **What is a good strategy for teaching ethnically diverse students? (Rigorous)**

    A. Don't focus on the students' culture
    B. Expect them to assimilate easily into your classroom
    C. Imitate their speech patterns
    D. Use instructional strategies of various formats

Answer D: Use instructional strategies of various formats

When teaching students from multicultural backgrounds, instructional strategies may be inappropriate and unsuccessful when presented in a single format which relies on the student's understanding and acceptance of the values and common attributes of a specific culture which is not his or her own. A good approach for teaching ethnically diverse students is to use instructional strategies of various formats.

11. **When teaching in a diverse classroom, teachers should: (Rigorous)**

    A. Plan, devise, and present material in a multicultural manner
    B. Research all possible cultures and expose the children to those
    C. Focus on the curriculum and whatever multicultural opportunities are built into it already
    D. Utilize single format instruction to present material in a multicultural manner

Answer A: Plan, devise, and present material in a multicultural manner

Curriculum objectives and instructional strategies may be inappropriate and unsuccessful when presented in a single format which relies on the student's understanding and acceptance of the values and common attributes of a specific culture which is not his or her own. Planning, devising and presenting material from a multicultural perspective can enable the teacher in a culturally diverse classroom to ensure that all the students achieve the stated, academic objective.

TEACHER CERTIFICATION STUDY GUIDE

12. **Because teachers today will deal with an increasingly diverse group of cultures in their classrooms, they must: (Average rigor)**

    A. Ignore the cultures represented
    B. Show respect to all parents and families
    C. Provide a celebration for each culture represented
    D. Focus on teaching the majority

Answer B: Show respect to all parents and families

To deal with a diverse group of cultures in their classrooms, teachers must show respect to all parents and families. They need to set the tone that suggests that their mission is to develop students into the best people they can be. They also need to realize that various cultures have different views of how children should be educated.

13. **What is an effective way to help a non-English speaking student succeed in class? (Rigorous)**

    A. Refer the child to a specialist
    B. Maintain an encouraging, success-oriented atmosphere
    C. Help them assimilate by making them use English exclusively
    D. Help them cope with the content materials you presently use

Answer B: Maintain an encouraging, success-oriented atmosphere

Students in an environment where their language is not the standard one can feel embarrassed and inferior and may also expect to fail. Encouragement is especially important for these students.

14. Jose moved to the United States last month. He speaks little to no English at this time. His teacher is teaching the class about habitats in science and has chosen to read a story about various habitats to the class. The vocabulary is difficult. What should Jose's teacher do with Jose? (Rigorous)

   A. Provide Jose with additional opportunities to learn about habitats
   B. Read the story to Jose multiple times
   C. Show Jose pictures of habitats from his native country
   D. Excuse Jose from the assignment

Answer A: Provide Jose with additional opportunities to learn about habitats

Students who are learning English should be exposed to a variety of opportunities to learn the same concepts as native speakers. Content should not be changed, but the manner in which it is presented and reinforced should be changed.

15. IDEA sets policies that provide for inclusion of students with disabilities. What does inclusion mean? (Rigorous)

   A. Inclusion is the name of the curriculum that must be followed in special education classes.
   B. Inclusion is the right of students with disabilities to be placed in the regular classroom.
   C. Inclusion refers to the quality of instruction that is important for student's academic success.
   D. Inclusion means that students with disabilities should always be placed in special classes.

Answer B: Inclusion is the right of students with disabilities to be placed in the regular classroom.

Inclusion, mainstreaming and least restrictive environment are interrelated policies under the IDEA, with varying degrees of statutory imperatives. Inclusion is defined as the right of students with disabilities to be placed in the regular classroom. Least restrictive environment is the mandate that children be educated to the maximum extent appropriate with their non-disabled peers. Mainstreaming is a policy where disabled students can be placed in the regular classroom, as long as such placement does not interfere with the student's educational plan.

TEACHER CERTIFICATION STUDY GUIDE

16. **What is one component of the instructional planning model that must be given careful evaluation? (Average rigor)**

    A. Students' prior knowledge and skills
    B. The script the teacher will use in instruction
    C. Future lesson plans
    D. Parent participation

Answer A: Students' prior knowledge and skills.

Teachers will generally have certain expectations regarding where the students will be physically and intellectually when they plan for a new class. However, there will be wide variations in the actual classroom. If the teacher doesn't make the extra effort to understand where there are deficiencies and where there are strengths in the individual students, the planning will probably miss the mark, at least for some members of the class.

17. **Which of the following is a true statement? (Rigorous)**

    A. Recess is not important to a child's development.
    B. Playtime is only provided in schools to help children release energy.
    C. Play has an important and positive role in child development.
    D. Solitary play is always an indication that a child has development issues.

Answer C: Play has an important and positive role in child development.

Too often, recess and play is considered peripheral or unimportant to a child's development. It's sometimes seen as a way to allow kids to just get physical energy out or a "tradition" of childhood. The truth is, though, that play is very important to human development. Play is an activity that helps teach basic values such as sharing and cooperation. It also teaches that taking care of oneself (as opposed to constantly working) is good for human beings and further creates a more enjoyable society.

TEACHER CERTIFICATION STUDY GUIDE

18. **Which type of learning involves the formulation of questions that convert new information into an active application of knowledge? (Rigorous)**

    A. Hands-on learning
    B. Guided reading
    C. Inquiry-based learning
    D. Teacher directed model

Answer C: Inquiry-based learning

A current trend in education is inquiry-based learning. It requires students to be actively involved in the learning process and in the construction of new knowledge. When students engage in inquiry-based learning, the learning process involves the formulation of questions that convert new information into an active application of knowledge.

19. **Which of the following is portfolio assessment most likely to encourage? (Rigorous)**

    A. Self-esteem
    B. Self-directed learning
    C. Conflict management skills
    D. Time management skills

Answer B: Self-directed learning

One of the main advantages of portfolio assessment for students is that it provides students with the opportunity to assess and reflect on their own work. This encourages self-directed learning.

Subarea II. Curriculum Development and Implementation

20. **Which of the following is the most important reason for integrating the curriculum? (Average rigor)**

    A. It increases ease of lesson planning.
    B. It meets the needs of diverse students.
    C. It breaks down barriers between subjects.
    D. It narrows the focus of study.

Answer C: It breaks down barriers between subjects.

The integrated curriculum is a method that teaches students to break down barriers between subjects. Major concepts are pulled from this broad concept, and teachers then plan activities that teach these concepts.

21. **Mrs. Potts is conducting a language development task with her students. She forms students into small mixed-ability groups. She then gives each group a discussion question. Each group is asked to discuss the question, while ensuring that each person has a chance to give their opinion. What approach to language development is this activity based on? (Rigorous)**

    A. Linguistic approach
    B. Cognitive approach
    C. Socio-cognitive approach
    D. Learning approach

Answer C: Socio-cognitive approach

The socio-cognitive allowed that determining the appropriateness of language in given situations for specific listeners is as important as understanding semantic and syntactic structures. By engaging in conversation, children at all stages of development have opportunities to test their language skills, receive feedback, and make modifications.

22. **A teacher attempting to create a differentiated classroom should focus on incorporating activities that: (Rigorous)**

    A. Favor academically advanced students
    B. Challenge special education students to achieve more
    C. Are suitable for whichever group of students is the majority
    D. Meet the needs of all the students in the class

Answer D: Meet the needs of all the students in the class

A differentiated classroom is one that meets the needs of special education students, the regular mainstream students, and those that are academically advanced. The purpose of the differentiated classroom is to provide appropriate activities for students at all levels.

23. **Why is it most important for teachers to ensure that students from different economic backgrounds have access to the resources they need to acquire the academic skills being taught? (Rigorous)**

    A. All students must work together on set tasks.
    B. All students must achieve the same results in performance tasks.
    C. All students must have equal opportunity for academic success.
    D. All students must be fully included in classroom activities.

Answer C: All students must have equal opportunity for academic success.

The economic backgrounds of students can impact the resources they have. Regardless of the positive or negative impacts on the students' education from outside sources, it is the teacher's responsibility to ensure that all students in the classroom have an equal opportunity for academic success. This includes ensuring that all students have equal access to the resources needed to acquire the skills being taught.

24. **A teacher is planning to get all of her students involved in sports for the purpose of helping develop hand-eye coordination and teamwork skills. What would be the most appropriate approach when planning the sports activities? (Rigorous)**

    A. Encourage competition among students so they become used to the pressure of competing.
    B. Ensure that students who dislike sports continue until they enjoy sports.
    C. Choose activities that are beyond the student's current abilities so students are prompted to improve.
    D. Maintain a relaxed atmosphere and remind students that the sport is designed to be fun.

Answer D: Maintain a relaxed atmosphere and remind students that the sport is designed to be fun.

Sports can be valuable in child development. Sports can develop motor skills, social skills, and personal interests. It is important that sporting activities for young children focus on the positive benefits such as the development of motor skills and personal interests, rather than focusing on competition.

25. Which is the best approach to the holistic teaching of a concept? (Rigorous)

 A. Start with the whole concept and then move on to the parts.
 B. Teach only the parts and avoid focusing on the whole.
 C. Focus only on the whole to avoid students becoming confused by the parts.
 D. Begin with parts until students have developed their own understanding of the whole.

Answer A: Start with the whole concept and then move on to the parts.

Holistic teaching of a concept should begin with the whole concept and then move to the parts. Let students observe the parts carefully and give them a chance to experiment on their own. This is usually done through play or learning centers in the classroom. When children internalize the small parts of the whole they can then grasp the whole concept.

26. Young children do not concentrate for long periods of time. Generally, young children should be changing academic activities every: (Rigorous)

 A. 5-10 minutes
 B. 15-20 minutes
 C. 20-45 minutes
 D. 45 minutes-1 hour

Answer B: 15-20 minutes

Students do not sit still and cannot generally focus on one thing for long periods of time. Good teachers know how to capitalize on the need of children to move and change topics. Generally, young children should be changing academic activities every 15-20 minutes. This means that if a teacher wants to fill a block of two hours for literacy learning in the morning, the teacher should have about 6-8 activities planned.

TEACHER CERTIFICATION STUDY GUIDE

27. **Providing instruction from various points of view, not only helps students academically, but it also allows them to: (Rigorous)**

    A. Work cooperatively and contribute to a team
    B. Develop the personal skill of being able to view situations from multiple viewpoints
    C. Become problem solvers with the ability to apply creative thinking to common problems
    D. Develop tolerance and patience

Answer B: Develop the personal skill of being able to view situations from multiple viewpoints

When the teacher actively and frequently models viewing from multiple perspectives as an approach to learning in the classroom, the students not only benefit through improved academic skill development, but also begin to adopt this approach for learning and contemplating as a personal skill. The ability to consider a situation, issue, problem, or event from multiple viewpoints is a skill that will serve the individual well in a wide range of situations.

28. **What area of differentiated instruction is a teacher focusing on when planning what material to teach? (Easy)**

    A. Process
    B. Content
    C. Product
    D. Assessment

Answer B: Content

The effective teacher will seek to connect all students to the subject matter through multiple techniques, with the goal that each student, through their own abilities, will relate to one or more techniques and excel in the learning process. This is known as differentiated instruction, and focuses on content (what is being taught), process (how the material will be taught), and product (the expectations placed on students to demonstrate their knowledge or understanding).

TEACHER CERTIFICATION STUDY GUIDE

29. **Which of the following best describes how different areas of development impact each other? (Average rigor)**

    A. Development in other areas cannot occur until cognitive development is complete.
    B. Areas of development are inter-related and impact each other.
    C. Development in each area is independent of development in other areas.
    D. Development in one area leads to a decline in other areas.

Answer B: Areas of development are inter-related and impact each other.

Child development does not occur in a vacuum. Each element of development impacts other elements of development. For example, as cognitive development progresses, social development often follows. The reason for this is that all areas of development are fairly inter-related.

30. **Teachers must create personalized learning communities where every student is a valued member and contributor of the classroom experiences. Which of the following are effects of a personalized learning environment? (Rigorous)**

    A. Decreased drop-out rates among marginalized students
    B. Increased learning affect for students
    C. Decreased unproductive student behavior
    D. All of the above

Answer D: All of the above

Researchers continue to show that personalized learning environments increase the learning affect for students; decrease drop-out rates among marginalized students; and decrease unproductive student behavior which can result from constant cultural misunderstandings or miscues between students. Personalized learning communities provide supportive learning environments that address the academic and emotional needs of students.

31. **What is a conflict resolution principle? (Average rigor)**

    A. Attack the person
    B. React immediately
    C. Find common ground
    D. Focus on the past

Answer C: Find common ground

One of the conflict resolution principles is "find common ground." This means that people should try to find something they do agree on as soon as possible. If an early compromise can be reached, the tension can often be resolved more quickly.

32. **What should a teacher do first when they notice a student appears stressed? (Average rigor)**

    A. Praise the student
    B. Hold a class discussion
    C. Inform the parents
    D. Ask the student what the problem is

Answer D: Ask the student what the problem is

The first thing a teacher should do when they notice a student appears stressed is to ask the student what the problem is. This simple step can often effectively reduce the student's stress.

33. **Johnny loves to listen to stories and points to signs all around the room that have letters on them. This suggests that Johnny: (Average rigor)**

    A. Will be a good reader
    B. Has good emergent literacy skills
    C. Has good phonemic awareness skills
    D. Understands grammar

Answer B: Has good emergent literacy skills

Enjoying stories and being aware of environmental print are factors in emergent literacy skills, not necessarily directly attributed to phonemic awareness, phonics, or future reading abilities. However, those students with good emergent literacy skills are more likely to be more successful in all of those skills than students who have poor emergent literacy skills.

34. Children having difficulties with spelling, reading accuracy, and reading comprehension skills are also likely to have difficulties with: (Rigorous)

    A. Cognitive skills
    B. Development factors
    C. Math skills
    D. Speech and language skills

Answer D: Speech and language skills

While students who have difficulties with speech and language skills often have difficulties with reading, the converse is also true. Students who are struggling with spelling, reading accuracy and comprehension may also have hidden difficulties with speech and language skills.

35. Children typically develop oral language by listening to: (Easy)

    A. Teachers
    B. Parents
    C. Peers
    D. All of the above

Answer D: All of the above

Children develop oral language by listening to others. This includes listening to teachers, parents, and peers.

36. Mr. Phillips has called a parent meeting with Maria's parents. Maria is struggling to acquire the necessary comprehension skills to maintain grade level standards. Maria's parents speak Spanish in the home and are eager and willing to do anything to help Maria succeed in school. Which of the following strategies below will help Maria, while maintaining and fostering the importance of her native language? (Rigorous)

    A. Encouraging Maria's parents to enroll in an English language course
    B. Making sure Maria speaks only English during classroom activities
    C. Encouraging Maria's parents to read and discuss books written in Spanish
    D. Ensuring that Maria's parents only speak English in the home

Answer C: Encouraging Maria's parents to read and discuss books written in Spanish

The foundations upon which comprehension skills are learned are not unique to one language. If Maria is indeed struggling with comprehension, it does not matter which language she uses to practice her skills. By encouraging Maria's parents to utilize their skills in their native language, they can feel a more active member of Maria's educational process and continue to embrace their heritage and native language.

37. In her kindergarten classroom, Mrs. Thomas has been watching the students in the drama center. She has watched the children pretend to complete a variety of magic tricks. Mrs. Thomas decides to use stories about magic to share with her class. Her decision to incorporate their interests into the reading shows that Mrs. Thomas understands that: (Rigorous)

    A. Including student interests is important at all times
    B. Teaching by themes is crucial for young children
    C. Young children respond to literature that reflects their lives
    D. Science fiction and fantasy are the most popular genres

Answer C: Young children respond to literature that reflects their lives

Children's literature is intended to instruct students through entertaining stories, while also promoting an interest in the very act of reading itself. Young readers respond best to themes that reflect their lives.

TEACHER CERTIFICATION STUDY GUIDE

38. Young children learning to write commonly grip the pencil: (Average rigor)

    A. Too far from the point
    B. With the wrong hand
    C. With too many fingers
    D. Too tightly

Answer D: Too tightly

A common problem for all young children learning to write is gripping the pencil too tightly, which makes writing tiresome. Usually the student learns to relax their grip as writing skill develops, but teachers can remind students to hold the instrument gently.

39. Mr. Adams uses a short story about early train travel as part of a history lesson. This shows that literature: (Average rigor)

    A. Can be used to expand students' vocabulary
    B. Can be used to build students' communication skills
    C. Can be used to help students empathize
    D. Can be used to enhance other areas of the curriculum

Answer D: Can be used to enhance other areas of the curriculum

"Learning across the curriculum" can be enhanced by using literature as another means to convey essential information. Using a short story with a subject related to history could be used to enhance the learning of history.

40. A classroom activity involves students writing letters to a mayor to ask for more bike paths to be built. What type of discourse are the students engaged in? (Easy)

    A. Exposition
    B. Persuasion
    C. Narration
    D. Description

Answer B: Persuasion

Persuasion is a piece of writing, a poem, a play, a speech whose purpose is to change the minds of the audience members or to get them to do something. A letter to a mayor asking for a bike path to be built is being writing to convince the mayor to do something.

TEACHER CERTIFICATION STUDY GUIDE

41. Ms. Smith considers the use of quality children's literature to be one of the most important qualities of an early childhood teacher. She is asked to justify her reasons behind this consideration to her principal. Which of the following is an appropriate justification? (Rigorous)

    A. There are many different types of children's literature, so there will be something to which every child can relate.
    B. Children's literature in early childhood classrooms provides the students with the opportunity to learn to read and process language.
    C. Children are like adults in many ways and need to be exposed to a variety of types of literature.
    D. Children's literature helps children improve their mental, social, and psychological skills and aids in the development in all of these areas.

Answer D: Children's literature helps children improve their mental, social, and psychological skills and aids in the development in all of these areas.

Modern educators acknowledge that introducing elementary students to a wide range of reading experiences plays an important role in their mental, social, and psychological development.

42. When teaching science, which of the following is a method of focusing on students' intrinsic motivation? (Average rigor)

    A. Adapting the lessons to students' interests
    B. Providing regular feedback
    C. Supplying rewards for the highest achievers
    D. Having regular science tests

Answer A: Adapting the lessons to students' interests

Teachers can focus on students' intrinsic motivation through adapting the tasks to students' interests, providing opportunities for active response, including a variety of tasks, providing rapid feedback, incorporating games into the lesson, and allowing students the opportunity to make choices, create, and interact with peers.

43. **What math principle is reinforced by matching numerals with number words? (Rigorous)**

    A. Sequencing
    B. Greater than and less than
    C. Number representations
    D. Rote counting

Answer C: Number representations

The students are practicing recognition that a numeral (such as 5) has a corresponding number word (five) that represents the same math concept. They are not putting numbers in order (sequencing), and they are not comparing two numbers for value (greater than or less than). In this activity, students are also not counting in order just for the sake of counting (rote counting).

44. **Recognizing if the word *fill* belongs in the word family of *bill, hill,* and *mill* or the word family of *king, sing,* and *wing* is an example of using what math principle? (Rigorous)**

    A. Pattern recognition
    B. Letter counting
    C. Counting by threes
    D. Identity property

Answer A: Pattern recognition

To choose the correct word family for *fill*, the student must recognize the pattern *-i-l-l* as opposed to the pattern *-i-n-g*.

45. **Students using a measuring cylinder are exploring what concept? (Average rigor)**

    A. Volume
    B. Weight
    C. Length
    D. Temperature

Answer A: Volume

The amount of liquid in a cylinder would be a measure of volume. A balance or scale would be used to measure weight. A ruler or meter stick would be used to measure length. A thermometer would be used to measure temperature.

TEACHER CERTIFICATION STUDY GUIDE

46. Science and technology are best described as: (Average rigor)

- A. Different names for the same thing
- B. Competing against each other
- C. Closely related and intertwined
- D. Independent of each other

Answer C: Closely related and intertwined

Science and technology, while distinct concepts, are closely related. Science attempts to investigate and explain the natural world, while technology attempts to solve human adaptation problems. Technology often results from the application of scientific discoveries, and advances in technology can increase the impact of scientific discoveries.

47. Which type of physical education activity is most likely to encourage appreciation of diversity? (Average rigor)

- A. Solitary activities
- B. Teamwork activities
- C. Competitive activities
- D. Creative activities

Answer B: Teamwork activities

One of the values that can be gained from physical education is appreciation of diversity. This is most likely to occur during teamwork activities, which often create opportunities for students to interact with other students they do not normally interact with. At the same time, students learn the value of the different skills that people have to offer.

48. Maintaining body weight is best accomplished by: (Average rigor)

- A. Dieting
- B. Aerobic exercise
- C. Lifting weights
- D. Equalizing caloric intake relative to output

Answer D: Equalizing caloric intake relative to output

The best way to maintain a body weight is by balancing caloric intake and output. Extensive dieting (caloric restriction) is not a good option as this would result in weakness. Exercise is part of the output process that helps balance caloric input and output.

49. Which of the following is the main source of energy in the diet? (Easy)

    A. Vitamins
    B. Minerals
    C. Water
    D. Carbohydrates

Answer D: Carbohydrates

The components of nutrition are carbohydrates, proteins, fats, vitamins, minerals, and water. Carbohydrates are the main source of energy (glucose) in the human diet. Common sources of carbohydrates are fruits, vegetables, grains, dairy products, and legumes.

50. According to Charles Fowler, why is it important for arts to be incorporated into the teaching of other subject areas? (Rigorous)

    A. It reduces loss of interest in the subject.
    B. It enhances the likelihood that students will retain the information.
    C. It provides a three dimensional view of the subject.
    D. It encourages the development of personal connections with the subject.

Answer C: It provides a three dimensional view of the subject.

Charles Fowler has argued that the best schools also have the best arts programs. According to Fowler, integrating arts with other subject areas gives a more complete view of the subject. Students then gain a more three dimensional understanding of the subject.

51. What should the arts curriculum for early childhood students focus on? (Average rigor)

    A. Judgment
    B. Criticism
    C. Interpretation
    D. Experimentation

Answer D: Experimentation

The arts curriculum for early childhood should focus on the experimental and discovery aspects of the arts. The focus should not be on perfect results, open creative processes with little judgment should be emphasized, and criticism should be minimal.

TEACHER CERTIFICATION STUDY GUIDE

52. What venues offer suitable opportunities for allowing students to view live performances? (Easy)

- A. Symphonies
- B. Dance companies
- C. Art museums
- D. All of the above

Answer D: All of the above

Live performances are an important part of learning arts and help to develop aesthetic appreciation of the arts. Local performing venues, art museums, symphonies, and dance companies can all provide opportunities for live performances.

Subarea III. Family and Community Relationships

53. Teachers and parents should be: (Easy)

- A. Enemies
- B. Friends
- C. Partners
- D. Strangers

Answer C: Partners

It is very important that teachers act like they are partners in the children's education and development. Parents know their children best, and it is important to get feedback, information, and advice from them.

54. Which of the following is NOT a right of parents? (Average rigor)

- A. To be informed of the teacher's concerns about their child
- B. To require the teacher to use the teaching method that works for the child
- C. To administer discipline to their child in the classroom
- D. Both B and C

Answer D: Both B and C

Since parents are entrusting the child to the teacher's professional care, they are entitled to know what concerns the teacher about their child during their absence. Parents do not have the right to mandate the teaching method used or to disrupt class by administering disciplinary consequences.

55. When addressing issues of concern in a parent-teacher conference, what is it best to focus on? (Easy)

   A. Likely explanations
   B. Personal opinions
   C. Statements from other students
   D. Observable behaviors

Answer D: Observable behaviors

When addressing issues of concern in a parent-teacher conference, teachers should focus on observable behaviors and on providing concrete examples.

56. What should a teacher begin a parent-teacher conference with? (Average rigor)

   A. Student weaknesses
   B. Positive comments
   C. Entertaining anecdotes
   D. Issues of concern

Answer B: Positive comments

A parent-teacher conference should begin with positive comments about the students. However, these should be accurate statements and not exaggerate the student's good points.

57. When dealing with a difficult family, what is most important for a teacher to display? (Average rigor)

   A. Strength
   B. Excitement
   C. Authority
   D. Patience

Answer D: Patience

When dealing with difficult families, teachers need to be patient. Teachers must also be aware that methods of criticism such as verbal attacks are not acceptable.

TEACHER CERTIFICATION STUDY GUIDE

58. **When considering a student's family, teachers should be aware that families: (Easy)**

    A. Can be in a range of forms
    B. Are commonly nuclear families
    C. Always have at least one parent
    D. Are always a positive influence on students

Answer A: Can be in a range of forms

When considering a student's family, teachers should be careful of making assumptions. Families take on a wide range of forms and can include single-parent families, step families, extended families, and many others.

59. **When communicating with parents for whom English is not the primary language you should: (Average rigor)**

    A. Provide materials whenever possible in their native language
    B. Use an interpreter
    C. Provide the same communication as you would to native English speaking parents
    D. All of the above

Answer D: All of the above

When communicating with non English speaking parents, it is important to treat them as you would any other parent and utilize any means necessary to ensure they have the ability to participate in their child's educational process.

60. **Tommy is a student in your class. His parents are deaf. Tommy is struggling with math and you want to contact the parents to discuss the issues. How should you proceed? (Rigorous)**

    A. Limit contact due to the parents' inability to hear
    B. Use a TTY phone to communicate with the parents
    C. Talk to your administrator to find an appropriate interpreter to help you communicate with the parents personally
    D. Both B and C

Answer D: Both B and C

You should never avoid communicating with parents for any reason. Instead, you should find strategies to find an effective way to communicate in various methods, just as you would with any other student in your classroom.

TEACHER CERTIFICATION STUDY GUIDE

61. **Which of the following is a sign of emotional neglect? (Average rigor)**

    A. Jealousy of other children
    B. Aggression
    C. Lack of attention to schoolwork
    D. All of the above

Answer D: All of the above

Signs of emotional neglect include jealousy of other children, aggression, lack of attention to schoolwork, and feelings of anger toward others. These can also be signs that a student has recently endured a family upset.

62. **Which of the following is the most likely cause of a child becoming easily agitated in class? (Average rigor)**

    A. Lack of sleep
    B. Lack of training in manners
    C. Being raised in a single parent home
    D. Watching too much television

Answer A: Lack of sleep

Symptoms of a lack of nutrition and sleep most notably include a lack of concentration, particularly in the classroom. Furthermore, children who lack sufficient sleep or nutrition may become agitated more easily than other children.

63. **What type of problems are children who have been abandoned or neglected most likely to have? (Rigorous)**

    A. Behavioral problems
    B. Medical problems
    C. Social problems
    D. Physical problems

Answer B: Medical problems

Children who have been neglected or abandoned often have medical problems. They may also experience problems due to poor nutrition. These problems can be addressed by schools by providing healthy school lunches and medical attention.

64. **Assigning an adult mentor to a student is an effective tool for addressing student achievement because: (Average rigor)**

    A. The mentor can reinforce learning through tutorial instruction
    B. It provides the student with an appropriate adult role model
    C. The mentor can help the student with the practical application of the lesson
    D. All of the above

Answer D: All of the above

Mentoring has become an instrumental tool in addressing student achievement and access to learning. Adult mentors work individually with identified students on specific subject areas to reinforce the learning through tutorial instruction and application of knowledge. Providing students with adult role models to reinforce the learning has become a crucial instructional strategy for teachers seeking to maximize student learning beyond the classroom.

65. **The NCLB Act requires schools to establish AYP. What does the acronym AYP stand for? (Easy)**

    A. Advocates for Youth Programs
    B. Adequate Yearly Progress
    C. All Young People
    D. Adequate Yearly Preparation

Answer B: Adequate Yearly Progress

Under the accountability provisions in the No Child Left Behind (NCLB) Act, all public school campuses, school districts, and the state are evaluated for Adequate Yearly Progress (AYP). Districts, campuses, and the state are required to meet AYP criteria on three measures: Reading/Language Arts, Mathematics, and either Graduation Rate (for high schools and districts) or Attendance Rate (for elementary and middle/junior high schools).

66. **Head Start programs were created in the early 1960's to provide for the needs of: (Average rigor)**

    A. Non-English speaking students
    B. Students with disabilities
    C. Low-income students
    D. Gifted students

Answer C: Low-income students

Head Start Programs were created in the early 1960's to provide a comprehensive curriculum model for the preparation of low-income students for success in school communities.

67. **Businesses are most likely to play an important role in supporting education in the community by: (Rigorous)**

    A. Providing work training as an alternative to school
    B. Encouraging students to increase their education
    C. Providing additional financial assistance to schools
    D. Allowing workers time off to attend school functions

Answer C: Providing additional financial assistance to schools low-income students

Businesses are an important part of the community and an important resource for schools. Businesses are most commonly a source of additional financial assistance. This can be by providing money directly, or by providing resources such as computers and other equipment.

68. The commitment that a community shows to its educational communities is: (Average rigor)

   A. Judged by how much money is contributed
   B. Something that doesn't matter much to the school
   C. A valuable investment in the future
   D. Something that will cause immediate gains

Answer C: A valuable investment in the future

The commitment that a community shows to its educational communities is a valuable investment in the future. While monetary gifts are valued, there are many ways for the community to invest in the school. Having an involved community will create a better school for all children and will eventually lead to improved academic results.

Subarea IV. Assessment and Evaluation

69. Which of the following are included in a student's permanent record? (Easy)

   A. Student's attendance
   B. Grade averages
   C. Immunization records
   D. All of the above

Answer D: All of the above

The student permanent record is a file of the student's cumulative educational history. It contains a profile of the student's academic background as well as other pertinent individual information including the student's attendance, grade averages, and schools attended. Personal information such as parents' names and addresses, immunization records, child's height and weight is an important aspect of the permanent record. All information contained within the permanent record is strictly confidential.

TEACHER CERTIFICATION STUDY GUIDE

70. **What are entry surveys, collections of reading and writing samples, and classroom observations examples of? (Average rigor)**

    A. Informal assessments
    B. Structured assessments
    C. Formal assessments
    D. Criterion-referenced assessments

Answer A: Informal assessments

There are many types of informal assessments used. These include entry surveys, collections of reading and writing samples, classroom observations, and notations about students' cognitive abilities as seen in classroom activities.

71. **Traditional assessment methods include the following: (Easy)**

    A. Multiple choice questions
    B. Questions that require self-reflection
    C. True/false questions
    D. Both A and C

Answer D: Both A and C

Traditional assessments are more inflexible with students choosing a prepared response from among a selection of responses, such as matching, multiple-choice or true/false. Alternative assessment is an assessment where students create an answer or a response to a question or task. Alternative assessment requires higher levels of thinking and may involve self-reflection about what was learned. It is also sometimes called "authentic assessment."

72. **What does a student's portfolio typically contain? (Easy)**

    A. Results of standardized tests
    B. Competed self-appraisal checklists
    C. Samples of work
    D. Results of all assessment activities completed to date

Answer C: Samples of work

A student's portfolio typically contains samples of work created throughout the year. These can be selected by the teacher, the student, or can be samples linked to learning objectives.

TEACHER CERTIFICATION STUDY GUIDE

73. **Flexible scheduling and use of mechanical aids are examples of: (Easy)**

    A. Alternative assessments
    B. Testing modifications
    C. Differentiated instruction
    D. Classroom observations

Answer B: Testing modifications

Testing modifications are changes made to minimize the effect of a student's disability or learning challenge on completing assessments. Testing modifications include flexible scheduling, flexible setting, alternate test format, and use of mechanical aids.

74. **Portfolio assessment provides what kind of opportunities for monitoring student progress? (Rigorous)**

    A. Formative
    B. Summative
    C. Both formative and summative
    D. Neither formative nor summative

Answer C: Both formative and summative

Portfolio assessment provides the opportunity for formative, or ongoing, assessment. It also provides the opportunity for summative, or culminating, assessment.

75. **The financial support that can be made available by community resources is best described as: (Rigorous)**

    A. The only financial support available
    B. Only available to students performing well
    C. A valuable additional source of funding
    D. Limited and rarely worth considering

Answer C: A valuable additional source of funding

Community resources can supplement the minimized and marginal educational resources of school communities. With state and federal educational funding becoming increasingly subject to legislative budget cuts, school communities welcome the financial support that community resources can provide.

76. **Portfolio assessment is especially useful for identifying:** (Easy)

    A. Quantitative changes
    B. Qualitative changes
    C. Behavioral changes
    D. Attitude changes

Answer B: Qualitative changes

One of the major benefits of portfolio assessments is that they can help identify qualitative changes that have occurred over time. These changes are often not as easily able to be identified using methods such as quizzes and exams.

77. **Which type of social skills assessment involves the teacher observing students in structured scenarios?** (Average rigor)

    A. Role play
    B. Teacher ratings
    C. Peer nomination
    D. Peer rating

Answer A: Role play

There are many ways to assess student's social skills. Role play is a method that involves the teacher observing students as they take part in structured scenarios.

78. **What are tests, exams, and a science project all examples of?** (Easy)

    A. Observation
    B. Informal assessment
    C. Formal assessment
    D. Norm-referenced assessment

Answer C: Formal assessment

Formal assessments are highly structured methods of assessing student performance. Tests, exams, and science projects are all examples of formal assessments.

TEACHER CERTIFICATION STUDY GUIDE

79. What type of assessment is a running reading record? (Average rigor)

    A. Observation
    B. Structured assessment
    C. Informal assessment
    D. Formal assessment

Answer B: Structured assessment

A running reading record involves the teacher using a coding system to record what students do as they read aloud. The running reading records provides information on the students' strengths and weaknesses.

80. Which type of assessment would be used to determine if students are meeting national and state learning standards? (Average rigor)

    A. Norm-referenced assessments
    B. Criterion-referenced assessments
    C. Performance-based assessments
    D. Observation-based assessments

Answer B: Criterion-referenced assessments

Criterion-referenced assessments are used to assess student learning goals as each student compares to a norm group of student learners. These are often used to determine if students and schools are meeting state and national standards.

81. Why are student records often a good indicator of student progress? (Easy)

    A. They contain information from several people.
    B. They show changes over time.
    C. They contain information gathered over a period of time.
    D. All of the above

Answer D: All of the above

Student records are often a good indicator of student progress because they contain information from more than one person, because they contain information gather over a period of time, and because they show progress over time as well as results at the current time.

TEACHER CERTIFICATION STUDY GUIDE

82. **When should a classroom management plan be implemented? (Easy)**

    A. When a parent requests one
    B. When behavioral issues are impacting students
    C. At the start of the school year
    D. On the first instance that undesired behaviors are observed

Answer C: At the start of the school year

A classroom management plan should be implemented at the beginning of the school year. It can then be analyzed and monitored for effectiveness throughout the year, and changes made if they are necessary.

83. **Which of the following should teachers remember when reading observations recorded by other teachers? (Average rigor)**

    A. Teachers may be manipulative.
    B. Teachers may be biased.
    C. Teachers may be dishonest.
    D. Teachers may be indifferent.

Answer B: Teachers may be biased.

When reading another teacher's observations of a student, teachers must be aware that the teacher may be biased. This could result in either a more positive or a more negative assessment.

84. **What should a teacher record in anecdotal records of a student? (Rigorous)**

    A. Assumptions about the student's interest
    B. Theories explaining the student's attitude
    C. Speculations about the student's motivation
    D. Observed behaviors of the student

Answer D: Observed behaviors of the student

Anecdotal records of a student should include observable behaviors. Anecdotal records should not include assumptions or speculations about the student's motivation or interest.

85. Which factor is it most important to consider when choosing structured assessment methods? (Rigorous)

    A. The ease of administering the assessment
    B. The benefits of observing students
    C. The opinions of parents on testing methods
    D. The purpose of the assessment

Answer D: The purpose of the assessment

The structured assessment methods used in class take into account two major factors. The first is the developmental stage of students, where teachers must choose assessment methods that are appropriate for the developmental level of students. The second consideration is the purpose of the assessment.

Subarea V. Professional and Program Leadership

86. Which of the following is a widely known curriculum model for early childhood programs? (Easy)

    A. Montessori method
    B. DISTAR method
    C. Success for All
    D. Voyager

Answer A: Montessori method

The philosophy and curriculum of the Montessori method is based on the work and writings of the Italian physician Maria Montessori. Her method appears to be the first curriculum model for children of preschool age that was widely disseminated and replicated. It is based on the idea that children teach themselves through their own experiences. Materials used proceed from the simple to the complex and from the concrete to the abstract and sixty-three percent of class time is spent in independent activity.

87. **Under the IDEA, Congress provides safeguards for students against schools' actions, including the right to sue in court, and encourages states to develop hearing and mediation systems to resolve disputes. This is known as: (Rigorous)**

    A. Due process
    B. Mediation
    C. Safe Schools Initiative
    D. Parent involvement

Answer A: Due process

Under the IDEA, Congress provides safeguards for students against schools' actions, including the right to sue in court, and encourages states to develop hearing and mediation systems to resolve disputes. No student or their parents/guardians can be denied due process because of disability.

88. **As teachers select instructional materials, it is important that teachers remember that: (Average rigor)**

    A. It is unlawful for students to study from textbooks or materials that are brought from home.
    B. It is unlawful for students to study from textbooks or materials that are more than 10 years old.
    C. It is unlawful to require students to study from textbooks or materials other than those approved by the state Department of Education.
    D. None of the above

Answer C: It is unlawful to require students to study from textbooks or materials other than those approved by the state Department of Education.

In considering suitable learning materials for the classroom, the teacher must have a thorough understanding of the state-mandated competency-based curriculum. According to state requirements, certain objectives must be met in each subject taught at every designated level of instruction. It is necessary that the teacher become well acquainted with the curriculum for which he/she is assigned. The teacher must also be aware that it is unlawful to require students to study from textbooks or materials other than those approved by the state Department of Education.

89. What is the most important factor in raising academic outcomes for all students as required in the NCLB law? (Rigorous)

    A. The curriculum model used
    B. The quality of instruction in the classroom
    C. The location of the school
    D. The number of years of experience the teacher has

Answer B: The quality of instruction in the classroom

The NCLB (No Child Left Behind) Act requires states to develop curriculum models demonstrating excellent academic outcomes for all children. The goal of any curriculum model is to provide consistency in instruction and create evaluation criteria for uniformity in programming. Researchers continue to show that most curriculum models produce effective academic outcomes when implemented as designed. However, there are limitations to how effectively the curriculum model is implemented in each classroom. Therefore, the quality of instruction for students by experienced educators will ultimately be what improves the academic outcomes for all students.

90. Which factor would it be most important to consider when developing an early childhood program? (Rigorous)

    A. The state standards and guidelines
    B. The interests of students
    C. The background of teachers
    D. The resources of the school

Answer A: The state standards and guidelines

One of the things that should be considered when developing an early childhood program is the state standard and guidelines. The curriculum should be based on these standards and guidelines, as well as taking into account the diverse needs of students and their families.

TEACHER CERTIFICATION STUDY GUIDE

91. According to IDEA, who must be involved in developing a child's IEP? (Average rigor)

    A. A medical doctor
    B. The school psychologist
    C. The parents or guardians
    D. The principal

Answer C: The parents or guardians

Under the IDEA, parent/guardian involvement in the development of the student's IEP is required and absolutely essential for the advocacy of the disabled student's educational needs. IEPs must be tailored to meet the student's needs, and no one knows those needs better than the parent/guardian and other significant family members.

92. Why should teachers view the websites of professional organizations like the IRA? (Rigorous)

    A. To find new video games for teaching children
    B. To chat with other early childhood educators
    C. To find strategies to improve early childhood education for students
    D. To post student's work for viewing by parents

Answer C: To find strategies to improve early childhood education for students

It is important to stay current with the latest research and teaching strategies to meet the needs of all children. The best information can be found in a variety of books, websites, or journal articles provided by professional organizations devoted to the education of young children.

93. A teacher notices that a student is sullen, and has several bruises on his head, arms, and legs. When asked, the student responds that he hit his arm getting out of bed that morning. The teacher should: (Average rigor)

   A. Attempt to get more information from the student
   B. Report the suspected abuse
   C. Inform the parents
   D. Wait and see if other signs of abuse become evident

Answer B: Report the suspected abuse

The most important concern is for the safety and wellbeing of the student. Teachers should not promise students that they won't tell because they are required by law to report suspected abuse. Failure or delay in reporting suspected abuse may be a cause for further abuse to the student. In some cases, a teacher's decision to overlook suspected abuse may result in revoking the teacher's license. Teachers are not required to investigate abuse for themselves or verify their suspicions.

94. If child abuse is suspected, what action should a teacher take? (Average rigor)

   A. Wait to see if the child talks about it again
   B. Talk to your supervisor about your concerns
   C. Call the child's parent
   D. Take no action unless there is proof

Answer B: Talk to your supervisor about your concerns

Child abuse can take many forms including physical, mental, and emotional. If any type of abuse is suspected, the best action is to immediately contact a superior at the school if abuse is suspected.

95. **When considering whether child abuse could be occurring, what types of abuse should teachers be aware of? (Rigorous)**

    A. Physical abuse
    B. Mental abuse
    C. Emotional abuse
    D. All of the above

Answer D: All of the above

While the symptoms of abuse are usually thought to be physical (and therefore visible), mental and emotional abuse is also possible. Teachers should be aware of all types of abuse, as they can all seriously impact student's wellbeing.

96. **Which skill would be most important for a senior teacher working with associate teachers and paraprofessionals? (Rigorous)**

    A. Delegation skills
    B. Problem-solving skills
    C. Conflict management skills
    D. Decision-making skills

Answer A: Delegation skills

The ability to delegate tasks is an important skill for teachers to have. Effective delegation skills allow a teacher to make the best use of paraprofessionals, associate teachers, and other individuals assisting in the education process.

97. **Which of the following is a sign of child abuse? (Average rigor)**

    A. Awkward social behavior around other children
    B. Bruises
    C. Withdrawn
    D. All of the above

Answer D: All of the above

Awkward social behavior around other children, bruises, and withdrawn behavior are all signs of child abuse.

TEACHER CERTIFICATION STUDY GUIDE

98. Students with disabilities may demonstrate difficulty in academic skills requiring a specialized education program. Which of the following is a program of special education intervention? (Rigorous)

    A. NTA
    B. IEP
    C. NCLB
    D. CIA

Answer B: IEP

Eligibility for special education services is based on a student having a disability (or a combination) and demonstration of educational need through professional evaluation. The IEP is the Individualized Educational Plan that delineates the intervention that the child will receive.

99. It is important to make a report when abuse or neglect is suspected because: (Average rigor)

    A. Failure to do so could result in revocation of certification and license
    B. Failure to do so could result in a monetary fine
    C. Both A and B
    D. None of the above

Answer C: Both A and B

The failure to report child abuse can result in revocation of certification and license and monetary fines. For state licensed personnel (teachers and school staff), failure to make a report when abuse or neglect is suspected is also punishable by the filing of criminal charges.

100. A positive classroom environment is a critical factor in creating an effective learning environment. Which of the following are factors in creating an effective learning environment for students? (Easy)

    A. Classroom rules prominently displayed
    B. Praise delivered by the teacher
    C. Teacher is in control of the behavior of all students
    D. All of the above

Answer D: All of the above

A positive environment is a critical factor in creating an effective learning environment. Verbal techniques for reinforcing behavior include both encouragement and praise delivered by the teacher. It is also helpful for the teacher to prominently display the classroom rules.

XAMonline, INC. 21 Orient Ave. Melrose, MA 02176
Toll Free number 800-509-4128
TO ORDER Fax 781-662-9268 OR www.XAMonline.com

MICHIGAN TEST FOR TEACHER EXAMINATION - MTTC - 2007

PO# Store/School:
Address 1:

Address 2 (Ship to other):

City, State Zip

Credit card number_____-_____-_____-_____ expiration_____
EMAIL _____
PHONE   FAX

ISBN	TITLE	Qty	Retail	Total
978-1-58197-968-8	MTTC Basic Skills 96			
978-1-58197-954-1	MTTC Biology 17			
978-1-58197-955-8	MTTC Chemistry 18			
978-1-58197-966-4	MTTC Elementary Education 83			
978-1-58197-974-9	MTTC Early Childhood Education 82			
978-1-58197-950-3	MTTC English 02			
978-1-58197-959-6	MTTC French 23			
978-1-58197-965-7	MTTC Guidance Counselor 51			
978-1-58197-972-5	MTTC Integrated Science 94			
978-1-58197-963-3	MTTC Library Media 48			
978-1-58197-958-9	MTTC Mathematics 22			
978-1-58197-962-6	MTTC Physical Education 44			
978-1-58197-665-6	MTTC Physics 19			
978-1-58197-952-7	MTTC Political Science 10			
978-1-58197-951-0	MTTC Reading 05			
978-1-58197-960-2	MTTC Spanish 28			
978-1-58197-9732	MTTC Special Education- Emotionally Imparioed 59			
978-1-58197-953-4	MTTC Learning Disabled 63			
978-1-58197-970-1	MTTC Social Studies 84			
			SUBTOTAL	
			Ship	$8.25